Latinos and Blacks in the Cities

LATINOS & BLACKS IN THE CITIES

Policies for the 1990s

Edited by Harriett D. Romo

Cosponsors
  IUP/SSRC Committee for Public Policy Research
    on Contemporary Hispanic Issues
  Joint Center for Political Studies
  Lyndon Baines Johnson Library
  Lyndon B. Johnson School of Public Affairs,
    The University of Texas at Austin

A volume in the Symposia Series of
  the LBJ Library and
  the LBJ School of Public Affairs

Library of Congress Catalog Card No.: 90-60692
ISBN: 0-89940-423-5
© 1990 by the Board of Regents
The University of Texas
Printed in the U.S.A.

Funding provided by the IUP/SSRC Committee for Public Policy
Research on Contemporary Hispanic Issues and the Ford Foundation;
the Joint Center for Political Studies; and the Lyndon Baines Johnson
Foundation

Cover and book design by David S. Cavazos and Ellen McKie

Photographs by Frank Wolfe, LBJ Library

CONTENTS

ACKNOWLEDGMENTS

Numerous people contributed to the success of the Cities in Transition symposium and to the publication of the proceedings. Members of the IUP/SSRC Committee, particularly Robert Reischauer and Frank Bonilla, provided suggestions on organization and context throughout the planning process. William Diaz of the Ford Foundation took a personal interest in the project and provided both financial and intellectual support to bring it to fruition. The staff at the UT Center for Mexican American Studies (CMAS), particularly Rose Turner and Linda Delgado, and Charles Corkran and the staff at the LBJ Library tended to every detail and managed the logistics of the symposium activities. Cynthia Russell, Cynthia Sanchez, and Rose Turner at CMAS, working with Marilyn Duncan, María de la Luz Martínez, and Helen Kenihan of the LBJ School Publications Office and freelancers Barbara Spielman, David S. Cavazos, and Ellen McKie, helped transform the symposium transcriptions into published form.

Planning Committee:

Harry J. Middleton, Director, Lyndon Baines Johnson Library and Museum

Milton Morris, Director of Research, Joint Center for Political Studies

Lawrence D. Reed, Assistant Executive Director, Lyndon Baines Johnson Foundation

Harriett D. Romo, Project Coordinator, IUP/SSRC Committee for Public Policy Research on Contemporary Hispanic Issues; Research Scientist, the Center for Mexican American Studies, The University of Texas at Austin

Max Sherman, Dean, Lyndon B. Johnson School of Public Affairs, The University of Texas at Austin

Latinos and Blacks in the Cities

Harriett Romo

INTRODUCTION

Harriett Romo: In 1968 President Lyndon B. Johnson authorized three pioneering commissions to analyze the problems in U.S. urban areas—the Kerner, Eisenhower, and Katzenbach commissions. The reports of those commissions threw a spotlight on our cities and recommended sweeping reforms. This book records the proceedings of a symposium held at the LBJ Library in late 1988 to investigate the condition of urban areas today, two decades after the commissions' reports. An important goal of the symposium was to bring together the diverse perspectives of scholars, policymakers, and politicians to present recommendations for policies in the 1990s. While there have been other conferences on cities and other meetings to reflect on what has been accomplished over two decades, the challenge to our panelists was to consider the condition of the poor within our cities and the role of minorities, particularly Latinos and blacks, in forming policies. Focusing on economic and community development, human services, income maintenance, and education and employment, the discussions recorded in these proceedings explore the political feasibility of various policy options and extract strategies for financing and implementing the recommendations proposed.

A primary purpose of the symposium was to bring together a number of the most talented Latino and black social scientists and analysts interested in cities and public service to determine which programs and policies work better than others and why. Our intention was to use their knowledge of Latino and black communities, programs, budgets, and existing political conditions to inform wise government policy. We drew upon the expertise of government officials at the local, state, and federal levels as well as analysts who are involved in the policy-forming process and asked them to make recommendations for innovative policies that can be implemented in the current political climate. We invited concerned citizens, organizations, students, and scholars to help identify some of the choices before us and to consider the possibilities and consequences of the implementation of our recommendations.

A Link with the Past
The Eisenhower Commission report, which focused on the causes and prevention of violence in our cities, emphasized that the "past has much to tell us about the present and the future." Therefore, in planning this

symposium, we determined to build upon an assessment of the changes that have occurred over the past twenty years and of how far we have come in meeting the needs identified in the 1960s commission reports. A strength of these proceedings is the potential to learn from the successes and failures of the policies and programs that arose from those earlier commission recommendations. Certainly, conditions are not the same in our cities in the 1990s as they were in the 1960s. Nonetheless, these historic commission reports provide a framework for identifying the enormous and enduring complexities, the vexing and multifaceted problems facing our urban areas, and the difficulties to be overcome in resolving them.

The Katzenbach Commission focused particularly on crime in U.S. metropolitan areas. Its recommendations were more than a list of new procedures, new tactics, and new techniques to fight rising rates of crime and violence. The commission called for a revolution in the way of thinking in America and recognized—as do these symposium proceedings—that "no single formula, no single theory, no single generalization" can explain or remedy the problems in our cities. The following proceedings are a compilation of our assessments of progress, the budget constraints we will encounter, new policy recommendations, and strategies for implementation.

Assessing Our Progress

Our attention to the problems confronting our cities is not to deny that there has also been tremendous progress in the past twenty years. As we begin the decade of the 1990s, more U.S. children are enrolled in schools than ever before and a greater number complete high school and go on to college than ever before. Our medical and computer technology advances have been phenomenal. Also, the economists participating in the symposium acknowledge that employment has increased tremendously among Latino and black youth, particularly in the private sector.

Assessing whether we have achieved the racial equality, opportunity, compassion, and vision called for in the 1960s commission reports, Nicholas Katzenbach, a former U.S. attorney general and undersecretary of state in the 1960s who was personally involved in the work of the commissions, looks back and concludes that the job of change is more difficult than the members of the early commissions thought and that racial discrimination is more pervasive than they assumed. Barbara Jordan, long familiar with the policymaking process, concurs with Katzenbach and eloquently asks us to think about the pledge we make when we say, "One nation, indivisible." She points out that we have failed to actualize the recommendations of those earlier reports because we have remained a divided people. Her assessment is that America is moving backward, not forward. Although the civil rights laws ended the formally sanctioned biases and laws forbidding racial discrimination in voting, public accommodations, employment, housing, and schools, today people are excluded from opportunities and power because of status, income, agenda, ethnicity, or sex. She is optimistic, however, because groups traditionally on the outside of the policy process can affect decisions by bringing the possibility of success or failure to programs and policies. Inclusion of all groups in the democratic processes, she proposes, must be accomplished through mutual trust and willingness to cooperate and by including in the initial stages of planning those who will be affected by policies.

Henry Cisneros, mayor of San Antonio at the time of the symposium, notes that it will be impossible to address questions of social justice in our society in the 1990s except through urban policies because the largest numbers of minorities will live in our cities. He and the other speakers emphasize that the strength and beauty of America is its diversity, and how we will deal with the emerging demographic changes in our country is a question of national survival.

These speakers and other panelists caution that, if we cannot meet our urban and racial problems by genuinely integrating this society, the United States will lose its position in world leadership. Even with the optimistic trends acknowledged by our experts, severe unemployment and schooling differentials remain severe between white and Latino and black youth. The high school dropout rates and low levels of literacy and math skills of those Latinos and blacks who graduate from our urban schools, coupled with the low rates of college education of minority youth, suggest that, unless conditions are changed to improve the economic and education prospects for our children who live in urban areas, these youth will be locked into low-wage, low-skill jobs and unable to provide the leadership and skilled labor needed in our cities in the future.

Katzenbach acknowledges that even the best-intentioned programs have complicated and, in some cases, even aggravated problems in our cities. Many government programs, such as improved transportation and rural utility expansions, have encouraged moves to the suburbs. Other programs, such as subsidized housing and welfare, have tied the poor to poor neighborhoods.

David Dinkins, now the mayor of New York City, points out that many past solutions to the problems of the inner cities have not been solutions that benefit the low-income black, white, and Latino residents in those cities. Instead, developers, real estate companies, banks, and the already affluent have benefited—largely because there has been little or no representation of these Latino, black, and poor white communities on decision-making and policy governing boards.

According to a report from the Joint Center for Political Studies, the number of elected blacks was up almost 6 percent in a single year in 1989 and up almost 50 percent more than a decade ago. Rates of increase among Latino elected officials show similar patterns. Recent elections giving the nation its first black elected governor and the blacks who won mayoral contests for the first time in predominantly white cities from New York and New Haven to Seattle demonstrate that Americans can take satisfaction in some progress. But there is little reason for complacency. In many cases, whites found reason to oppose moderate, nonthreatening minority candidates such as Douglas Wilder and David Dinkins, and there is a heightened ethnic consciousness in city and state politics.

The National Association of Latino Elected and Appointed Officials has data showing that Latino and black elected officials represent less than 2 percent of the total elected officials. Minority appointees in the federal executive branch represent a dismal number. There are few blacks or Latinos in positions responsible for formulating long-term policy objectives and few Latino or black policy analysts. Panelists Harry Pachon and Lena Guerrero argue that these networks of elected and appointed Latino and black officials are essential to carry out the goals proposed at this symposium and to formulate long-term policy objectives to improve life in our cities.

A New Generation of Americans
The Eisenhower Commission noted that a new generation of Americans is emerging, and, as this symposium has confirmed, that generation is increasingly Latino, black, and Asian. The Census Bureau reported recently that during the past decade the nation's Hispanic population grew more than 39 percent, from 14.4 million to 20.1 million. The increment results from Hispanics born in this country as well as from continuing immigration. The majority of those Hispanics live in three states—California with 34 percent, Texas with 21 percent, and New York with 12 percent. Florida, with its growing Cuban and Central American immigrant population, also has a substantial proportion of the nation's Hispanic population, with 8 percent. The concentration of these Latinos is predominantly in urban areas, and Latinos and blacks are becoming the majority of the population in a number of our major cities.

Several factors have worked to make this population of Latinos and blacks disproportionately disadvantaged. Paul Peterson points out that the nature of poverty has changed, and today it is principally in our central cities. The poverty rate in the United States is much higher than that in European countries and is particularly concentrated among children, more so than in any other industrialized country. A substantial body of economic research conclusively shows that the trend toward growing inequality of household income is paralleled by a growing inequality in the distribution of wages. The number of poor people, estimated to be approximately 13.1 percent by the Census Bureau, remains well above the levels of poverty in the United States two decades ago. In fact, the Center for Budget and Policy Priorities reports that the median family income of Hispanics under the poverty level fell 10 percent from $7,238 in 1978 to $6,557 in 1987 after adjusting for inflation. Moreover, the high numbers of Latino and black children living in poverty, the increasing number of single mothers with children who get little financial support and have few child-care resources, and the increase in poverty among married-couple families with below-poverty wage jobs represent growing crises in our cities. Participants in this symposium argue that a more equal distribution of poverty among ethnic groups is not acceptable. Others suggest that perhaps the economic growth of this country is dependent upon existing and growing pockets of poverty. Panelists warn that poverty conceptualized in terms of limitations of choices is not congruent with a country that respects the common good and aspires to be "one nation, indivisible."

Edwin Melendez and Bernard Anderson provide examples of how the prospects for economic mobility for low-income blacks and Hispanics have been diminished by the elimination of jobs in the auto industry, in steel factories, and in other manufacturing industries. For many of those in the labor market, opportunities have been affected by the increase in high-skilled jobs in the professions, finance, information processing, accounting, and education that require college degrees, which they do not have, and by the proliferation of low-skilled, low-wage jobs in the service sector. The result is an increasingly high rate of unemployment since the 1960s. Latinos and blacks face unemployment rates that are more than double those of whites. Both Melendez and Anderson agree that the current employment and training programs are inadequate. The structure of the programs has not provided opportunities for those most in need of them, training periods are too short, very little actual training is provided, the emphasis on job placement favors the most skilled applicants, and participants are channeled into low-wage, dead-end jobs.

The Kerner Report, which was a response to racial disorder in American cities in 1967, ominously warned that the nation is "moving towards two societies, one Black, one White—separate and unequal." Nationwide scholars present disturbing research findings that suggest that the Kerner Report's warning may indeed be true. Gary Orfield, one of our panelists, shows persuasively that cities such as Chicago are becoming increasingly segregated and that segregation breeds increasing inequality. A black or Latino living in a neighborhood that is predominantly poor and ethnically segregated is more likely to live in a neighborhood with poor schools, deplorable housing, fewer and inferior jobs, limited economic resources, poor conditions for successful small businesses, and higher rates of poverty, drug abuse, and crime. The residents of those communities are trapped in schools where more than half the students drop out and the achievement of those who remain is substantially below the national average.

Several of our panelists point out that middle-class minority families as well as the white population are increasingly detached from these urban, inner-city institutions, making it ever more difficult to direct resources toward institutional change. Richard Nathan argues that three institutional areas are critical to any urban agenda—the schools, the welfare system, and the corrections system—and, if we are to make substantial changes in the quality of life in our cities, we must demand that administrations build confidence in those institutions. Several of our panelists discuss the problems of transforming large urban bureaucracies and the difficulties of turning experimental programs and imaginative new ideas into systematic approaches to change.

Budget Constraints

The recommendations of the commissions of the 1960s demanded far-reaching improvements in our institutions and unprecedented levels of public funding. As the Kerner Commission pronounced, the scope and costs of its recommendations also called attention to the fact that there can be no higher priority for national action and no higher claim on the nation's conscience than improving basic circumstances—health, safety, housing, education, and jobs—for all who live in this country. This claim, made in the midst of the Vietnam War, called for high levels of domestic spending. For four decades now, military spending has ranked first in our national scale of priorities. The conduct of wars and foreign affairs, the building of "Star Wars" technology and bombers, the growth of the economy, and the conquest of space have consumed attention and devoured federal expenditures. Efforts in civil rights, medical care, housing, employment, and education have been subordinated to capital gains, technology, and tax benefits for the wealthy. The result has been an enormous and alarming budget deficit and an equally enormous deficit of unmet social needs and deeply felt social injustices.

The budget constraints faced by future leaders of the United States are a recurrent theme in this symposium. The country has experienced a decade of sustained economic growth but not substantial expansion. The proposals for improved human services made in the proceedings will be even more difficult to implement if the country experiences an extended recession. The policy analysts who have been closely involved in budget decisions and program costs, such as Robert Reischauer, Paul Peterson, and Dick Nathan, do not paint a pretty picture in terms of allocation of additional federal resources in the current fiscal climate. Reischauer and Peterson argue that budget deficits are a serious problem that is cutting into our domestic agenda. Peterson argues that accumulating huge deficits and eliminating social programs while calling for a balanced budget amendment to the Constitution has been a brilliant political strategy that has allowed conservatives to control the policy agenda. Reischauer cautions that competition for new resources among groups with different priorities will be fierce in the 1990s and will necessitate setting priorities and emphasizing people-oriented policies with a broad appeal to the American middle class.

Other panelists, such as Robert Valdez and Frank Bonilla, argue that budget constraints will be moot points if the majority of our population has poor access to health care and if the majority of our future workers lack the skills to be competitive in a world market. Bonilla claims that investment in people must be a priority so that U.S. residents can meet the needs for literate, skilled, and well-trained workers in the global marketplace. Valdez illustrates that the crisis is one of organizational capacity, political will, and social conscience, not financial constraint due to budget deficits. Our discussions highlight various strategies to invest in human development without depleting the national treasury and ways to press for a firm commitment to a society concerned about human needs.

Recommendations for Action

The Kerner Commission, while pessimistic about the direction the country was headed—toward a nation divided by racism and inequality— also concluded that such a division is not inevitable. The commission identified the principal task as "one of identifying the alternatives and pressing for a national resolution to injustices—or risk destruction of basic democratic values." Our symposium participants agree that we have not yet witnessed the destruction prophesied but neither have we acted upon what needs to be done to make this nation "one nation, indivisible."

Guadalupe Valdés warns that the solutions to urban education problems cannot place the needs of the black community and the Hispanic community at odds with one another but, instead, must join forces for the kinds of things that all children need. Along with radical changes in teaching as an occupation, she proposes quality standards and performance accountability that can be achieved through a targeted school improvement plan that focuses on schools with high social and economic distress, underachievement, and linguistic complexity.

Rafael Valdivieso takes a two-generational approach that includes both short-term interventions and long-term prevention. Data presented by Valdivieso show that we now have more Latino children with mothers who are school dropouts than Latino children with mothers who are high school graduates. Valdivieso would make programs directed at improving the life chances of children focus on improving the job skills, parenting skills, and life chances of their parents as well.

Gary Orfield calls for detailed reform at the school level as well as the institutional level. He argues that we must address the structural questions of poverty, segregation, and institutional organization that affect achievement at every level within urban school systems.

Margaret Simms calls for setting priorities and determining which level of government can best implement our proposals. Variations in fiscal capacity across states mean vast variations in the standards of programs and opportunities. As a way of resolving these inequities, Simms proposes that we accept the need to expand public-sector activities in medical care, education, housing, and child care. In recognizing the need for regional and ethnic group variations in programs and policies, she cautions us not to overlook the question of the common societal good.

Economist Lynn Burbridge urges that our policies provide incentives for self-sufficiency through housing subsidies, child care, medical benefits, and good-wage jobs. She proposes that we move away from the concept of poverty programs to a policy of family programs.

Carol Thompson, a city manager who must deal with policies on a day-to-day basis, points out that the success of any program depends on appropriate funding levels and retention of effort for a significant period of time to allow the programs to accomplish their goals.

Possibilities for Implementation
The political trend toward decentralization, which has accelerated in recent years, has meant more money for state and local programs and a greater voice for those who live in our cities. Milton Morris points out that many state and local governments are more creative and more aggressive now than in the past in developing programs and policies because of the increasing presence of minorities in state legislative offices and as mayors and city managers. He suggests that solutions are likely to come at these levels, and the future of our cities depends to a great extent on Latino and black coalition building. Morris argues that we have to be unwilling to accept the constraints imposed by present political

situations and politics of the budget. Our future leaders must be prepared to lead the struggle in shaping values and in initiating and implementing policies that reflect those values. Cisneros challenges us to bring together diverse people together who combine a sense of mission with a responsibility and determination to harness economic growth and make it work for those outside the economic mainstream.

The 1960s commissions made clear that solutions demand the participation of schools, businesses, social agencies, private groups, and individual citizens, as well as government. Our symposium participants draw this ring of responsibility even broader and point out that, with the increasing economic interdependence of nations in the world today, our urban problems demand solutions that are international in their scope and in their consideration of cause and effect. Our government structure is also more complex and our citizenry more ethnically diverse today than twenty years ago. This means that policies for the 1990s must include local and state initiatives as well as leadership from the federal government and must address the needs and perspectives of individuals from different cultural and social class backgrounds. The proceedings of this conference suggest that we know a good deal about how to solve some of the problems facing our cities. Latino and black scholars are providing an impressive body of research that presents convincing answers to some of the important social problems facing urban areas in the 1990s. It is the responsibility of this generation of Americans to address those problems with innovative policies and to build on the strength of our cities and their multiethnic populations.

Now, after two decades and with the promise of a new presidential administration, these conference proceedings represent one small effort to reopen the discussion about what our government should be doing, where it should be allocating its resources, and how the obstacles can be surmounted to actualize a better life for us all. It is our hope these deliberations will stimulate each of us to continue the commitment sparked by those historic commissions to improve the policies affecting our cities.

Nicholas Katzenbach

PART I

What Have We Learned since the Presidential Commissions of the 1960s?

Introduction
Harry Middleton

What Have We Learned about Problems in Metropolitan Areas since the Presidential Commissions of the 1960s?
Nicholas Katzenbach

Discussion

PART I

Introduction

Harry Middleton: The turbulent 1960s produced many memorable images that were etched into the national consciousness. One of those is the image of a defiant governor, in a doomed effort to block the enrollment of two black students at the University of Alabama, being faced down by the United States government at the college door. In that dramatic confrontation, which was preserved on the front pages of the nation's newspapers, Mr. Katzenbach represented the U.S. government as the old order of segregation crumbled there on Alabama soil. He was then deputy attorney general of the United States. He went on through the administrations of John Kennedy and Lyndon Johnson to become attorney general and then undersecretary of state, and he made his mark on the history of that time. The part of his service that is most pertinent to cities in transition was as the head of a presidential commission on law enforcement and the administration of justice. The commission's report, issued in 1967, was a landmark event. It recommended sweeping reforms, many of which go to the heart of issues and concerns of the U.S. cities. He looked deep into the problems that plagued the American society, and the insight he gained gives him unique credentials to serve as our keynote speaker.

What Have We Learned about Problems in Metropolitan Areas since the Presidential Commissions of the 1960s?

Nicholas Katzenbach: President Lyndon Johnson was a political animal skilled in the pragmatic arts of negotiation and compromise, and it wasn't always easy to know his personal views on any particular issue.

But I do know that there were fundamental beliefs that guided him through his presidency and, I suspect, through his life. One was a conviction in racial equality and the other was a conviction in the importance of education, good education for everyone. His Great Society may have been a little of a campaign slogan, maybe an idealistic dream of a man who didn't often indulge in dreams. But, achievable or not, it was a dream worth dreaming—an ideal of racial equality, opportunity, compassion, and vision worth striving for. Of course, we have not achieved it. Perhaps we never will. But surely we should always try to keep that goal in mind and never give up and never succumb to a belief that we are not all in the same boat and that we can achieve a great society through some kind of selfishness.

This symposium, I hope, will help to rekindle that dream and move it by whatever steps, small or large, toward reality. What have we learned about problems in the metro areas since the presidential commissions of the sixties? As you remember, the three presidential commissions—the Crime Commission, focusing on crime in the streets; the Kerner Commission, focusing on the causes of racial riots of the time; the Eisenhower Commission, focusing on the causes of violence in the wake of the King and Kennedy assassinations—all found common ground in the ghettoization of our urban society.

Crime, riots, and violence all had their roots in the poverty, the joblessness, the hopelessness of slums—slums made politically more difficult to remedy because their population was primarily black or Latino. As the Kerner Commission so eloquently phrased its basic conclusion: "Our nation is moving towards two societies, one Black, one White, separate and unequal." The commission went on to say: "What White Americans have never fully understood, but which the Negro can never forget, is that White society is deeply implicated in the ghetto. White institutions erected it, White institutions maintain it, and White society condones it." Blunt, harsh, true. One thing we should have learned since the sixties is the truth of those statements. Have we? As one who participated in the Kennedy and Johnson administrations, I take pride in what was accomplished by way of breaking down the caste system that existed in parts of the country and chipping away at the racial discrimination that existed and still exists throughout much of our nation. I believe that we understood then that breaking the back of formerly sanctioned biases through laws forbidding racial discrimination in public accommodations, voting, employment, housing, and schools was only a beginning, a premise on which to build.

We knew that much more had to be done, that success would require fundamental changes in attitudes, and that leadership, determination, the will to succeed, and an awful lot of good hard work was necessary.

That was the common message of all three commissions. And it seems to me as correct today as it was then. I do not mean that we have learned nothing in more than two decades; we have learned a lot. One thing we have learned is that the job is more difficult than we thought. We have learned that racial discrimination is more subtly pervasive than, frankly, most whites had assumed. And, if we are willing to open our eyes, we have learned that the problems are worse today than they were twenty years ago. Yes, we have made progress in race relations; the middle-class black population has grown and prospered. Those are the beneficiaries, I believe, of the antidiscrimination laws. But those laws have not helped the inhabitants of segregated black ghettos that exist in so many of our cities. We have indeed moved further toward those two societies, black and white, separate and unequal.

It was, of course, understandable that in the atmosphere of the sixties, with its emphasis on eliminating the most overt and scandalous and offensive aspects of racial discrimination, the importance of those aspects may have been exaggerated. But it is, I think, to the credit of those administrations that they perceived elimination of overt discrimination as a necessary but not sufficient factor in creating the just and equal and color-blind society that this country has always claimed and aspired to be. Although it didn't seem so at the time, I believe that, comparatively, what we did was a piece of cake. To LBJ's great credit, his Great Society didn't rest on so formal a base. It may have floundered on the costs and the destruction and the disruption and argument of Vietnam, but it always contemplated equality in far more realistic than formal terms.

To speak of equal opportunity for black youths of central cities and white youths of suburbs is only an exercise in cynicism. The commissions of the sixties were focused on the solution of problems of racial inequality in a particular context, both understandably and probably rightly so. Racial prejudice across this country bears it. It would, I submit, be enormously difficult to solve the problems created by a changing society, even if we had no problems of race whatsoever. I think it's that additional burden that has caused us so often to flounder and equivocate.

In all countries, the pace and content of technological progress give shape and direction to where people live and where people work, to urban development in cities, towns, villages. The smokestack economy of the late nineteenth and early twentieth centuries concentrated on jobs, especially entry-level jobs, in large urban centers. We can see that happening elsewhere in the world today. These were centers of commerce and industry, located on oceans, seaports, rivers, canals, railroads. It was to these cities that the immigrants from Europe flocked; it was these cities that attracted surplus farm labor; it was these cities that attracted unskilled blacks from the rural South. Some cities have much in common; all cities have important differences. It's hard to avoid too much generalization, but it can be terribly misleading. I am aware of that, and indeed I insist that there must be different solutions in different places. There isn't a simple answer. And the fact that there isn't a simple answer greatly complicates the search for political resolution, because of the structure of our political system in this country.

Some of our current problems have become worse because we have not fully appreciated that uniform solutions can help in some cases and hurt in others. As we have moved and continue to move from the smokestack to the service economy, what had to be geographically concentrated for sound economic reasons has now become increasingly deconcentrated, also for sound economic reasons. Technology and its diversification have made concentration no longer necessary, nor even desirable. The automobile, the airplane, the computer, telecommunications, automation, the portability of technology—all contribute to forms and levels of deconcentration.

Even where concentration continues to have benefits—perhaps financial centers with access to money markets, access to record information, access to expensive lawyers and deal makers—is a far different kind of concentration than the smokestack economy of the past. No entry-level jobs these. The entry-level jobs that do exist—the messengers, the fast food establishments, the taxi drivers—are fewer in number and increasingly dead end. And, worse than that, they emphasize inequality and tend to perpetuate it.

Jobs have in many cities, particularly in the Northeast and the Midwest, moved to the suburbs. While deconcentration proceeds at different rates in different places, we find the highest-paid, highest-skilled jobs tending to move out. We also find the bulk of entry-level jobs moving out along with them. What industrial activity remains today is increasingly located away from central cities: retail trade in the shopping centers in the suburbs, corporate headquarters daily moving to office parks in bedroom areas.

I mention what is probably obvious merely to point out how this development—which has been substantially greater and faster paced since 1968 than before and faster paced, I think, than we contemplated—has greatly complicated both our urban and our race problems. Left behind in the cities are the poor, the unemployed, and, in most of our major northern cities, inadequate education, inadequate job opportunities, inadequate housing, increasing homelessness, disease.

Promises of nondiscrimination sound hollow. They are hollow when the fundamental opportunities do not exist. Is it any wonder that such conditions breed violence and crime? Is it any wonder that opportunities to succeed seem better on the nether side of the law? We didn't find that surprising in the sixties, and we shouldn't find it surprising today.

Perhaps law and order can be achieved through more police and more prisons and more courts and more get-tough policies, but all three commissions in the sixties rejected repression, unleavened by realistic hope, as inconsistent with a free society. Nothing that we have learned since suggests to me that they were wrong in that conclusion. Viewed in historical perspective, it becomes increasingly obvious that many of the best-intentioned programs have complicated, perhaps even aggravated, problems of urban change. On the one hand, federal programs totally unrelated conceptually to race have encouraged, even made possible, moves to the suburbs and beyond: rural electrification, highways, mass transportation, aid to higher education, even water purification and environmental programs, have all served to geographically allocate amenities much more evenly and have permitted us to run away from other problems. On the other hand, other well-intentioned programs—subsidized housing and welfare programs, as they have been conceived and administered—have too often served as handcuffs, tying the urban poor, primarily blacks, to their ghettos.

It is, after all, important to remember that residence is the most important determinant of access to education and access to jobs. As I said, I do not believe that in the sixties the pace of change was fully appreciated, and I am certain that the consequences of many programs conceived with the best of intentions were not foreseen. It is a political fact that moving jobs to people has always been more popular than moving people to jobs, at least when the people are black and poor. Creating better housing and rebuilding cities through urban renewal programs have had occasional success, but they do not always serve, as one would hope, as seeds for future development. Indeed, private renewal in many instances has served to displace renters and may simply worsen polarization. Gentrification certainly helps the gentry. And the city? Yes, more income for the city. It does precious little for the urban poor. I do not oppose it. It's a limited process, which may, as one scholar has suggested, create "islands of renewal in seas of decay."

I hope, therefore, that we are prepared to face and accept the fact that our urban problems and their resolution are inextricably tied up with problems of race. And, unhappily, that is a very important political fact that whites are too reluctant to face and blacks too eager to exploit. I begin with the pragmatic premise, as I said, that there will be and should be different solutions in different places. A workable strategy, it seems to me, has to be geared to a host of local considerations, which may vary, and such a strategy needs local input and ultimately needs local support.

Federal standards consistently applied across the board are not going to work. Federal subsidies may promote, but they can not provide, local leadership. And a federally financed program, such as urban renewal, may work reasonably well in some circumstances and perpetuate problems in others.

Of course, federal money is needed and so is federal leadership, at an inspirational and purposeful level. But the solution of the nitty-gritty problems is going to depend on local leadership, both public and private. And I emphasize the private. Multiple suburban governments are rarely, I might say, the source of imaginative and courageous programs. You have to work for solutions, and that calls today for a peace negotiation that is probably more complicated than that of Mr. Reagan and Mr. Gorbachev in the Cold War.

Suburban governments have long been insensitive—perhaps hostile is a better word—to urban problems and to the welfare of metropolitan areas as a whole. Take the single most important example, residential housing. The restrictions that exist, however nondiscriminatorily applied, have far more to do with concentrating minorities in central cities than do the objective forces of change in technology and the economy. The fact that suburbanization has nothing to do with race is proven by the ability of middle-class blacks to join the barbecue society. The fact that it has everything to do with race is proven by the barriers to low-cost housing.

Racial prejudice? It's easy to perceive it as such. Blacks often do. But what seems racial hypocrisy at best may simply be concern about other matters, about the value of what is probably the biggest investment most Americans ever make, their home. Many who have fled the city, with its problems, perceive the move as a migration greatly affected by race. They see, rightly or wrongly, their savings, their modest success, the schooling of their children going to hell in a hand basket as the poor, mostly black, invade. And I think they feel helpless in their own way just as blacks feel helpless in theirs. Those are powerful emotions that can only be dealt with by an understanding born of political leadership at the local and, of course, the national levels. I sense the shortage of both in terms of vision and commitment.

I wonder if I dare quote in these times the Pledge of Allegiance: "One nation under God, indivisible, with liberty and justice for all." People in the suburbs are willing, though reluctant, to subsidize the urban poor through state and federal taxes for welfare programs, but what they seemingly oppose—and what we must overcome if we are to achieve anything—is the coherent metropolitan plan for housing and education, which truly eliminates race as a factor.

We have a long way to go politically. Oddly enough today, one obstacle, though perhaps not yet a serious one, may be the political perspective of the increasing number of black urban mayors and council members, so interested, understandably, in solving their own budgets. I do not for a minute blink at the political difficulties of this task. To point to federal budget deficits is in my view a cop out, an unwillingness to face squarely the fact that poverty and race are, like it or not, unhappy though it may be, intimately connected. In the 1960s, under the leadership of President Johnson, we at least made an effort to face that problem squarely and honestly, but, distracted by Vietnam, then by Watergate, by space, the Cold War, and faced with the intractable nature of prejudice, we have, I submit, turned our backs on the future, our future, all of our futures.

The Kerner Commission sought three possible outcomes, or strategies, with respect to the problem of separate and unequal societies. It urged the strategy of racial integration in metropolitan areas, coupled with federal spending to encourage both integration and enrichment of city life. It feared—it warned against—the strategy of continued segregation and poverty that would result from a do-nothing policy. In between, perhaps the middle course, its members saw the possibility of some federal enrichment but no significant integration.

I believe that we followed the middle course in the 1970s and discovered that it was not working very well in most places and that it was expensive. If the suburbs continued to be treated as separate, unrelated entities that, in effect, segregated housing and segregated schools, it could not be expected to work. And given the failure of that middle course, our response in the eighties has been to do exactly what the Kerner Commission feared it would be—continued segregation and continued poverty—and what a tragedy!

Let me conclude on this note. If this country doesn't face up to its urban and race problems by genuinely integrating this society, we will, in the not-too-distant future, lose our leadership in the world. We cannot afford the waste or the divisiveness of racially separated societies. As our economy moves further and further into high-tech service, we need an educated citizenry. This is not a radical idea.

If we cannot achieve it—and we cannot without meeting the residential and educational problems head-on—then either we will fill those jobs with immigrants from Europe or Asia or Latin America or we will export those jobs to other countries. What we must do, therefore, is concentrate in particular on our young people, because they are the future, all of them.

Discussion

Aramia Garcia, IBM: I have a concern about the responsibility that corporate America has toward the inner cities. Corporations are asking for special rates for utilities and causing the inner city to become poorer while they live in the outskirts and only come to town to use the golf course. I would appreciate your comments.

N. Katzenbach: Well, I think that corporations do have a responsibility in that regard, but I do not think that anybody is telling them what they should do, why they should do it, and how to fulfill that responsibility. It seems to me that it's not sufficient for the mayor to say, "Don't leave town," and then offer a lot of economic subsidies to prevent them from leaving town. It's not really sufficient unless you are working on some kind of policy, some kind of plan that incorporates that.

In New York there was a great success in Bedford-Stuyvesant—a lot of money was put into that community, and a lot of talent was put into it, and it worked reasonably well. Whether that can be replicated, whether that is a broader solution or just a solution to a small segment of Bedford-Stuyvesant, I do not know.

I think if you want to harness the power of corporations in terms of their jobs, in terms of what they are doing, you have to do it in the context of a plan that addresses the area you are dealing with. If you do not, I think corporations are going to see their policies as more narrowly confined to taking care of their existing employees and providing benefits to them and so forth, which is not an unreasonable position.

Mary de Ferrier, Hispanic Women's Network of Texas: Your speech particularly discussed the biracial issues of blacks and whites and their problems. With your background, this is the expertise that you have. However, in Texas, with our Hispanic community predicted to be the largest minority group not only in the state but also in the country, we deal with the same kinds of problems—the social issues of poverty and lack of education. How should the next president of the United States change the infrastructure of the educational system in this country to improve benefits for all children?

N. Katzenbach: I could not be more dedicated to efforts to provide decent education for all children, because the child who becomes an adult without a decent education is going to be expensive to this society for the rest of his life, and he is living longer and longer.

You are not going to exist as a contributing citizen of this country unless you get education. I cannot think of anything that is more important for the government—all governments—to attempt to achieve. The problem is that to achieve such an education is going to take more than just improving the educational system. I do not think you can look at education apart from residences, houses, homes, homelessness, where people live, who they associate with, and so forth. I think it is all part of that problem. You can just pour money into a school system that exists in a sea of decay and hopelessness and still not get a very good school system. You have to deal with the problem in a broader way.

If I were to select one focus of attention, it would be the young people and schools, thinking back, that tell us a little bit about LBJ's convictions. It was the work that he did as a young person with Mexican Americans that gave him that perception of how important education was and how important nondiscrimination was throughout his lifetime.

Henrietta Jacobson, City of West Lake Hills, Texas: You mentioned the need for different solutions for different kinds of cities, and I wonder if you could give some examples of what you had in mind and whether you envision enabling legislation at the federal level to achieve that flexibility.

N. Katzenbach: The reason I say different needs in different cities is that I think cities in the West and Southwest have problems that are easier to resolve than the problems faced by the far-older cities of the East Coast, the Northeast, and the Upper Middle West. These problems are far more difficult to resolve. You could do more rehabilitation in cities in the West and Southwest than in the Northeast where the exodus has gone as far as it has. The area from Washington, D.C., to Boston, Massachusetts, is really one city, but it is divided up in different ways.

The other point that I would make is that there must be leadership in the federal government, because you might get leadership to resolve problems in some state governments and none in others. I would like to see a federal government that plans on a regional basis, that looks at what might be done within some reasonably defined region, proposes that plan, and then finances the plan within the region as well as with federal assistance. Involve the local governments, the local citizenry. Ask them to tell us what's wrong in their area and focus attention on the problems. You will not get local political leadership unless you have some federal or state leadership.

From the floor: One of the ironies of history, if you will, is that, although Lyndon Johnson understood Mexican Americans and developed an understanding about poverty out of the Mexican American experience, in his administration the 1965 Voting Rights Act was not extended to the Southwest. Instead, enforcement of voting rights focused primarily on the black population in the South. It was not until 1975 that the government began to address southwestern issues and issues of the Latino population of the United States.

In many ways your comments suggested a black/white perspective. Are Latino issues similar to or different from black issues in American society? If they are different, how would you suggest one approach them? If they are not different, why would you think that?

N. Katzenbach: There are a great many similarities in problems. The only difference—and it may be a significant difference—is that, historically, language has been less of a barrier in this country than color has been, and there are numerous reasons in our history for that. Other than that, I think the problems—and probably almost all of the solutions—are the same. If you could solve the black/white problem, you could solve the other problems. I think race is a more difficult issue.

Let me defend the coverage of the acts passed under LBJ. The problem was not to allow the 1964 Civil Rights Acts and 1965 Voting Rights Acts to be overloaded in ways that were going to hurt politically. The effort was to focus on the most important issues. I will never forget the marvelous congresswoman from the state of Washington who led the struggle for equal jobs for women throughout her career. When it came to the employment part of the 1964 Act, she did not put the employment amendment in, because she felt that blacks had a bigger problem, and she did not want to overburden the bill. The amendment was, in fact, put in by Judge Smith of Virginia, who also miscalculated the situation. I think the reason that we did not do more was not for lack of comprehension of the problem. It was a political decision to see if we could get a foot in the door and have the votes to pass. That was landmark legislation.

Sherry Sylvester, Eisenhower Foundation: I was impressed with your reiterating the conclusions of the commissions that repression will not work in dealing with many of the inner-city problems. But if you look at the proposals of candidates Dukakis and Bush to deal with the problems of drugs in the inner city, which are major problems there, you find that programs of repression are the options presented on both sides. I wonder if you could suggest a more progressive direction that we might go in dealing with drug problems.

N. Katzenbach: Well, I have no quick solution to the drug problem, and I am not running for office, so I am more able to say that repression will not work. I think you can couple tough law enforcement with other ways of giving hope to people, giving opportunity to people. There are private programs that have worked a little for a few people in various areas, but I think you will resolve the drug problem when you have created two things: opportunities for jobs, on the one hand, and hopefulness for people, on the other. Drugs today are the escape mechanism for those who are using them. The ability to be a success if you deal in drugs is also an escape. You make money; it's easy, and it's corrupting.

Diego Vigil, University of Wisconsin, Madison: Today you regularly see news about gangs in the urban areas. During the 1960s I was involved in the Great Society programs in Los Angeles and worked in the teen posts. They were widespread throughout the Los Angeles area. I know for a fact that part of the Great Society program was working. There was less gang violence then. There was also an accompanying program with the teen posts known as NYC, Neighborhood Youth Corps, that provided jobs and other outlets for the youths in those barrios and ghettos of Los Angeles.

Which of the Great Society programs would you say would work today if the incentive and resources were put behind them?

N. Katzenbach: One of the most successful programs that we ever had in this country was Head Start. An important component of the Great Society initiatives that you mentioned was a willingness of people to get in and work with those programs. A program is going to work if the people who are its beneficiaries, the recipients of it, feel that there are other people out there who care and who are devoting energy and talent to try to help them.

It is terribly important to have both public and private programs. I get very depressed when I see the best of our young people, the brightest of our young people, seeing how many billions of dollars of stock they can buy and sell in the course of a day, and how much money they can make. It seems to me that we have encouraged enormously a give-me generation. There were satisfactions in the Peace Corps and satisfactions in the Job Corps that went well beyond what those programs accomplished in terms of public attitudes. Those programs are important.

Joan Moore, University of Wisconsin, Milwaukee: You have given a great deal of thought to this issue of regional areas and the nature of cities and suburbs. From a legal perspective and from a legislative perspective, what could the federal government do to improve conditions in the cities? Leadership at the federal level can provide moral direction. At a more pragmatic and instrumental level, what might be implemented if there were a federal will toward overcoming the problems of the cities? If the federal government were to focus on cities versus suburbs or central cities versus metropolitan outer-ring areas?

N. Katzenbach: The problem is difficult because we have a crazy political system in terms of municipalities, townships, counties, states, and then the federal government. It is difficult to do anything on a regional basis. In some areas you can run airports on a regional basis and toll bridges, but that's darn near all. They make money. That is the primary reason you can do that—because they make money. You have to have the federal government involved, and the only incentive that I can see is dollars, and money makes it an enormous political problem.

As soon as the federal government gets into the decision-making process and starts saying, "Here is what we ought to do within the region," you have people who are not from the region, not locally involved, who may or may not know regional needs. Or you get people from the locality who do know regional needs, but each has his or her own particular ax to grind and therefore, may not look at the bigger picture. The decisions become political problems one must deal with. It takes an enormous amount of leadership. I would like to see involvement by the federal government; I would like to see federal initiative taken within two or three areas with a lot of money in those areas and see what happens. However, selecting the areas is difficult.

Evelyn Hu-Dehart, University of Colorado, Boulder: I was born and raised in China, and I came to this country around the time that President Johnson come into office. Professionally, I am a Latin Americanist, so I have also lived and worked in many different countries in Latin America. Much of what you said, and much of what has been coming out in the press about recent census and economic and income analyses, gives me a sinking feeling that we are experiencing something called underdevelopment in this country; that the United States of America, at least certain parts of it, such as the big cities, are resembling what we call Third World cities and Third World countries.

What I am concerned about is whether we are entering an era in this country in which we are going to see a population that is dispensable and disposable and that no amount of tinkering with what we have in place in our structure, no amount of public policy reforms, is necessarily going to change that situation. I am concerned that we are actually perpetrating some kind of cruel hoax by suggesting that educational reforms will change the conditions in our cities that you described so well. I have been a college professor for twenty years, and I am dealing with these issues, but sometimes I wonder if I am not being entirely honest when we suggest that the solution lies in public policy or other kinds of reforms. We ought to address—and this is the difficult thing—more-profound solutions and engage ourselves in these solutions.

N. Katzenbach: I agree that there is the danger that you point out and that we may be creating the kind of society that you describe. That is what the Kerner Commission was concerned about. If we let that happen, God knows what effect it is going to have on the politics, values, and future of this country.

I am less pessimistic than you about programs' working, but they may not work. I am not a pessimist. I have only taught ten years, so I have ten more years to go before I get that pessimistic. Programs may not work, but you have to try. You have to do the best you can do, because we have many other values in our society: values of freedom and liberty and choice, which fundamentally depend on a reasonably affluent society. If we do not do something about solving the problems of poverty and the problems in our cities, we will in fact become more repressive; we will, in fact, change the politics of this country. I do not want to see that happen, but I think there is a real danger. Nobody thought we could get a Civil Rights Act in 1964. We got it. You can make this political system work, but it takes a lot of oil to do it.

Maria Garza-Lubeck, IUP/SSRC Postdoctoral Fellow: I would like to ask you a question that many groups that profess to be interested in the education of minority children, educational opportunity, and economic development continue to ignore or fail to bring to the forefront.

I take issue with your earlier statement that language is not as much an issue as race. I have been in schools in Texas and elsewhere, and I have seen elementary children and secondary children punished for speaking Spanish in school. Can you give us some idea as to why this English-only movement has grown, and why people that profess to be interested in all of the issues that I raised earlier are not at the forefront saying, "We need bilingual education for these children"? We know from common sense that children learn better if they are guided from what they know to what they do not know. Language issues represent an enormous problem that is not being given the attention that it should be given by educators and other public policy people.

N. Katzenbach: I would say two things: If I were in your position, I would take issue with my statement, too. But I do not take issue with it. You have an interest, and you are right to emphasize the discrimination that comes with respect to language. I do not know why the English-only movement has grown or what the force behind that movement is—I guess only English is spoken in the suburbs.

TOP (Left to right): *Arturo Madrid,*
Gary Orfield. RIGHT (Left to right):
Guadalupe Valdés, Rafael Valdivieso

PART II

Education and Employment Practices

Introduction
Arturo Madrid

Unrealistic Rhetoric and Realistic Reform in Education:
A Critical Perspective
Guadalupe Valdés

Closing the Gap for Young Latino and Black Families:
An Urban Education and Training Agenda
Rafael Valdivieso

Policy Analysis
Gary Orfield

Discussion

PART II

Introduction

Arturo Madrid: The media have publicized the 1980s as the decade of the Hispanic, but there has been considerable disappointment in that decade. Certainly it has been the decade of Hispanics if the decade is seen as a period in which Hispanics ceased being an invisible population in America and entered the consciousness of the leaders of American society. Nonetheless, this has not occurred for all Hispanics and has not occurred to the same degree for all Hispanics. If the decade is seen in terms of issues that have historically been dealt with as private problems—such as low income, poverty, homelessness—and are now seen as public issues, then certainly it has been the decade of Hispanics. What is clearly lacking, however, is an understanding of the needs, the status, and the concerns of the Hispanic population. This conference is an important step forward in that regard.

Guadalupe Valdés, our first panelist, comes from El Paso, a part of the United States settled before Plymouth Rock. Latinos have been part of the American reality without being part of the American consciousness; we have been part of the American problem without being permitted a voice in the American solution. Guadalupe Valdés has coauthored her paper with Bernard Gifford, dean of the Graduate School of Education at the University of California, Berkeley.

Rafael Valdivieso has historical antecedents in Puerto Rico, which had a historical presence before America was settled but has only recently become part of the American consciousness. Dr. Valdivieso is currently vice president of programs and research for the Hispanic Policy Development Project.

We have asked Gary Orfield to comment on the papers presented. Dr. Orfield is from the University of Chicago and became a hero to Hispanics a few years ago when he took on the United States government and challenged the way the courts were prepared to reconceptualize the status of children and adults of minority background in American public life.

Unrealistic Rhetoric and Realistic Reform in Education: A Critical Perspective

Guadalupe Valdés: Before beginning, I want to say that Bernard Gifford is a black man, and I am a Chicano woman. We struggled to come to solutions that would not place the needs of the black community and the Hispanic community at odds with one another and would encourage both communities to join forces for the kinds of things that we know our children need, whether they are black or brown children.

It has been nearly five and one-half years since the National Commission on Excellence in Education issued its landmark report, *A Nation at Risk: The Imperative for Educational Reform*. In terms of specific policy recommendations, the report was unremarkable, calling for reforms in five distinct areas. If the commission did not manage to distinguish itself through the formulation and presentation of a collection of recommendations for educational change and reform, it did manage to differentiate its effort from the efforts of other study groups that had covered the same policy terrain through its style of presentation, mainly by casting its findings and recommendations in blunt and pugnacious language.

As we all know, *A Nation at Risk* was quickly followed by a number of studies and reports elaborating on the themes of crisis and collapse in the nation's public schools. Between April 1983 and mid-1988, no fewer than one hundred blue-ribbon governmental study commissions, modeled along the lines of the National Commission on Excellence in Education, had issued their own agendas and recommendations for educational reform.

All in all, we would have to argue that the jury is still out on the enduring impact of *A Nation at Risk* and its progeny. Certainly, in the last five years, the debate over the direction and quality of the nation's schools has been better informed than usual, and it has been spirited and ongoing. For this, *A Nation at Risk* must be given its just credit. More important, this debate has left its mark on the nation's politics. In the 1988 presidential campaign, both candidates vied for the right to be known as the "education president," a contest that would have been unimaginable in 1980 or even in 1984.

Important also are the trends in school reform that can be traced to *A Nation at Risk*. The first and, we would argue, the most dominant trend to have emerged in the wake of the report is what we will call the trend toward quality standards and performance accountability. This trend is clearly reflective of a view that educational reform is impossible absent the articulation of a consistent set of performance expectations applicable to all students and the imposition of a consistent set of student performance indicators applicable in every school setting.

The second trend to emerge is not so much a trend as it is a logical outcome of the first. Strongly influenced by the report's ominous predictions of national economic and social disaster, nearly all the commissions, panels, task forces, and study groups that issued reports in the immediate wake of *A Nation at Risk* called upon governors and state legislatures to impose those reforms on local school systems from the top down and, moreover, to hold tightly onto the reins of accountability.

Implicit in trend two is the view that reform is likely to be thwarted absent policy and administrative imposition force-fed to the educational establishment by strong and determined executive leadership. This view is based on the assumption that schools have lost their capacity for self-analysis, self-evaluation, and self-correction of widely recognized faults.

Of course, one problem with trend two, a form of policy absolutism, is that its successful application to the real world is dependent on there being a widely held consensus within the three distinct worlds of policy, administration, and practice on what specific steps need to be taken in order to improve the quality of education in schools. Of course, as we have already implied, the real world of school districts and schools does not respond in such a straightforward fashion to external pressures for reform. This gap between public pronouncement and public debate about how change should take place and the reality of everyday life in real schools is not at all difficult to understand.

This reality, then, has in turn led to a reaction to reformist assumptions of a different type. Following the initial surge of approval for the policy prospectus presented in *A Nation at Risk,* with its implied acceptance of the Top Down Three-Cycle model of school change, many would-be school reformers have had to confront the possibility that the Top Down Three-Cycle model might not be the best way to generate policies that stand a chance of producing enduring reform and change in the schools. One result of the second look at the policy prescriptions presented in *A Nation at Risk* is that some new trends in school reform have begun to emerge, which we will label "second-stage trends in school reform."

One of the second-stage trends that we feel warrants a thorough review, because of its potential for significantly improving everyday educational practices at the classroom level, is the new and radical analysis of the nature and structure of the teaching occupation. Suggested reforms in this area place great emphasis on the need for radical changes in the nature of the teaching occupation, far beyond the routine cosmetic changes called for in *A Nation at Risk*.

Another second-stage trend that has begun to emerge with increasing frequency is the growing emphasis on the unique educational requirements of students of population groups whose needs are sufficiently distinct to require policymakers to give serious consideration to formulating specific targeted educational policies designed to address these needs. In particular, within the last three years, an increasing amount of attention is being focused on the necessity for education reform efforts to take into account the special needs of students who do not fit the standard student model undergirding the rationale behind the policy prescriptions imbedded in *A Nation at Risk*.

The topic we have been asked to address argues implicitly for approaches that have emerged in the second stage of school reform. These approaches direct attention not to the larger processes of educational policymaking as a whole but rather to the formulation of specific educational policies designed to address the unique educational needs encountered in large city school systems by minority and poor youngsters. Putting things plainly, our concern is not with grand policymaking schemes but with the particular needs of children who are poor, who are a minority, who live in the big cities, and who, if educational policies continue to be developed in the future in the same manner as they have been in the past, are likely to end up labeled as educational failures.

Consistent with the views of the policymaking process we have presented, we will argue that general educational policy proposals, built on the assumption that all students have the same educational needs and that all educational policies are equally effective for all students, have the effect of ignoring the pressing educational needs of the big city school systems. In an attempt to focus on the specific problems encountered in urban schools, we propose the implementation of a targeted school improvement plan and policies that would support the targeted school improvement plan. This school improvement plan would be designed to bring about change in inner-city schools, and it would be implemented across the country in major urban centers. While generally guided by certain organizing principles, each urban school district, in conjunction with state-level agencies, would have discretion in the exact design of particular programs.

Essentially, the targeted school improvement plan would address the following major components: (1) the school structure, (2) the core curriculum, (3) language and literacy, (4) teacher empowerment, (5) effective principals, (6) the recruitment of teachers and principals, (7) parent involvement, (8) school and university collaboration, and (9) an educational opportunity evaluation. In order to decide which schools would be targeted for this improvement, we would use three indices.

They would be first, an index of social and economic distress, which would be measured by the percentage of school pupils who reside in neighborhoods where the rates of youth crime, youth unemployment, school dropout, teenage pregnancy, infant mortality, welfare dependency, housing abandonment, and other indicators of social and economic distress are well above the normal average for the entire city. The second index used in choosing such schools would be reading underachievement or lack of achievement measured by the percentage of school pupils who score in the bottom quartile of the reading test. The third index would be linguistic complexity, which would be measured by the percentage of school pupils who have limited proficiency in English (LEP). Schools with a significant percentage of LEP pupils would have great educational need. The targeted school improvement plan itself is described as follows:

Component 1. The School Structure
The plan would entail changes in the structure of the racially impacted schools with high numbers of students at risk. Structural changes are needed to foster the quality of teacher-student interactions so that classroom learning environments are conducive to student academic achievement, especially in the form of the early acquisition and continued development of language and literacy skills. The improvement plan would include school restructuring so as to improve the quality of classroom instruction and of the school learning environment, especially in the area of language and literacy.

Six categories for restructuring are recommended:

1. First, new early-childhood education programs should be instituted at each of the target elementary schools. Restructuring emphasizes that these early-childhood educational programs exercise experience-based activities, parent involvement, and low student-teacher ratios.

2. New and expanded counseling and guidance programs should be instituted in each of the target elementary schools. These programs would be staffed by counseling and guidance specialists, paraprofessionals, select high school students, and volunteers, all of whom would be specially trained to work effectively with students at risk.

3. Remedial curriculum libraries should be established at each target elementary school.

4. Each target elementary school would have an after-school program staffed by trained volunteers, including parents, paid personnel, and carefully selected and trained high school students. The volunteers and paid staff should provide language and literacy tutoring enrichment activities to children on a one-to-one basis.

5. At target middle schools and secondary schools, the school day would be restructured to include extended blocks of time (as opposed to periods less than one hour long) in order to promote intensive, high-quality instruction in language and literacy.

6. At all target elementary, middle, and secondary schools, reductions in class size would be made. Reductions in class size should be differentiated by school and by grade level, depending upon the particular language and literacy needs of the students and the instructional resources available to the school.

Component 2. The Core Curriculum
The targeted school improvement program plan would call for the review of the core curriculum and for the development of a new curriculum based upon the results of that review. Special attention would be paid to language and literacy at all levels of schooling.

Component 3. Language and Literacy Mobilization
In all of its components, the improvement plan would concentrate the forces of school districts and state departments of education on the students' early acquisition and continuous development of language and literacy skills. Language and literacy skills are requisite to all other types of learning. They are the enabling skills. They enable communication, learning, and thinking in many subject areas.

Component 4. Teacher Empowerment
The plan would offer new programs of preservice and in-service teacher training. These programs would be designed to empower teachers to recognize and develop their skills, knowledge, and abilities as professionals responsible for the schooling of students from diverse racial, ethnic, linguistic, and economic backgrounds and educational needs.

Component 5. Effective Principals
An effective principal is the key to effective education in every school. Without principals who have the time and the ability to provide instructional leadership and who are willing to take risks, to learn, and to make changes, the school improvement plan will ultimately fail. Simply calling upon principals to report compliance with the plan will result in the continuation of the educational status quo. To facilitate effective school leadership by principals, the targeted school improvement plan would call for an increase in the administrative staffing of targeted schools and for the creation of a form of leadership that would be drawn from the principals of these schools.

Component 6. Recruitment of Teachers and Principals

The plan would call for the development of a coordinated and systematic effort to recruit teachers and principals who have records of effectiveness in working with students from diverse backgrounds or who demonstrate promise of establishing such records of excellence in the targeted schools.

Component 7. Parent Involvement

The importance of parent participation in educational activities to children's learning is undisputed. The improvement plan would call for the coordinated and systematic strengthening and renewal of efforts from all parents in the education of children attending the target schools. We strongly believe that the improvement plan should call for close communication between the teachers and principals of target schools and the parents of the children attending such schools. A parent involvement class should be developed, implemented, and assessed by each target school. School plans may include the following elements:

1. The scheduling of teacher-parent-counselor meetings during the evening with child care provided.

2. The establishment of a hot line with bilingual staff for parents who seek assistance in helping their children with homework.

3. The design of learning activities for parents and children to do at home together.

4. The development of family learning centers.

Component 8. School-University Collaboration

The targeted school improvement plan would call for the coordination of educational improvement and reform efforts with community services. In addition to the beneficial effects on learning, the coordinated delivery of educational and community services would result in efficiency payoffs to taxpayers.

Component 9. Educational Opportunity Evaluation

The plan would include close attention to the monitoring and analysis of the implementation and outcomes of the educational improvement and reform efforts over a five-to-seven-year period. Specifically, we recommend that a two-part evaluation study be conducted. One part of the evaluation should consist of an ethnographic study, and one part should consist of a quantitative study. When the five-to-seven-year period comes to a close, the evaluation results should be used to determine which aspects of the plan should be incorporated permanently into the programs of school districts.

Traditionally, school improvement evaluations have been quantitative in nature, with student test scores at the center of analysis. However, standardized tests, even at their best, are fallible and only partial indicators of academic achievement. Additionally, they are not at all able to provide information about higher-order thinking, creativity, effort, persistence in the face of adversity, commitment to justice, concern for the common good, or any of the other human qualities that our society values and that the improvement plan would attempt to promote. Nor are standardized tests suitable instruments for identifying the ambiguities, unacknowledged contradictions, and conflicts involved in every major educational change effort.

Clearly, the purpose in focusing on the improvement plan is to suggest that, in order to address the needs of inner-city children in the 1990s, we must make certain that our policies are not merely unrealistic rhetoric, but that they are developed and articulated in such a way that true reform in education can take place.

Closing the Gap for Young Latino and Black Families: An Urban Education and Training Agenda

Rafael Valdivieso: The problems of education for urban minorities cannot be exaggerated. The legacy of unresponsive politicians, entrenched interest groups, and a separate and, in many ways, unequal education is reflected in the relative powerlessness of minority communities in cities throughout the country. The schooling of children has been made difficult by the ills of urban poverty, depressed neighborhoods, stifling bureaucracies, and demoralized teachers.

When one speaks of public education, particularly public urban education, one is speaking of the education of minorities. The majority of the minority populations in the United States are located in metropolitan areas: overwhelmingly, the majority population of urban areas and particularly urban public school districts are minorities. While the education problems persist, there is change on the political landscape in these cities. In many cities we now have black and Latino mayors and elected officials. In fact, in a city today, most politicians, whether minority or Anglo, cannot be elected without minority votes. Moreover, there is change afoot among school systems. Many are now administered by black and Latino personnel. Many school systems are undergoing radical restructuring, both on the school system level and on the local school or school building level. However, there are no easy solutions, and it is going to take some time to solve the problems that have taken a long time to come about.

My primary focus is on about one and a half million Latino and black young adults, eighteen- to twenty-four-year-olds, who have not completed high school and also the faction of those who did complete high school but were poorly prepared, as well as about a million and a quarter children under the age of six. Of particular interest is the group of students who graduated from high school in 1982 or who were dropouts from that group. Why this focus? The intent is to determine what happened to those individuals over the subsequent four years. This perspective will provide a sense of the depth of these problems in terms of the undereducation of young minorities in our cities. These groups live in poverty, and these young adults are raising these children. Thus, my proposal is that the next administration take a two-generation approach of short-term interventions and long-term prevention programs.

Four years after the scheduled graduation date in 1982, we find that, among the blacks, about one-third of the female graduates who were A and B students are now mothers, about one-half of those who were C and D students now have children, and almost two-thirds of the dropouts are mothers with young children. For young black adults in this cohort, the greatest problem is the number of unwed mothers. This problem is not just one affecting dropouts; it is also pervasive among those young black women who made good grades in school. In fact, pregnancy rates among this age group are sufficiently high to assume that this condition must have affected the college-going rate of blacks, which has declined during the last six to eight years. That is how pervasive the problem is.

For the Latinas, we find that 18 percent of those who graduated with an A and B student record are now mothers. Forty-one percent of the Latina graduates who were C and D students are now mothers, and a staggering 71 percent of the Latina dropouts are now mothers with young children. For the Latina population, the high birth rates are masked by their high rates of marriage, although there are also high rates of divorce.

The surprising and alarming information presented by these statistics is that in this country we now have more Latino children with mothers who are dropouts than Latino children with mothers who are high school graduates. Overall, more Latina dropouts than black dropouts have children. In fact, among sixteen- to twenty-four-year-olds in 1987, there were 263,000 Latina dropouts with children compared to 247,000 black female dropouts with children.

When one considers the economic and social predicament of black and Hispanic females, combined with the pervasiveness of school dropouts among Latinas and the sharp declines in wages of young people, it is understandable why there is such a devastating amount of poverty among young adults and children in this country.

The most recent statistics from 1987 show that the poverty rate for black children who live in households headed by persons under thirty climbed to 61 percent, while the poverty rate for Hispanic children rose to 53.4 percent. In short, of all these black and Latino children, well over half now live in poverty. These figures justify a two-generation approach to policies for dealing with the poverty affecting Latino and black children in urban areas.

To deal with the backbone of the dropout problem in this country, we must reach young parents, particularly young mothers, through programs that serve their children. This approach would entail a community-based effort and ideally would comprise education and training for the young adults, preschool and child care for their children, and affordable housing and social services for the whole family. These comprehensive services would be delivered by community-based organizations and public institutions, such as community colleges, in partnership with the private sector. In addition, supporting funds would come from all levels of the government. Federal education training initiatives are only a part of this solution. Most of these initiatives are not new but are enhancements of existing legislation and programs. Funding for comprehensive service programs would assist low-income people in general in this country. However, if Congress could pass a focused program of comprehensive service for urban minorities—if that were politically feasible— the price tag would be smaller.

The following components would provide the bases for a two-generation approach:

The Job Training Partnership Act (JTPA)
In the JTPA there are two specific initiatives. One would be to increase and add intensive training slots for unskilled young adults over twenty-one years of age, who form the largest pool of dropouts. Geographic areas with chronically unemployed people as well as high dropout rates would be targeted. The emphasis would be on intensive investments in the skills of individuals least likely to succeed on their own.

The other part of the JTPA would be to increase the training for youth in general. That is, increase training programs for those young people who qualify under Title II(A). In this initiative, funds would be directed toward the youth with the most severe deficits rather than those who are the easiest to employ. Another component would be to expand the Job Corps to provide a number of additional positions in this program.

Welfare Reform
New legislation directing welfare reform will be family oriented in terms of family support. States are required to establish education, training, and child-care provisions for welfare recipients. Under such require-

ments, mothers and children in a two-generation approach can be trained at the same time, in the same programs.

Jobs for Employable Dependent Individuals (JEDI)

JEDI would target for job training those youth most likely to become long-term welfare recipients, such as unmarried teenage mothers or those over 21 who have been on welfare more than two years. This bill would enhance the use of job-training funds. Trainers would be awarded a bonus for each year, up to three years, that a trainee remains working, and the bonus would increase the longer the person stayed on a job.

Head Start and Other School-Based Programs

In a two-generation approach, support for Head Start would be doubled to include the parent and child in learning activities. Numerous studies and evaluations have documented the benefits of preschool education. However, one must not confuse preschool education with the need that many parents have today for child care. These are two separate programs, both important for encouraging better job skills and work opportunities for young, poor families.

Other two-generation initiatives could be designed for elementary- and secondary-level students as well as postsecondary students. One is an expansion of Title One, or Chapter One, of the Elementary and Secondary School Improvement Amendments of 1988. A very interesting provision in the Chapter One legislation for new money is that, if 75 percent of a school's enrollment is under the poverty level, the school can receive money as general aid and use the money any way it chooses as long as its test scores remain elevated. There is also a provision that rewards a school if test scores improve.

This type of legislation—and right now that provision would affect only about 15 percent of the schools—is the kind of funding strategy that cities can expect to see in the nineties, that is, unregulated funds going directly to schools. Funding would be developed categorically in Washington and targeted, but once the funds reached the school level, money could be used as general aid. In this form, federal funds would not be intrusive and would support the restructuring and school-based reforms that are occurring at local and state levels.

Postsecondary Initiatives

TRIO programs (Upward Bound, Talent Search, and Educational Opportunity Centers) counsel, tutor, and reach out to targeted high school students and college-aged disadvantaged individuals. Research demonstrates that those who have participated in such programs in the past are twice as likely to graduate from college as are low-income students who have not participated. To encourage student retention at the post-secondary level, student financial aid should be grant-based aid. Loan-based aid should be reserved for postbaccalaureate college education or professional programs.

Higher Education Act

A new provision in the Higher Education Act allows a program of special child-care services for disadvantaged students. This should be particularly successful in recruiting and retaining the black high school graduates who had good high school records but who also have children.

In conclusion, these initiatives rely on proven programs and do not require experimentation. We can move forward immediately with these proposals. In addition, a number of other programs in vocational education could be more closely linked to a two-generation approach. In any case, the price tag for this package would be about $6 billion a year during the next five years, which is about $30 billion in new monies.

By the turn of the century, one-third of all children and youth in the United States will be minorities. The white population is aging and shrinking in number. In contrast, the minority population is growing. These demographic facts bear repeating over and over. These facts must become a part of our thinking and planning. If we do not begin major education and training initiatives, and if we do not undertake their implementation soon, where will the workers for this nation's future job market come from? Who will support the many dependents of today's young families? Who will support the baby boomers who begin to retire early in the next century? Who will provide the stewardship for our country?

These are very real policy and political issues that we as a nation do not seem to want to face. More than ever, we need national leadership in these matters.

Policy Analysis

Gary Orfield: It is a pleasure to comment on these contributions and to note some of the common themes. Additionally, I will suggest ideas that were not included in these particular presentations.

I think the authors share a common perception: that there is a very serious threat to urban minority children, which is indeed true. Every measure shows that that is true. Furthermore, central-city populations are becoming predominantly minority. If we look at the twenty-five largest school districts in the country, presently they serve 30 percent of the nation's Hispanic children, 27 percent of the black children, and 3 percent of the white children. In other words, the institutions that are crucial for minority children are becoming irrelevant to whites. In some cases, they are becoming irrelevant to middle-class minority children in the suburbs as well. These urban school districts are desperately troubled institutions that have not been helped much with recent public policy.

We have evidence of self-perpetuating and perhaps accelerating social decay. More and more children are growing up poor, and families with single parents or, in too many cases, families with two working parents cannot get above the poverty threshold. Poverty has increased in our society and it is, to some extent, the direct foreseeable consequence of a number of social policies that we have adopted, such as not raising the minimum wage.

We have a deep web of poverty and inequality that is not much affected by general economic growth. Although we are in a period of substantial economic growth after a terrible recession, poor people, particular low-income minority children, have not recovered. The numbers of such children benefiting from the economic growth are few. There is little movement out of poverty that comes from the general fiscal stimulation policy that, classically, both liberals and conservatives have advocated.

Something is occurring that is unique and disconnected from the rest of this society, and it is very serious. This process involves a growing part of our entire population. There is an increasing inability of Latinos and blacks to create and maintain families that can provide the minimum essentials for children. Since 1968 the number of whites in the U.S. public school population has decreased by 16.5 percent, the number of blacks has increased by 20 percent, and the number of Hispanics has more than doubled. We are going through a huge transformation, and our institutions are not producing success for the portion of our population that is growing. That threatens the future of this country. Anybody who thinks about the future has to take these patterns into very serious consideration. The United States is a deeply multiracial society with an increasing self-perpetuating isolationism and inequality.

What ideas have been presented for dealing with these patterns? What are the intellectual bases, factual problems, and advantages of each? Some things are encouraging. Experience has already proven that some things will work, and the problem is that we are just not implementing them. There is good evidence of success for some policies that have been tried in the past and for some that are presently being implemented, although they have been only partially and often not well executed. Head

Start is an example of a program that has been successful. Chapter One has fairly good, although indirect, evidence of positive effects.

Minority students have increased in achievement in basic skills since the late 1960s. In the Job Corps there is strong evidence of positive effects from drastic intervention with highly disadvantaged young people. In other words, quite a few programs are out there, bits and pieces at least, that we know made a difference. Minority access to college soared between the middle 1960s and the middle 1970s, almost reaching equality for a brief year or two in the middle seventies, but minority college access has plummeted since the late 1970s. Financial aid is drastically down. Additionally, weakened civil rights enforcement has had a substantial effect on equality. In policy discussions in the 1980s, there is little discussion about attacking basic racial barriers as part of the policy for opportunity. That is one area that should receive greater attention in policy recommendations.

Gifford and Valdés, describing how we build on an effective school's model of educational improvement, convey a model that is widely shared around the country among educational reformers—community-based educational reform at the school level with participation by the faculty and community, with substantial new resources channeled to schools, smaller class sizes, preschool and after-school programs, summer school, support mechanisms, additional counseling, additional administrators, and more of everything. These are radical experiments in school reform occurring in a few school districts, in Miami Dade County, for example. These are important bases for experiments, but there are major problems in our urban schools that must be considered.

In the situation where central city schools are left virtually all minority and, increasingly, all poor, those schools depend on resources from the state and federal governments. This dependency occurs at a time when city representation, both in the state capitals and in Washington, will decrease after the 1990 census. In these cases the middle-class minority population as well as the white population is increasingly detached from those urban, inner-city institutions. This situation presents serious political problems. Teachers' unions also present institutional problems. In some cases, new teachers cannot be brought into central-city schools in large numbers because of seniority systems. In other cases, because of high turnover rates, urban school districts do not have experienced staffs. Staffs are most unstable in the lower-income, minority schools where the majority of teachers request transfers out. Principals are able to hire better, more qualified teachers in suburban schools than in central-city schools. Planning is based on financial crises in central-city education. There are other institution-wide problems. For example, there have been nine teacher strikes in the last eighteen years in Chicago, an urban school district that serves more than two-thirds of the minority children in the state of Illinois.

In order to think about school-level changes, we must think about the macroforces that affect the whole structure that make these changes possible or impossible. As we broaden our policy agenda, we must think about changes that address problems at the depth of the barriers we are confronting. We must think about broader changes as well as school-level changes. School-level changes beyond one or two schools are very difficult to accomplish without broader changes in terms of resources, organization, and a variety of other things.

What was presented by Valdivieso, in addition to some parallel recommendations for preschool programs, was a number of proposals that relate to a more targeted and intense job-training program. These proposals suggest the opposite direction from that taken when the administration adopted the Job Training Partnership Act in the early 1980s. The 1980s' JTPA emphasizes high placement at low costs. The program, as enacted, encourages selectivity in the pool of trainees and superficial short-term training. The objective is to get the trainees out some place so they become an employment statistic. A recent report shows that half of the people who are placed through JTPA are gone from those jobs in just thirteen weeks and that there is decreasing access by minorities to those training programs.

The Job Corps, which is perhaps the only program that demonstrates strong evidence of positive long-term effect, is very expensive and has been attacked repeatedly because of its expense. This program, however, works and should be expanded.

We need renewed college-access programs. We have almost entirely lost the progress made between the middle sixties and seventies toward closing the college-access gap between minority poor and white middle-class and well-to-do students. We have almost returned to where we were before the Great Society programs. This represents a tremendous crisis in a society where the rewards for college education are growing very rapidly, and the number of jobs that can support a family and do not demand a college education are shrinking as quickly.

When we are thinking about policy—and as a political scientist I like to think about policy—we should first think about undoing the damage that has been done. That is clear. That should be the first stage in the policy agenda.

The JTPA was misguided reform in terms of access for disadvantaged minority youth. There is no question about that. JTPA encourages behavior in job-training systems that is exactly the opposite of what has proven to be most beneficial. A priority should be to expand the Job Corps and change the incentives from quick placement to long-term success in the job-training system. Current federal aid for higher education covers a much smaller percentage of college-going costs than it did in 1980, and colleges across the country are responding to the lack of federal and state support by raising their tuitions. The result is that tuition is rising much faster than incomes and vastly faster than incomes of low-income minority people, who are increasingly impoverished. One of the basic results is a sharp decline in college access. That problem is very expensive to address. It would cost billions of dollars just to return to the situation of 1980 in terms of coverage of college costs.

Civil rights is another area in which much damage must be undone. Civil rights enforcement has been abandoned almost 100 percent in the United States in the 1980s. All over the country, the Justice Department is attempting to resegregate public schools. There has been no significant civil rights enforcement in our society in the 1980s. Judicial appointments during the 1980s have resulted in courts that increasingly throw out structural challenges to discrimination. Thus, the United States is becoming increasingly minority and increasingly unequal. When we design policies to address these urban and metropolitan problems, civil rights enforcement has to be part of those policies.

State education reforms must be addressed on a larger level than that of the school. Some reforms, particularly raising graduation and admissions requirements for college, which have been common reforms throughout the United States, are having a very negative effect on the success of minority students. If that negative effect is not counterbalanced by achievement gains—and thus far data do not indicate that minority achievement has increased substantially—the result is negative effect without any real gains.

Policy analysts must scrutinize the consequences of these school reforms. Ironically, school reforms with negative consequences for minority students are not being enacted just by people who are hostile to minority students. Many minority administrators in central-city school systems proposed and implemented more rigid policies, particularly in the area of grade retention. Most big cities adopted grade-retention policies in the late 1970s and early 1980s. This policy is producing an increasing dropout rate in a number of big cities, despite the fact that educators have known for a long time that grade-retention would have that effect. With this example in mind, it becomes urgent that policymakers and scholars analyze the unanticipated consequences of politically popular reforms.

An implicit decision has been made, as a society, to concentrate minority students in community colleges. Few are transferring from those minority community colleges and succeeding in getting degrees in four-year universities. Many states are directing four-year universities to drop remedial programs and to concentrate that function in community colleges. It can be anticipated, based on past patterns, that such policies will have a predictable negative effect on minority opportunity.

The first imperative is to reverse some of these negative decisions that have been made recently, often with good intentions but with already discernible negative results. We must also focus on some of the broader issues, and we have only briefly addressed some of them here. Basically, we must think of each stage of the education and training process as a stage with particular sets of problems.

At the preschool stage, for example, there is an agenda for preschool educational programs and quality, affordable day care, although the agenda is acted upon in a half-hearted way in some cities and states. Preschool education at least has a body of supporters and momentum as an important policy for Latino and black youngsters.

At the early elementary stage, there are numerous models for basic skills programs that have been developed in bilingual education and other initiatives, thanks to Chapter One. The knowledge base is emerging that will allow policymakers to identify positive and proven ways to improve basic skills acquisition in the early elementary grades. What is required now are targeted programs with actual enforcement strategies, for the enforcement of programmatic changes that improve minority education has been in a serious decline during the era of the 1980s.

Numerous interesting proposals for restructuring the distribution of functions within school districts have not been evaluated carefully. Most central cities are engaging in strategies that involve some restructuring of responsibilities, and those proposed changes must be carefully analyzed and thoughtfully implemented.

School desegregation should be seriously considered again. We know we have educational systems in our metropolitan areas where 90 percent of the minority children in the central city are in schools that are inferior to 90 percent or more of the schools that white children attend. There exists an incredible stratification. While self-initiated help is essential, these disadvantaged schools cannot pull themselves up. We must also think about how to get people across barriers of privilege and opportunity. We must get "disadvantaged" students successfully prepared for college in schools where 90 percent of the students go to college, instead of where 85 percent drop out. We must have schools where the challenge and stimulation necessary to prepare a student for a reasonable chance at college prevail.

The reform agenda must continue from the early elementary grades into the middle and secondary school levels. What happens when a student learns basic skills by the third grade because of improved programs and schools but transfers into a rotten middle school and a chaotic high school? The reform effort in the 1960s targeted basic skills and has not progressed since then into effectively looking at how to improve middle schools, high schools, community colleges, and college equality issues. We must expand our agenda to give equal attention to each of those successive levels. The Carter administration was reaching in this direction toward its end, but, unfortunately, those issues have disappeared from the political agenda since that time.

We must intensify efforts to prevent students from dropping out of school. This requires more than merely a couple of million dollars per state. It requires serious efforts that deal with counseling, early identification of problems, summer school rather than grade retention, teen pregnancy and child-care programs, and other policy changes. There is no reason why we cannot lower the high school dropout rate in our big cities from its true rate of 40 to 50 percent by at least 10 to 15 percent with the kinds of incremental things that we already know how to do. We know that dropouts have no future in the American economy. It is evident that their lives are destined to be tragic and their children's lives are destined to replicate those of their parents. Data have shown this to be true. Changing these patterns should be a priority of extreme importance. We should try to redirect those negative patterns through high schools, through graduate degree equivalency (GED) training, through adult education, through job training that emphasizes high school completion, and so forth.

In college access, again, we must focus on each level, beginning with making students aware of financial aid. Evidence from Chicago shows, for example, that most minority students in the central city in their senior year who think they are ready for college— which is laughable given the curriculum they have had, but nobody has told them any different— those who think they are going to college have not even applied for financial aid or applied to take the national tests required for entrance into most colleges and universities. Information must get to these students with sufficient time to allow them a reasonable chance of making it. They are not given the basic information about what they need to know or what they must do to get into the system. The worlds of the privileged and those who are not so privileged are so separate that the very worst victims believe that they are being given the skills and opportunities to prepare themselves for college. They do not hit the rock until later on when they drop off the edge.

In the higher-education area, an intensive examination of the conditions and mechanisms for graduation and retention is needed. Policies of the 1970s succeeded at increasing the enrollment of minority students in college, but the reforms were less successful at increasing the numbers of those students who received degrees. This area represents a very important agenda for policy development and research.

Mr. Katzenbach presented an image of the late 1960s, a realization that our society was coming apart, especially in the metropolitan areas where more than 80 percent of blacks and 90 percent of Hispanics live and go to school. Many of the predictions of increased violence and separation have come true. During the last twenty years, blacks have become more segregated, and inequality, as William J. Wilson shows in his new book *The Truly Disadvantaged*, has become much more profound, the separation much deeper. Hispanics have become much more separated from the mainstream of the society in every metropolitan area and subject to the same kinds of pressures that blacks have experienced. Sadly, no one has paid much attention to what is happening, particularly in education after the early grade levels in elementary school.

New policy initiatives must focus on these large inequalities in our society once more. The presentations included here address some of the issues that must be drawn together to create an agenda for detailed reform both at the school level and at the individual institution level. Additionally we must address structural questions that affect every level within these systems.

Discussion

G. Valdés: I agree with what Dr. Orfield said and, in essence, the structural changes that must be made. Providing a plan or coming up with policies to change schools is difficult when you believe you cannot really change schools without changing the rest of society. This presents a tangle. In fact, we started by asking what kinds of policies would have to be there to try to eliminate the causes of the differences that we see in children, rather than trying to remedy those differences when we see them. The other issue, alluded to earlier, is that, unless we discuss how blacks and Hispanics can collaborate and, in fact, can become partners in an effort that involves us both, we are not going to make progress. The problem is a racial one—one of racial prejudice and ethnic conflict. Few scholars or policymakers discuss ethnic conflict or deal with questions of racism among Hispanics and blacks. Hispanics are seen as people of color by the majority population but often refuse to see themselves as people of color. They pretend they are not a racial minority but an ethnic minority and all that that difference implies.

Another issue in response to Hispanic groups that want to solve everything by saying, "Let's have bilingual education," is that if you have bilingual education in ineffective schools you will have ineffective bilingual education programs. Thus, arguing for bilingual education is not going far enough.

Finally, we had some reservations about suggesting local control, because local control has been used in detrimental ways against Hispanic groups. Local control has been one of the means schools districts have used to avoid implementing the regulations and remedies that resulted from the *Lau v. Nichols* decision. Thus, Hispanics are reluctant to see local control as an effective route to educational reform unless we have allies. It is evident from our experience with school districts in the past that relying mainly on local control means losing some of the gains that have been made in school reform.

R. Valdivieso: I struggled with a dilemma—where do you start? Is it best to focus on the large structural problems or on the problems of a specific group? My policy proposals do focus on a specific group—the adolescent and young adult school dropouts and their children. This focus does not imply that there are no other problems in other populations that need to be dealt with. It is critical that we offer some recourse to these young adults, whom we tend to forget. Policymakers say, "Well, they dropped out of school," and the dropouts fall into a dark hole. But these youth are the parents of the children who are now entering elementary and preschool. It is critical at this point to try to lessen some of the damage that has already occurred. Gary Orfield has been a champion in the area of civil rights enforcement and desegregation, which is an important area. However, each of us must take an initiative with the school building down the street or the community center around the block and build with what we have. Nonetheless, the narrower perspective sometimes prevents us from seeing that larger perspective, which scholars and policy analysts, such as Dr. Orfield, have so eloquently kept in front of us over the years.

A. Madrid: There were two comments that you made, Dr. Orfield, that raise several questions. First, you discussed the problems of reform at the local level and the need for macrosolutions. I would like for you to elaborate on the kinds of changes that need to be implemented at the macrolevel. Second, there are any number of new initiatives that have the support of the body politic: preschool education, early elementary interventions, restructuring the schools, et cetera, but there are continuing issues that do not have particular support and attention. The latter include issues that you seem to believe are critical, such as the targeted programs, for example, that are in disrepute and school desegregation, which has been criticized by the minority populations as well as the white populations who support neighborhood schools. Moreover, I question the emphasis on school dropout programs. Dropouts are only a symptom of the real problems of lack of achievement and attainment. These minority students often drop out for good reasons, because there is not much good going on for them in the schools.

G. Orfield: If you attempt to change the society from the schools, you have to begin with the realization that schools are much more likely to reflect the society of the families that they serve than change society. There are important reasons why that is true. The two most important things about schools are the children who are in a particular school—the families that stand behind them and the kinds of experience and background they bring with them—and the staff and teachers who are in that school. Both of those groups are much less empowered at low-income minority schools than in middle class schools.

Thus, with that approach, reform begins with tremendous problems. In low-income minority schools, the level of student competition is less and teachers' expectations are lower. Even the minority personnel in those schools tend to be middle-class minority people, because, by definition, they must have teachers' degrees. And, as a result of social-class differences, they do not always understand or relate to the children who are in their schools. Families themselves have low expectations, and there tend to be relatively few families who have been successful. Low-income families move very frequently, so an individual school holds a child for only a short time. In many central city schools there is a 50 percent or more turnover in population each year.

No school, no matter how well it is run, can change a child's life in a few months if that child then transfers to another school. In any case, many children have very disruptive lives. They have untreated medical problems; they have very serious family problems at home; they are not nourished adequately. These are problems that a school cannot solve by itself.

Our data show that if you look at the income of children who come to a particular school, you can predict with a terrifying level of probability how well the school is going to work. A recent study has examined all the high schools in the five largest metropolitan areas in the United States, and we find a correlation of approximately .8 to .9 between the percentage of students who are on free lunch or AFDC and low achievement scores. A much lower correlation of .5 is considered a strong relationship, and correlations this high are seldom found. The correlation between the percentage of black and Hispanic enrollment and the percentage of low-income students is approximately the same order of magnitude; in other words, it is incredibly high.

So, if we are really going to change opportunity, we have to think about income, employment, health care, and other factors as well as schooling. Focusing on schooling in itself is not adequate for social change. If we focus on schooling, we must begin realistically thinking that middle-class children are going to be in schools that are functioning better on average, that are going to have better-prepared teachers, that are going to have higher expectations, that are going to have more connections to the next level of education than schools that serve poor children. Thus, one important strategy is to determine whether or not some of the poor children can be enrolled in those schools that function well.

What the school reform movement is attempting is to create aspects of middle-class schools in conditions that are not middle class. That represents an important effort, especially since we have such an extremely high level of stratification. Moreover, we must also design ways to provide opportunities for those children to attend the mainstream schools and make it possible for their families to move into communities that are more connected to opportunity in the society. The Katzenbach Commission emphasized this approach when it said, "Residential segregation is the basic dimension that has replaced *de jure* segregation laws as a rock-hard basis for inequality in the society." Thus, to bring about significant change, we have to think much more broadly about the issue of school reform and determine why schools are unequal and why all the other reform efforts of the last twenty years, which have embodied many of these ideas, have not succeeded beyond the level of increasing some basic-skills achievement. When we search beyond the minimal increases in basic skills, we only find special cases that are not replicable on a large scale. That is because there is a deeply rooted inequality reflected through the schools. Americans, who believe firmly in democracy and equal opportunity, tend to think the schools can change on their own initiative, and that may not be possible.

The second question posed by Mr. Madrid was that there are certain reforms that are supported by the establishment in the society and certain that are not. Why is that, and can anything be done about it? Of course, the reforms that are supported are the ones that ask the institutions to reform themselves with little external assistance and do not disrupt the rest of society in any way. This suggests that there is a magic formula that does not cost too much and can be incorporated on a large scale. The reforms that are not supported by the establishment are the ones that call for initiating major transformations, changing the experience of middle-class children, making access to suburban enclaves possible for disadvantaged students, and shifting power and advantage. As we found in the South, when major reforms were imposed, they were not supported by the establishment.

Instigating policy changes is incredibly difficult. One of the first steps is that Latino and black intellectuals and researchers have to be thinking and talking about policy reforms. They must not be limited by what blue-ribbon Wall Street firms or established policy institutes think is a good idea for reforming minority community schools. Another first is for researchers to fully describe the inequalities as well as the nature and the success of radical and moderate interventions. A third step is to identify ways, through both legislation and the courts, that local organizations and other groups that will support them can begin to get some more broadly conceived efforts in operation, at least on an experimental basis. There is a program in Chicago, for example, that, under court order, has moved a couple thousand extremely low-income families to the outer suburbs. The low-income children are doing very well in the schools and have had few difficulties, contrary to almost everyone's prediction. Innovative ideas such as this should be considered as one of an array of possible options.

Where there is common interest among the established institutions and the minority communities, we must take advantage of the opportunity. This common interest exists on some issues, like preschool education, early childhood programs, basic-skills instruction, and so forth. On other issues there are no common interests, and these reforms are inherently conflictual. In these instances we are talking about changing the socialization system of our society and opening up opportunities. This will not occur on a large scale in an effective way without conflict. Nonetheless, we cannot make substantial changes if we limit reform to the issues that everybody agrees on.

Manuel del Valle, Attorney: My basic concern is with policies that tie progress, program participation, or school improvement to testing. Essentially, I have been involved in numerous cases involving testing litigation. I find testing to be woefully unpredictable and truly invalid for minority populations, certainly for Hispanics and blacks. Thus, I see severe difficulties when new money or progress in a given school is linked with the testing paradigm. Linking test scores to improvement and reform seems woefully inappropriate.

In terms of the overall civil rights enforcement picture, the pessimistic portrayal punctuates a point. Those involved in fair labor standards litigation, nonetheless, are quite busy. The picture is more complex than it seems, as usual in the area of civil rights. While much remains to be done, as a person with legal training and a legal practitioner for some fourteen years, I do not recommend the legal system as the most appropriate way to achieve anything other than piecemeal reform.

My basic concern is how to measure the progress and changes we are proposing. The issue of college access, for example, is exceedingly important. Very few Hispanics seem to reach four-year colleges, let alone Ivy League colleges. We lose many, many talented young men and women each year because of the lack of minority faculty. The picture painted by the presenters of the lower levels of educational reform are mirrored at the higher levels. There seem to be more complex problems facing us in the future.

Finally, the question of minority access to higher education is always coupled with the question of discrimination in employment with respect to minority faculty. Many of the researchers and scholars participating in the symposium are faculty persons who may at some point be subjected to review in the existing tenure system and will be denied tenure because of varying points of view. Thus, there is an array of issues that must link education and employment in order to find a workable solution.

A. Madrid: Part of the question raised deals with an accountability paradigm that has been emphasized in the last few years. It is an appropriate issue to discuss, since some of the targeted schools programs include rewards or accountability based on improvement in student test scores.

G. Valdés: I said that there should be both an ethnographic evaluation and a quantitative study of school-improvement plans. Traditionally, school-improvement evaluations have been quantitative in nature; however, standardized tests, even at their best, are fallible and only partial indicators of academic achievement. Additionally, standardized tests are not at all capable of providing information about higher-order thinking skills, creativity, effort, persistence in the face of adversity, or other important factors. My position is very definitely similar to the one that Mr. del Valle has taken. To the degree that we continue to base decisions on standardized achievement scores, we are clearly looking at inadequate information for a great many reasons.

Bernard Gifford chairs a blue-ribbon commission on testing and public policy that is funded by the Ford Foundation. This commission has done a great deal of work in trying to delineate the issues of testing, not only in the schools but also in employment and in the military. I am writing a long report for that commission addressing bilingualism in testing. I look at bilingual processing and how these processes might affect people taking tests when they have two linguistic systems. We are not looking just at superficial items of language or word choice in a test item, which is how others have looked at bilingualism and testing. We are examining cognitive processing in bilinguals. I would be the first one to agree that, unless we do something about testing as the only measure of achievement, we are not going to progress very far.

R. Valdivieso: Possibly Mr. del Valle was referring to my comments on the new Chapter One legislation, which does tie test scores to the continuation of general aid funds to schools. But the requirements are minimal. The new legislation requires that student test scores do not decrease, that, at the least, they stay at the level they were when the money was appropriated. If, in fact, test scores go up, schools should not be penalized. Thus, schools that do well and have increased students' achievement test scores would be able to continue to receive funds. I have the same perspective as Guadalupe Valdés about the inadequacy of standardized test scores. I do believe, though, that we should hold school people accountable for school outcomes. The argument is over what those outcomes should be and how to measure them.

G. Orfield: Testing is a very important issue. We have gone test crazy in this country since the school reform movement, and test scores have become the only dimension of measuring improvement in many school systems. Some people believe the emphasis on standardized test scores is driving out the teaching of higher-order thinking in the early elementary grades and causing teachers to overemphasize basic skills.

Test systems are very manipulable. Every state is reporting itself over the national norms, for example. Many central-city school districts are producing extremely misleading test results based on out-of-date norms. As a consequence, people who are disadvantaged cannot get true measures of how disadvantaged they are, even along the unreliable standardized test metric.

The most dangerous part of the emphasis on testing is the way it is used in college admissions, especially in highly stratified admission systems like California's. In the University of California system, a test plays an absurdly important role. The admission process is producing a system in which the 50 percent of the minority students who are high school graduates are only one-third as likely as Anglos to be eligible to get into the university system.

Until the tests have a lot more predictive power for college performance than they do—and Richard Duran's Educational Testing Service monograph shows they have especially weak power for Hispanic students—we cannot legitimately stratify access to higher education with a heavy emphasis on testing. This is especially true if the tests have totally foreseeable racial consequences. This is a policy issue that should be examined very, very closely.

Josephine Segura, Hispanic Women's Network of Texas: Obviously, the contributors have presented good proposals, but their recommendations do not really represent any new concepts. The concepts that have been suggested have been implemented in the past. Of most concern to those in agencies are such questions as, What is it going to cost? What is it going to cost me? Who is going to pay for it? Who is going to benefit? Who are going to be the beneficiaries of these programs? We need to concentrate on these questions because we are not doing a very good sales job, obviously.

You suggest that these programs would cost about $6 billion. That is a minute investment in terms of their benefits. Nonetheless, when a president sees this recommendation, the first thing he is going to say is, "What is it going to cost me? Is it going to cause congressional legislative action? Can I get it passed? And what's it going to cost me politically?" These are the realistic factors that we must consider when we make these proposals.

Estevan Flores, University of Colorado, Boulder: My recent work on the question of AIDS and distressed areas for the truly disadvantaged suggests that, in essence, many of the same variables— high unemployment, propensity to live in areas where crime rates are high, drug usage, et cetera—are present when addressing different problems.

I was impressed with the President's Commission on AIDS hearings when researchers brought to the commission's attention that the frequency of AIDS as it affected minorities is correlated with the same variables discussed in relation to educational disadvantage. I have never held education as the panacea for minority socioeconomic equality, although I have worked very hard on committees on educational improvement. The question I pose is, if we were to reduce our dropout rate, or get achievement levels up to par, or have college enrollments on an equal level with the majority of society, what are these educational improvements going to provide for the individual? Given the economic status of the United States at the present time, what is going to be available for Latinos and blacks in the next decade if we do have improvements in educational achievement?

A. Madrid: It is important to note that the average black with a college degree earns three times as much as the average black dropout in this country. It does make a major difference. Another important question to ask is if everybody earned college degrees, would there be jobs for them?

But at the present time, based on data we have now, it makes a very large difference for employment rates, income, and many other outcomes in people's lives to have that college degree.

From the floor: I live in Austin, Texas, where our schools have recently been resegregated. We have sixteen readily identifiable minority target schools. My reason for being here is to question your emphasis or target schools. A target school is very convenient. You have a large population of people who need help. Would it be possible, instead of perpetuating the usefulness of segregated schools, to give help to individuals, to allow funds to follow individuals who need help, rather than identify and concentrate large populations with special needs in segregated schools?

I do know that this has been a trend in mental health in Texas. As the large institutions are being phased out, there has been a great effort to bypass the vested interests of existing institutions and channel the funds and the services to the individuals who need the help wherever they are located, rather than to the institutions who used to receive it. Would it be possible to aim help at individual students no matter where they are enrolled, rather than to target segregated schools?

G. Valdés: Certainly, I recognize the tension within the plan of targeted schools that we presented, and I think Gary Orfield has alluded to that. Are we talking about not having integrated schools? Obviously, we have the reality of overcrowded urban schools where, in fact, segregation is a fact of life. In our plan we simply said, given that we have segregation and overcrowding and given the resistance to changing it, then let's do the best we can do with that.

Certainly, in the best of all possible worlds, it would be wonderful if we could deal one-on-one. You are talking about many, many children one-on-one. You are talking about the training of many, many teachers, tutors, and paraprofessionals to deal one-on-one. If we are willing to spend the money, I think it would be wonderful.

G. Orfield: There is no reason why you could not do exactly what you propose in a situation like Austin's. Austin did have a reasonable desegregation plan and abandoned it exactly where it is most beneficial and easiest, in the early elementary grades. I filed an affidavit against the abandonment of that plan in this case. I think the return to neighborhood schools is a major mistake for the city. This resegregation is also occurring in Oklahoma City and Norfolk and several other cities right now, partly under the leadership of the U.S. Justice Department. You can have identification of individual students. In desegregated school districts

Title One targeting has to be reconceptualized so that the students who need special services are identified flexibly and there is more flexibility in using the funding.

There are white children in schools that were not targeted who can also be reached, who have the same kinds of problems as the underachieving minority children. We do need a different approach, and it has been worked out in some school districts. Also, I agree with Guadalupe Valdés that this issue is not going to be the basic problem in the Oaklands and San Franciscos, and so forth, in the near future. We are experiencing the reality of intense segregation, and we must devise ways to identify massive compensatory resources, which do not exist at the present time. None of our political leaders is proposing to provide them, either.

Barbara Jordan

One Nation, Indivisible: True or False, Rhetoric or Reality?

One Nation, Indivisible:
True or False, Rhetoric or Reality?
Barbara Jordan
Discussion

PART III

One Nation, Indivisible:
True or False, Rhetoric or Reality?

Barbara Jordan: The subject I will be addressing is one you will recognize. The words are familiar ones, "One nation, indivisible." True or false, rhetoric or reality? Now, you know those words, "One nation, indivisible," come out of the Pledge of Allegiance to the flag of the United States of America. I have felt that this symposium would be a proper forum for me to pose this question, because you have planned discussion panels, and you are framing issues, and you intend to send memos proposing policy initiatives to the next president of the United States. We have a candidate for president who has wrapped himself so tightly in the flag that he has almost choked his judgment and his thought.

I know that this is not a partisan event, and I certainly would not make it such. I am not calling names here—but, you see, when you wrap yourself very tightly in something, it sometimes can cut off circulation, and sometimes what your mouth says does not get action from the brain if you are too tightly encapsulated.

So, I want you to think about "One nation, indivisible: true or false, rhetoric or reality?" I want you to think about these words and what they mean and whether they are true or whether they are just some of the stuff we say mindlessly and thoughtlessly.

One nation. We want to be one. We want to be single. We want to have a single end, a single goal, a single purpose. We would like that. We would like for that single end, goal, purpose, to be the common good. That is what we would like. What a great day it would be if for just an instant we could suppress our preoccupation with self, with private wishes, private desires, private gains, and private profits. What a great day it would be if for just an instant we could forget about I, me, and think about us, we, community, the public interest, the common will.

The reports that helped spawn this conference—the Kerner Commission, the Katzenbach Report, the Eisenhower Commission—were presented two decades ago. Those reports identified wrongs and made certain suggestions for ways we could correct those wrongs. We were very serious about those undertakings and the follow-up of those reports. We were serious about it, and we have failed in the action that we planned to take to actualize the recommendations of those reports. We have failed.

Why do I say that? I say we have failed because we are a divided people; we are separate. We seem to speak the rhetoric of one nation of community, but it seems to be very illusory, very illusory. The people who come to power have been more concerned with exacerbating our divisions than healing our wounds. Think about that.

If we are the inclusive society, the inclusive government we say we are, then all people, individually and collectively, should have a say. Everybody ought to have a say if we are this all-inclusive people. There should be no one excluded from the paths to power, no one; no one excluded for reasons of status, income, agenda, or any of the other extraneous litany of things that keep people from rising to the top.

There are numerous things still with us historically, traditionally, customarily, that prevent us from joining together in community. I regret to say that, but it is so. We don't like to admit that. We would rather beat our breasts, salute the flag, and say that we are all one, all-inclusive; all-inclusive, liberty and justice for all. We would like to believe that. We say it. We say it, but reality gives the lie to what we say. Reality gives the lie to our denial. Now what reality am I talking about at the present time?

The Commission on Minority Participation in Education and American Life was established in the fall of 1987 by the American Council on Education and the Education Commission of the States. The impetus for the formation of that commission was a shared deep concern over the faltering pace of minority advancement. A report issued by the commission was entitled *One-Third of a Nation*. The report took its title from something Franklin Roosevelt said more than fifty years ago, "I see one-third of our nation ill-clothed, ill-housed." That's where the "one-third of a nation" comes from in that title.

But let me read to you the jarring indictment in the introduction of that report. It says: "America is moving backward, not forward, in its efforts to achieve the full participation of minority citizens in the life and prosperity of the nation. In education, employment, income, health, longevity, and other basic measures of individual and social well-being, gaps persist; and, in some cases, the gaps are widening between members of minority groups and the majority population."

The report continued, "This is an intolerable"—an intolerable—"conclusion. We call for a renewed commitment. A renewed commitment by all of the American people to the idea of equality and the inclusion of all people in the productive, the constructive, the substantive life of a nation." This call from this most recent commission is not a call for new policy. The call is for a reinvigorated commitment, a reinvigorated public policy, a public policy that would include everybody in it and leave no one out. This is what is requested.

There are those who question the sincerity of anyone calling for a renewed commitment to the inclusion of all people. There is suspicion in the response of others outside, looking at the people who draft reports. Why is there suspicion about sincerity in the call for renewal? The suspicion is there as a result of the failure of those who draft the charter to consult the very people who will be affected by whatever action is taken in their behalf. The people who are affected want to be consulted about ways and means to bring about implementation of a renewed public policy.

Any effort leading to a successful outcome of this renewed policy must include in the planning the people who are going to be impacted by the policy. Groups and single individuals who are going to be most intimately affected by the policy must be included in the planning stages. These persons who are going to be affected can impact and influence the outcome.

Now, how can a group—blacks, Hispanics, whoever—how can a group traditionally on the outside of the policy process affect the decision on such a broad-based policy as inclusion of all people in the workings of this country? How can the "outs" influence the "ins"? What clout can they bring to persuade others to include them, from planning to completion? They cannot bring money, because they do not have wealth. They cannot bring status, because they do not have status. What they can bring is the possibility of success or failure. The outs can cause a policy to fail if they do not desire to cooperate with those who are implementing the policy and trying to bring about change. Success or failure can be determined by those who are outside; their cooperation or refusal to cooperate can make the difference in the successful outcome of a policy. The outs must make it clear that there can be no success without them. That, you might say, sounds threatening. No, it is not really threatening. It is the only reality the outs can bring with them: "We will cooperate if you let us be a part of the initial process from beginning to end, but, if you don't include us, count us out." That is the stick that the outs can present to the ins, "If you want to be successful, talk to us. If you want your policies to fail, exclude us."

The policy of inclusion of everybody can be implemented if the participants trust each other and are willing to cooperate with each other. The policymaking process should be based on mutual trust and cooperation in pursuit of that common end, that common goal, that unity of purpose. Distrust and lack of cooperation equals stalemate and failure.

Robert Reich, at the Kennedy School of Government, recently edited the book *The Power of Public Ideas*. Reich wrote a chapter in that book entitled, "Policymaking in a Democracy." In that chapter Reich says that policy is made one of two ways: Intermediation of interest groups, on the one hand, and maximization of net benefits, on the other hand. On the one hand, intermediation of interest groups requires extraordinary negotiating skills and interpersonal relationships handled with care. On the other hand, the policy of net maximization, net benefits, requires the cold calculation of who wins and who loses.

Where do researchers come in when policy is made in one mode versus the other? Researchers may report what they see, what they know, all that is knowable, and the nuances that may be encountered. Researchers may help clarify the policy question and explain possible alternatives. Researchers can crunch the numbers. But that's about all the researchers can do. Researchers, in my opinion, have little impact on policy outcome.

So can we become one nation, indivisible? I think the answer to that question is, we must become such a nation. We do not have a choice. We must become such a nation because the alternative consigns us to a nation of permanent unrest, permanent instability. That in my opinion is un-American.

Discussion

Arturo Madrid, Tomás Rivera Center :   Professor Jordan, I would like to address a question to you about discourse and what you have been describing as a discourse of exclusion, a vocabulary of exclusion. How has that discourse of exclusion been functioning, particularly with the 1988 presidential election?

B. Jordan: The tragedy is that many of those who could be contributors in a meaningful way to the political process, because they are outside the process, have been excluded. People who could put thought and content into words are not here in the main. We have seen, as a consequence, a presidential campaign that has turned so many people off that the surprise may be that nobody is going to vote. People are disenchanted with the failure of the candidates to deal with the issues in a substantive and coherent manner. People are turned off by the advertisers, the packaged events, and are becoming nonparticipants in a very large way. This is a result of the failure to bring to the inside those people who could deal meaningfully with the issues we care about.

I am making a sweeping assumption here that the majority of the American people would like to hear a thoughtful discussion of the issues we care about. I do make that assumption, and I do think it is a correct assumption. A presidential election is an important event, and it should not be trivialized. I fear that in a number of instances presidential campaigns are being trivialized. You can hear proposals handed down that are so lacking in what you would call common sense, you break out in a big laugh when you hear them. That comes from only one side of the spectrum, however.

From the floor: How would you articulate the diversity of the United States in this oneness approach that you talk about?

B. Jordan: When I say "oneness" or "wholeness," or "indivisible," I do not mean for one second to denigrate the pluralism that is a part of the beauty of this country. What I am saying is, we take this pluralism, this mosaic, this diversity, all of these different people, and we try to meld them together for the public good. I believe that we can do that in a sensible and sensitive way without for one moment denigrating the diversity that is a part of the greatness of our country.

From the floor: Without adversely affecting the majority, what could or should Jesse Jackson do in the final stages of the presidential campaign?

B. Jordan: You don't want me to answer that. Seriously, I feel that the best thing that Jesse Jackson could do would be to talk to his supporters and convince them that there is something worth voting for on the eighth of November, and that that something is the Democratic party under whose banner he ran. He is supposed to be registering voters and getting them excited about the campaign, but we have trouble finding him—I have trouble finding him. If Jesse Jackson got out there and got his supporters excited about the Democratic party and ready to vote, at this stage I do not think that would adversely affect the majority, because people are fairly hardened in their positions. I believe that anybody who is going to vote for the Democratic party knows that they are going to do that, and Jesse Jackson has caused probably as much defection as he can cause. We are moving into another phase now. I do not think that would adversely affect the fortunes of the Democratic party.

David Dinkins, Manhattan Borough President, City of New York: I feel the need to speak because I was chairman of Jesse Jackson's campaign in New York not only in 1988 but in 1984, as well. I rise because you say you have not been able to find Jesse Jackson. Well, I have found him. He was in New York last Saturday, as well as the Saturday before. His theory is to put out one thousand young people, each of whom should come back to New York with at least one hundred persons registered to vote. And he makes the argument, and most eloquently, that we do not need any money to register people. Nobody is going to register us but us. He says this; he says it again and again, to throngs of people all over the United States. I think it is, perhaps if I may say, a bit unfair and inaccurate to suggest that he is not at work. I have seen him in my state, and I read the press from elsewhere.

I think that in terms of encouraging our people, meaning the people of the United States, to vote, those who might be inclined to vote the Democratic ticket, there are many, many arguments for voting. We have but to point to the Supreme Court. There are three justices who will be eighty in the time of the next presidency, and that alone, it would seem to me, is enough to offer to people who say, why? Why should we vote? For what should we vote? I find those reasons effective in trying to persuade some people. There are many, many other reasons. We can persuade our conservative friends, sometimes referred to as Reagan Democrats, that when we talk about infant mortality and housing and education, on and on and on, it is possible to be graphic in demonstrating that these things are, in fact, cost effective. It costs us less in the long run to attend to problems of children and youth, although the motivation for many of us is more humane.

Gerard Farrell, Daily Texan, Austin: Coming from New York City, as does Mr. Dinkins, I have witnessed firsthand the effects of gentrification. With the recent announcement that Austin, Texas, is the fifth fastest growing city in the United States, and since the subject of the symposium is the changing cities, how do you feel gentrification will have an effect on the lower-income people in Austin, with more people coming in to work in the high-tech fields, and jobs opening up for people that have degrees and advanced training? What is going to happen to the other people? Are they just going to fall through the cracks?

B. Jordan: They are going to fall through the cracks if someone does not do something to prevent them from falling through the cracks. There must be a policy designed to take the people who cannot participate in this boom, which is certainly going to occur, and train them and get them ready to do something.

We do not have policies in place to catch these people and keep them from falling through the cracks. Unless some policy is devised for that purpose, that is what will happen. They will fall, and they will become a part of the underclass, and then the outcasts, and we will lose their services in the mainstream for the rest of their lives. That is not an acceptable alternative for the successful achievement of a strong economy of this city or of this state. There is no one focusing on such policy now, and there ought to be one now. Perhaps a new administration will come with new ideas for how one protects and saves its citizens.

G. Farrell: You referred to the power of the "outs," who, if not involved in the formation of policy, can cause the policy to fail. Hasn't this been the complaint of the "ins," that, because they are unwilling to go along with the policies that have been implemented, the outs have, in effect, brought about the failure of whatever programs have been initiated? The reason often given to explain the failure of social programs is the nonparticipation, the unwillingness of the people who rely on the programs to go along with them.

B. Jordan: What I am urging is, when developing a program, bring the outs in initially. Bring those who are going to be affected by the program to the table when you say, "I think we have a problem." Let them in at the point of having an idea, and then work from the idea forward. Don't wait until you have a *fait accompli*, a done deal, and present it as a done deal to the outs. If you include people initially, in the beginning stages of whatever program you are trying to develop, it is very likely that they will stay attached to the program, very likely.

TOP (Left to right): *Ernesto Cortés* (back to camera), *Robert Valdez, Lynn Burbridge, Carol Thompson.* BOTTOM LEFT: *Ernesto Cortés.* BOTTOM RIGHT: *Robert Valdez*

PART IV

Human Services and Income Policies

PART IV

Introduction

Ernesto Cortés: I am not used to being a moderator. Some people think there is nothing moderate about me, but I am going to try to fill the role assigned. I want to say briefly that I hope the comments of the panelists are in the spirit of the speech given by Professor Jordan, because I do think it is important, given my own perspective and bias, that people who are poor, who are considered outside the decisionmaking process, ought to be able to make decisions, particularly about matters that affect them.

However, that process is not quite so easy as it seems. One of the things we have to deal with is that a culture has developed, or has been imposed upon people, that has taught them how to be nonparticipants. That is not turned around overnight. Just as you can teach someone to be competent, just as you can teach someone to be effective, you can also teach someone to be dependent, to be passive. Those obstacles, those attitudes that have been inculcated culturally, not just personally, are not individual failures. They are cultural failures and political failures and are not easily overcome. They require careful thought and training and development. They require the rebuilding of some institutions. And those institutions have to be democratic institutions as well as mediating institutions. Our culture is not particularly good at nurturing such institutions, particularly as we begin to suburbanize and unravel the core institutions of family, church, and neighborhood, which have always mediated our cities and our public policies.

The first panelist is Robert Valdez, who is assistant professor in the School of Public Health at UCLA. He is a resident consultant with the Economics and Statistics Department of the Rand Corporation, and is coauthor of *Californians without Health Insurance: A Report to the California Legislature.*

Mr. Valdez will speak on the issue of health care, or the lack of it, and need for it.

Health Care for All in the Year 2000?

Robert B. Valdez: Human services, as all of you know, are largely provided in our society at the local level in our cities and in our counties. The cities and counties bear the human and the fiscal burden of a national government that has largely abandoned responsibility for direction and funding of human services.

Future actions to reduce the federal deficit threaten to strand cities, leaving them with the chore of providing for the poor and for the middle class. By phasing out financial support for human services at the national level and by increasingly requiring municipal governments to shoulder the full responsibility of providing and financing these services, the relationships between the levels of government in our federal system are being reshaped. Given this changing set of responsibilities for human services, it is important to recognize several problems in providing these services in the urban environment of the United States or, for that matter, any urban environment.

First, the concept of an urban environment or a city, as many of us call it, continuously evolves. Technical definitions of the city that are based on geographic or political or historical criteria fail to provide the flexibility and the scope necessary for serving ever-changing human service needs today. Such definitions hinder the ability of a system to provide needed services.

Second, socioeconomic, cultural, and ethnic diversity coupled with mobility create unique challenges for providers of services and for the financing of these services. Cities, I would like to argue, are constantly in transition. These transitions have resulted in a haphazardly constructed urban landscape, often with multiple overlapping governmental jurisdictions. Cities accommodate large numbers of diverse residents, and, as a result, problems of air and water pollution, substandard housing, physical decay, and garbage and sewage disposal emerge. With these issues in mind, we must have a set of guiding principles for any effort to restructure the responsibilities for human services programs. Let me offer a few of those guiding principles.

Human service programs should meet at least three goals: First, they must meet basic human survival needs. Second, they must assure people an equal chance to compete in the marketplace. And, third, they must improve the local environment in which people live.

The Reagan administration deserves credit for the strong push toward a more decentralized program authority within government. It also deserves credit for emphasizing the importance of private sector participation in addressing social problems. But the Reagan administration has failed to provide the guiding principles for reestablishing local program responsibility and ensuring adequate financing for these efforts. The phaseouts of federal funding force states and localities to raise their own revenues to meet human service needs that have been abandoned by the federal government. These abandoned programs include programs for nutrition, disease control, basic health, and minimum shelter.

I would like to use as an example of one of these human service needs the issue of access to medical care. Access to medical care provides an excellent example of human service problems faced by cities in this transition of responsibilities. It also represents a major problem for many groups in our society, not just the economically disadvantaged. For significant segments of our society, access to health care is often inadequate or nonexistent. When it is available, it is offered through the efforts of county or city government. Access to health care is also a double-edged issue; it is relevant to both social equity concerns and the issue of social cost dependency.

Numerous studies point to the influence of health, ill health, on the ability of people to find and maintain a place in the labor market and to gain self-sufficiency. The consequences of inadequate health insurance coverage for our society are well documented. Yet an effective and efficient health safety net remains an unfulfilled promise.

The stresses and strains on cities can be illustrated by looking at four major cities in the United States: Los Angeles, New York, Chicago, and Houston. I have chosen these cities for illustration because they represent different geographic, economic, and social regions of the country. Also, each is home to a large and growing Latino population. Furthermore, over the last eight years, these four major cities have experienced dramatic increases in the number of people without health insurance coverage.

The two largest cities in the country, Los Angeles and New York, have added 1.1 million people to the pool of uninsured citizens in the country. More than a quarter of Los Angeles' residents and a fifth of New York's residents do not have health insurance. Although less dramatic, cities with highly unionized work forces, such as Chicago, have also experienced considerable increases in this insurance problem. Houston presents an unusual example of a city that has seen an overall decline in the proportion of uninsured in the last eight years, largely because of population flight. Nonetheless, despite its overall decline, the city still faces huge health insurance problems among its diverse populations.

In Houston and in Los Angeles, as well as other southwestern cities, over 40.9 percent of the Latino population is uninsured. These rates are two to three times those of Anglo residents in the same locale. Even in the industrialized and unionized cities of the North and Northeast, Latinos are more likely to be without health insurance than other residents. In New York, 27 percent of the Latinos are without health insurance. In Chicago, 29 percent are uncovered.

Among Anglo and black residents, the lack of health insurance coverage is not a trivial problem, either. In Los Angeles, for example, 18 percent of the Anglo adult, nonelderly population lacks health insurance coverage. In New York and Chicago, 13 percent of this group are without any protection against the costs of illness. The black population of these cities is at great risk of health and financial ruin because of the costs of illness. In Los Angeles and other southern and southwestern cities, more than a quarter of the black population lacks any kind of health insurance coverage—Medicare, Medicaid, or private. At least a fifth of northern black residents also lack any kind of protection.

Despite Medicaid—a human service program initiated under the Johnson administration to provide adequate access to medical care for the poor—one-third to one-half of all poor residents in Los Angeles, New York, Chicago, and Houston are without health insurance of any kind. These individuals along with the near poor, those living just above the poverty line, increasingly rely on the charity services offered by cities, counties, health care professionals, and health care institutions. Even among the lower middle class, 20 to 30 percent are without health insurance and, in a time of crisis, either rely on services available through the city or create bad debts in their own community facilities.

We know that individuals without health insurance use the health system less often than those with insurance even when they are sick. Yet the uninsured and the underinsured have worse health and a greater likelihood of low-birth-weight babies, hypertension, and other chronic diseases that require long-term attention. Usually, the long-term attention is gained in locally provided, publicly funded facilities. These illnesses and tragedies increase social dependency costs and reduce opportunities for attaining self-sufficiency.

The strain of the growing number of uninsured and those relying on the Medicaid system puts the cities at considerable risk. In Los Angeles, where more than half of the Latino residents are either uninsured or on Medicaid, the only places available to serve them are public facilities. The county's health care system is besieged from all points: crowded public hospitals, emergency room closings, trauma networks destroyed, mental health clinics closing because of lack of funds. Access to medical care is problematic for citizens of other cities as well.

For the uninsured, the lack of health insurance can mean personal tragedy. The uninsured are less likely to receive various kinds of preventive services, which could slow or prevent serious problems from occurring. When these serious problems do occur, leading to stroke or heart attack, treatment creates a larger cost for health care providers and for the taxpayer. Under the weight of the uncompensated and undercompensated medical assistance, municipal budgets strain to meet other human service needs that cities have historically provided their residents, including garbage disposal, street cleaning, and fire and police protection.

Health insurance and health care are big businesses in the United States. This is demonstrated by the total outlays for health care in this country, which this year will surpass $550 billion. Yet, in spite of the numerous private and public programs in existence, more than one in six Americans lacks health insurance of any kind. Most of the uninsured are young, healthy, employed persons, or their children. Increasingly, attention at the state level has focused on broadening coverage available through the workplace, especially for the working poor, the temporarily employed, and dependents who have to go without insurance even if the head of household is insured. Despite the improvements that increased coverage in these areas would bring, I believe the answer lies in looking not at the total amount spent on the medical arsenal but at the distribution of the financial burden and at how the health insurance system in our society is structured.

The problems are shared by government and by private institutions. In 1935 we developed our alternative to a universal entitlement system: the employee benefit health insurance through the public employment sector. In 1965 we sought to protect the deserving poor from the cost of illness with Medicaid. With 37 million uninsured people in the United States and millions more inadequately insured, and the employee benefit system losing its ability to provide adequate coverage even for the middle class, our major human service challenge is to move from this crazy patchwork of a medical care system toward one that provides coverage for all. The challenge is to devise a system that delivers care through arrangements that neither encourage wasteful expenditures nor withhold needed care nor bankrupt our cities.

A framework will have to be proposed by the next administration and enacted by the Congress to establish universal entitlement and equity in the financing of and access to medical care. Whatever scheme emerges from the current chaos, our crisis is clearly one of organizational capacity, political will, and social conscience and not one of financial constraints in the guise of the federal deficit.

What model should we think about? What options are open to use for universal coverage, universal entitlement? I would like to propose a public utilities approach, in contrast to the inequitable employment-based insurance coverage in the current system. It is a concept that is still being formulated. The program would entitle all people within a region access to the health insurance provided by the health "utility" company of that region.

E. Cortés: Without any further ado, I would like to introduce Lynn Burbridge, who is a research associate in policy analysis for the Urban Institute, formerly at the Joint Center for Political Studies, and a member of the Board of Directors of the National Economic Association.

Human Services and Income Policies: Current Trends and Future Directions

Lynn C. Burbridge: If I were to state what I feel is the critical problem of this decade, it is a real increase in inequality in this country. This is quite extraordinary because we are talking about increases in poverty rates for blacks and Hispanics at a time of a much touted economic recovery. While there are problems with minorities who have lower education attainment levels, those levels have risen over the years. There have been clear gains by subgroups within these populations, but the gains that have occurred for some have been undermined by losses experienced by others. This can be simply illustrated by taking a look at income distributions. The percentage of black families with real annual incomes of less than $5,000 (in constant, inflation-adjusted dollars) increased by 36 percent between 1970 and 1985. The percentage of black families with incomes of $50,000 and over increased by 56 percent over the same period. The percentage of black families in the middle of the income distribution declined. The result is growth on the high end, growth on the low end, and decline in the middle.

Obviously, it is not that a great number of black families are in the high income group, but that there has been great growth at the upper income level and significant growth at the lower levels. Altogether, 45 percent of black families have incomes below $15,000 a year. This increasingly large percentage of low-income families remains in spite of years of efforts to improve the situation of blacks and other minorities.

Three reasons have generally been given in the literature for the high poverty rates. One explanation focuses on demographic changes, primarily the rise in female-headed households, or the so-called feminization of poverty. The problem with that reasoning, of course, is that many of these female-headed households were poor before they become female-headed households. Thus, there must be other reasons.

A second group of hypotheses have focused on economic changes. Essentially, theorists have focused on declines in manufacturing, the switch to the service sector, and the flight of jobs from the urban areas. There is serious discussion regarding the importance of these factors. But what is evident is that the average wage rates for manufacturing are much higher than for service jobs. Manufacturing jobs have, in fact, declined. And, if we analyze real wages, real wages for service jobs have declined between 1970 and 1980. They have not for manufacturing. Most two-parent families have been able to keep up in spite of declining wages by increasing the number of people in the family who work. Both parents are now in the work force. Single-parent families do not have that option, and, as an unsurprising result, when we analyze family incomes as opposed to individual incomes, there have been dramatic drops in the real income of female-headed households in recent years.

An interesting aside is that, at the same time there has been a drop in real income, there has been an increase in the emphasis placed on education. The data suggest that the gains in educational attainment have not really paid off. There are numerous reasons for this trend. Some say that educational credentials are used to ration jobs. Others say that the switch to service jobs has placed a greater emphasis on education because there is a greater need for people who deal with the public to be able to speak English or, if they are native speakers, to speak English well. Thus, education has been used as a proxy for ability to comport yourself well on the job. The point is that, whatever gains have been made in education, they have not come quickly enough to compensate for the changes that have occurred in the emphasis placed on education.

The third reason often given for the increase in inequality is public policy. Public policy has been blamed by both conservatives and liberals. Conservatives feel the welfare state has decreased incentives for people to work and therefore has increased poverty. Liberals feel that gaps in the safety nets, particularly evident in recent budget cuts, have increased poverty.

Most of the published literature does not indicate that Aid to Families with Dependent Children (AFDC) benefits have substantially increased the number of female-headed households, and recent cuts in benefits have not helped to decrease poverty but in fact may have increased the numbers of families below the poverty threshold. If the conservative argument held, there should be a decline in poverty with the cuts in welfare programs that have occurred.

I want to focus on two public policy issues that I believe are key. One is that the largest transfer programs are not those that serve the poor; they are programs that serve the elderly. This reality is very often forgotten. Social Security, retirement programs, and medical programs consume about 81 percent of federal transfers. Public assistance is about 6 percent of all transfers. If you add food stamps and housing vouchers, only 13 percent of all transfer programs are specifically targeted for the poor. Although the emphasis in recent years certainly has been on the programs targeting the poor, the media give the impression that these programs are devouring the budget. I am not opposed to programs for the elderly, but it is important to remember where the majority of the transfers are going.

Second, not only have there been drastic cuts in transfer programs, but some of the biggest cuts have come in federal grants to state and local governments. Between 1980 and 1985, for example, there was a 38 percent cut in community regional development programs and a 37 percent cut in education, employment training, and social service program monies going to state and local governments. These programs are very important, for disparities create not only inequality between individuals but also inequality between regions. The original purpose of providing federal grants and aid to state and local governments was to help ameliorate some of these regional differences.

In the past few years, I have studied state differences in programs for employment training, particularly employment training for welfare recipients. Two key factors determine the success or failure of the programs that states have. One is the political commitment in that local area, and the other is the fiscal ability of that area to do something. There is a big difference between the programs that a state with a 3 percent unemployment rate, like Massachusetts, can establish and the programs that a southern state or a state in the Midwest with a high unemployment rate can finance. Consequently, when assistance to local areas is cut, these cuts increase the inequality across regions, which in turn affects inequality among families.

The fourth issue is discrimination. Some observers feel that discrimination is not as significant as it was in the past. The evidence is clear, however, that discrimination is an important variable in explaining inequality, especially as it affects minorities. There is a larger debate over whether discrimination has affected increases in inequality over time. There are those who will propose that in light of gains made by some members of minority groups, you cannot argue that discrimination has, in fact, increased. If you look at discrimination in a very narrow sense in terms of job segregation, it would be difficult to make an argument that prejudice has increased. But if you look at discrimination in a broader sense, in a much more political sense, I think it has to be cited as a very important factor.

Especially when making transnational comparisons, race and ethnicity become significant factors in poverty. In the United States, poverty is associated with race: blacks are poor; Hispanics are poor. Thus, it is much more difficult to get a consensus on what public policy should do about poverty when poverty is associated with minority groups in a pluralistic society, in comparison to dealing with poverty in more homogeneous societies. Comparisons of policies in the United States with policies in countries in Western Europe suggest that it is much easier to put forth a progressive policy agenda in homogeneous societies. In diverse societies race plays a very important role in policy agendas.

Two routes can be taken to reduce inequality. One is to increase productivity. The other is to broaden the social safety net. Both are needed since there is no guarantee, even in the most productive economy, of prosperity for all. There are always going to be pockets of high unemployment. There are going to be low-wage jobs that do not pay enough to keep a family going. Regardless of how productive the economy is, social programs will be necessary. What I propose is a focus on crosscutting policies.

The first issue is minimum standards. There has been discussion about federalism and the concern that local areas know better what their needs are than does the federal government. Certainly, in recent years, when there have been major federal cuts, some states and local areas have been extremely innovative and have done quite marvelous things. In fact, in the past eight years some of the best innovations in social policy have come from the state and local levels. Nonetheless, there are also extreme differences across states and local governments in the kinds of services and safety nets provided to the poor.

There is little justification—and this has been pointed out in a recent study by the Center on Budget and Policy Priorities—for AFDC benefit levels that range from 15.6 percent of the poverty level in Alabama to 83.8 percent of the poverty level in California. Several attempts have been made, of course, to establish minimum standards for AFDC. These efforts have not succeeded, but that does not make them any less important. We must think in terms of minimum standards for states, because some states will only do what is expected of them. Other states will do more than is expected. The question then becomes, What are the minimum standards for social policy programs?

The second issue is indexing. Again, I am talking across programs, not just benefit programs but minimum wage programs as well. A significant proportion of the growth in inequality can be explained by the erosion of benefits and minimum wages due to inflation. Yet few attempts have been made on Capitol Hill to do anything about it. I think we have to think in terms of indexing.

The third issue is incentives. There is a big concern throughout the United States about welfare dependency. In recent travels around the country visiting various programs that provide services to welfare recipients, we heard the same story over and over and over again—the incentives are not there to get people off welfare. Wages are too low, the housing costs are too high, child care is too expensive, and medical benefits do not exist in a lot of small firms. I heard the same story from conservative jurisdictions and liberal jurisdictions, from local areas with low unemployment rates and from local areas with high employment rates. This issue was predictable wherever I went.

The fourth issue is to move away from the concept of poverty programs. The poor are not the only people receiving transfer benefits, and that fact needs to be reiterated again and again and again. Instead, we should think in terms of a family policy that incorporates programs that help all families—programs from AFDC to unemployment insurance to SSI to disability insurance. Different families will, of course, have different needs, but under a universal family policy, no one group will be stigmatized and isolated as "welfare" recipients. This approach can involve making use of already existing universal programs, such as the tax system, to provide benefits similar to the earned income tax credit for the poor.

Similarly, a universal youth policy should include all youth who participate in government programs, from the student loan programs to the Job Corps. Finally, there should be an emphasis on a full-employment policy, so that when employment training programs for the disadvantaged assist the poor in finding jobs, their jobs would not be at the expense of other Americans.

E. Cortés: Our third speaker on this topic is Carol B. Thompson, city administrator and deputy mayor for operations in the government of the District of Columbia. She has served as director of economic development and consumer and regulatory affairs, and heads the district's historic preservation effort.

Policy Analysis

Carol B. Thompson: It is a real pleasure for me to participate in this symposium. Normally, I am out there on the front line working on how to administer these programs and how to assure that the programs have an impact on those who need the services most.

I think it is very important that both Mr. Valdez and Ms. Burbridge acknowledge racial discrimination and inequality as key variables in the problems that are confronting us now. Both acknowledge what Burbridge clearly identifies as the widening of the gap between the haves and have-nots, the growing inequality among blacks, and a higher overall poverty rate in spite of lower unemployment rates. Further, it is noted in both papers that the poor, the near poor, and in some cases the middle class, particularly those with children, do not have access to the resources or the opportunities or the abilities to attain self-sufficiency, and that these circumstances do impact all of us.

Mr. Valdez points out that the poor and others without health insurance coverage have worse health conditions, increased social dependency costs, and reduced opportunities. These conditions result in the public health system being besieged from all points, which increases the cost for health care providers and, ultimately, for the taxpayers. Ms. Burbridge says that increasing concern about lack of skills among high school graduates, particularly minorities, creates a necessity for us to ensure that children within affected families are not denied access to the same opportunities for health, housing, and education as other young people.

They both talk about a crisis but also indicate that there is an opportunity for making a difference. Mr. Valdez says that our crisis is clearly one of organizational capacity, political will, and social conscience and is not solely one of financial constraints in the guise of the federal deficit. Ms. Burbridge recognizes that states with political commitment and resources can simply do more than states without the will and economic base. Both address the need for federal leadership. According to Mr. Valdez, there is a need for guiding principles to reestablish local program responsibility and a need to ensure adequate financing for such efforts. He also has addressed the need to reconsider and eliminate categorical restrictions that exclude certain groups. Ms. Burbridge discusses the need for greater federal commitment for such programs as Head Start, the Job Corps, loans and grants for college education, and training programs.

Both, I think, set forth challenges. Ms. Burbridge says that the challenge is to improve social welfare programs in the context of major budget deficits. Mr. Valdez says that we must move from a crazy patchwork quilt of current medical care systems toward one that provides coverage for all and minimizes or eliminates wasteful expenditures without withholding needed care or bankrupting our cities. He argues that we must develop a framework that establishes universal equity in financing and access to medical care. Ms. Burbridge makes an important point in emphasizing that a key to the discussion of policy solutions is the reality that poverty programs and policies generally considered as minority problems and solutions must be recast as problems that affect all U.S. citizens. These issues do impact us all and must receive the attention of the broader communities.

Both succeed in laying out facts and figures that describe the dramatic picture of human need and inequality in our cities. They present ideas and general proposals that are key elements of any approaches necessary to increase or redirect limited resources. These ideas must be considered as we develop effective social welfare policies and programs and create opportunities for those who need to achieve self-sufficiency.

I would like to take the opportunity to make some comments as an administrator in a city that is very progressive: I believe we are investing a considerable amount of our money in programs that will create opportunities for self-sufficiency, and we receive criticism for doing just that. The welfare reform legislation that has just been passed, although not perfect, provides cities and states with an opportunity to convert income support systems into systems that are more meaningful for welfare-dependent families. Success of those programs will depend in large part on appropriate funding levels and retention of this effort for a significant period of time.

The Work Incentive (WIN) Program, which has been repeatedly criticized, had great potential. The problem is that cities' and states' efforts were crippled by uncertainty of funding from year to year. Unfortunately, welfare reform legislation will not provide assistance to a significant number of poor residents in need of training, child care, and health care. In the District of Columbia nearly one of every two poor adults of working age holds a job. Those poor cannot benefit from the current welfare reform.

The District of Columbia has an excellent start on development of comprehensive child care strategies. Over four hundred children are in city-funded child care programs run by the Department of Human Services or the Department of Recreation. We have four day care facilities for D.C. government employees: one at D.C. General Hospital, another in Superior Court, two in our Department of Human Services, and another is on the way in a new municipal building. The city provides scholarships for residents to be trained as childhood development specialists in cooperation with the city's university. We are spending $16 million annually for child care subsidies, but still the demand for affordable day care far exceeds the supply. Short-term child care initiatives in D.C. and other cities need to be expanded. There needs to be greater utilization of sliding fee scales to expand the pool of day care dollars. Working closely with developers and employers, the city government is committed to offering on-site child care. The government must assist by helping with the design of facilities, identifying day care providers for management, and efficiently administering the licensing process.

The D.C. government has created imaginative legislation that allows the city to appropriate local dollars for human service needs. We are spending more per capita for resident employment and training than any other jurisdiction in the country. The local share for the program has exceeded the federal dollar amount since fiscal year 1985. The use of local dollars empowers us to establish eligibility guidelines that are more liberal than federal requirements. Thus, programs, such as our summer jobs program, are open to many more of our residents. Local dollars are also appropriated to meet the housing needs of low- and moderate-income families through such programs as our Tenant Assistance Program and the Home Purchase Assistance Program.

Because of a strong commitment to investing in our people, city government in the District of Columbia promotes academic and vocational excellence and provides financial incentives in these areas. Although the program received criticism this spring, the mayor did provide $1,000 to each high school valedictorian and salutatorian and, on the junior high level, $500 each to the valedictorian and salutatorian. We expanded the program to provide $1,000 for D.C. residents graduating in the top 10 percent of their class. Our philosophy is to put the money on the front end and not on the back end, because we do pay for inadequate educational training one way or the other.

Since health care is costly and the delivery systems are so complex, I am less confident about our ability to resolve this challenge in the short term. We can, however, begin by making fundamental choices about how health dollars are spent. In the District of Columbia, Medicaid expenditures represent 32 percent of all dollars spent for the poor, a significant portion for long-term care for the elderly and disabled. We are now exploring redirecting some dollars to provide reduced-cost medical care for people in their homes. Overall there must be commitment from the federal government, the local government, the state government, the private sector, and the health care industry to come to the negotiating table and make sacrifices for a better life for all of us.

It is difficult to plan for future human service needs in the same way that we plan for capital development or infrastructure needs. It is also impossible to plan for social services today in the same ways that we have in the past. Who would have predicted five years ago that we would have the AIDS problem, or the extent of homelessness that exists in our cities, or the drug abuse that drains human services budgets?

The city government and the people in the District of Columbia remain confident that investment in people will ultimately become a priority, because businesses now understand that a major element of our economic survival and the changing global economy is people: people who are literate; people who are skilled; people who are trainable. Our competitive edge is on the line, and promoting opportunities for those most in need will create better opportunities for all of us.

Discussion

L. Burbridge: I have a question for Ms. Thompson. The new welfare reform law has been touted as a major initiative for welfare reform, but when I look at it I do not find, except for a few provisions, that there are significant differences from what existed many, many years ago under the WIN Program. Is there any sense from local government about the impact of the new law?

C. Thompson: I do not think the welfare reform legislation goes nearly as far as, or in the directions, we wanted it to go. It does, however, provide some opportunities and gives more flexibility to local jurisdictions to do things that they need to do.

Robert Reischauer, Brookings Institution: With respect to Robert Valdez's tantalizing suggestion that he favors a public utility model for health care, I would like to know what this is, and how one plugs into it. I would like to suggest that I think the medical proposal put forward by Dukakis, and the one being followed in the state of Massachusetts, while not perfect, is certainly a step in the right direction.

E. Cortés: I have been told by people who should know, but perhaps do not, that one of the reasons the Massachusetts program works is that there are very few people who do not have health insurance in the state of Massachusetts, some 10 to 20 percent. The reason that we are concerned here in the Southwest is that approximately 40 to 50 percent of the people here are without health insurance. One out of every five Texans, for example, does not have health insurance. In the Rio Grande Valley virtually no one has health insurance.

Consequently, to focus on an employer—as the one responsible for carrying the health insurance benefits (which I have no objection to per se)—is politically a very onerous task. This approach is much more difficult to implement in places like Texas and Louisiana, particularly with the high unemployment rates those states are experiencing at the present time, than it would be in states like Massachusetts. Therefore, it is somewhat of a cop-out to talk about that model as a model for the country. Would you mind addressing that issue?

R. Reischauer: First of all, it would be an overstatement to say that what Massachusetts is doing is working, because it has not gone into effect yet. We will not really know how successful that approach is for two or three years.

Massachusetts was able to institute a program like this because (1) the fraction of uninsured is low; (2) the state is terribly rich; and (3) it had a system in which the uncompensated care costs of hospitals were being shifted to large employers that provided health insurance, so that there was a built-in constituency among big employers to do something about this—to, in a sense, socialize the costs so that they would not have to bear the burden.

I do not think anybody would argue, Mike Dukakis included, that the proposal is the end of the problem. The question is, is it a first step, given the budget constraints and the political constraints in this country? Is it possible to implement in the next few years? I think there the answer is yes. The Massachusetts plan is basically a proposal in which employers would have to provide some form of basic health insurance. If they did not, they would then have to pay a tax, like an unemployment tax, which would go into a trust fund that would buy health insurance for the uninsured, so that everyone who had a job working more than half time for more than a period of a month or so would have some basic form of health insurance.

The concerns about that approach are, first, what are the costs to society at large? Those costs come in two forms. One is disemployment. The plan raises the costs of hiring an individual; therefore, employers will hire fewer of them. And, second, will the costs be shifted forward in the form of higher prices that all will bear?

My response to the first concern is that the disemployment effects are exaggerated. Most of the uninsured people work in occupations and industries that produce nontradeable goods. Nontradeable goods are not the kinds of products the Japanese make; they are goods produced at McDonald's or Wendy's, for example. Hamburgers will not be delivered from Japan, so we do not have to worry so much about disemployment in these industries due to raising the costs of hiring.

With respect to the prices, there is no question at all that prices would be raised. But is that argument a strong one for not offering health insurance? For example, we are going through a high inflation period, and it is unlikely that anyone will argue that General Motors or the University of Texas or the Brookings Institution should drop health insurance for its employees. Those employers are shifting costs to the rest of society. Why should it be different for other employers?

R. Valdez: You did an excellent job of responding for me. That was just to give equal billing, since you said I have a pox on both camps. On the one hand, the Dukakis plan, as you suggest, is perhaps a first step. I say my job is not necessarily to agree with the plan, but to point out the fact that it inherently continues one of the major problems, the structure of the health insurance system in the United States. The problem is that this approach is dependent upon employment and is employment related.

Some argue that one of the reasons we are in the present situation is that we have seen the U.S. industrial base shift, and the current health insurance benefit program was designed during a period in which we had a different industrial base. As the industrial base has shifted and different types of jobs, such as those in the fast food industries and others like them, have become more prevalent, the employment mechanism is no longer a viable mechanism for providing health insurance. That particular approach accepts the current medical care system with all of its inequities and all of its inefficiencies.

On the Republican side, the Bush proposal takes an approach to social concern that relies primarily on the concept of charity, and charity predominantly from private institutions. That is the thousand lights he frequently refers to. After push came to shove, an expansion of Medicaid was discussed but no details were offered. You can buy into Medicaid, but Medicaid is different in the different states and also the District of Columbia.

The public utility model that I briefly mentioned is not completely defined. The basic component of such a model would be a sense of universal entitlement to a health insurance system in all regions of the country, available to all people by virtue of the fact that they are residents in those areas. Each area would have its own utility, in a sense, its own set of systems, so that the area can define what kind of medical care is needed and make the hard medical choices, such as whether to spend more money on transplants or whether to spend more money on immunizations. Those decisions would be made at the local level and would cut across the jurisdictional lines. The problems of such a jurisdiction have been raised already, as in the dilemma of having many cities that have grown into one another and municipal agencies and governments that overlap.

R. Reischauer: Did you mean something like the Canadian Health Insurance? That is about as close to a current model as is available. But you cannot transfer a model from one country to another, so it is not fair to say a Canadian model. I would not call it that.

John Jeffries, New School for Social Research, New York City: I would like to make a comment about this discussion and then pose a question based on some of the things that Lynn Burbridge had to say on which I agree wholeheartedly.

One thing that is very interesting about the whole poverty and inequality debate is the extent to which poverty, in a very real sense, has been redefined by those people who examine it for a living. Conceptually, poverty has implied for a very long time a lack of income or a very low income as a result of being out of work. Increasingly, poverty is more complicated in the United States, because there is also a poverty that implies wages: the working poor. And so now the combination of these two types of poverty raises complex questions for the programs designed to address poverty and demands reconceptualizing of the problem.

Poverty and inequality, in particular, are very often perceived as anomalies in the American economic system. We are puzzled by the fact that there is poverty and there is economic growth. For some reason the two things seem incongruent with one another. Analysts are concerned that poverty can exist and economic growth can exist concurrently. Their coexistence, I would suggest, implies that poverty is not an anomaly to the economic system on which we are dependent. In fact, one can argue that economic growth of any magnitude is, in fact, dependent upon existing, and perhaps growing, pockets of poverty.

If that is in fact a perspective, I ask you to bear with me for the moment. Let us assume that that is our way of looking at the problem. Then the issue of intervention programs takes on a different perspective. If poverty and inequality are intrinsic to the economic system on which we depend, that is, poverty and inequality are essential to that system (and I know it is not popular to talk about essentialism in these postmodern times), then that raises questions about the type of intervention programs to be pursued and their ends. The question then becomes, what is the extent to which poverty and inequality are disproportionately borne by black and Latino labor force participants and citizens? That is, there seems to be a lot of poverty relative to all the other poverty that must exist, because the system needs poverty in black and Latino communities.

The question then becomes, as analysts and policy people, would we be satisfied with a more equal distribution of poverty? Should that be the focus of programs that attempt to intervene and intercede? That's one perspective.

Another perspective would obviously imply something about the construction of programs that address the more fundamental issue of inequality and poverty as being essential. Would we as analysts, or should we as public policy people, be prepared to argue that we would be a lot happier with a distribution of poverty that is more equal? Poverty is not acceptable. I do not think I could ever argue that it would be.

E. Cortés: Well, let me ask the question differently. If we were in Mexico, and there were no Indians, and a lot of people were impoverished and illiterate, would we be happy because everybody who is poor is Mexican?

L. Burbridge: I do not think you can argue that poverty is okay if it is equally distributed. On the other hand, you can argue that when poverty is concentrated within a certain group the ramifications go beyond that particular group. A 30 percent poverty rate among blacks affects the entire society in terms of the disintegration of the family and the other consequences of poverty. So it is a tricky question to answer. I would argue that we must attack poverty wherever it is. But the concentration of poverty within a particular group is very, very, very serious and can be very dangerous to the economy.

E. Cortés: I never conceptualize poverty in terms of income. I have always thought about it in terms of choices and limitations of choices.

Evelyn Hu-Dehart, University of Colorado, Boulder: As a working mother, I want to talk specifically about the delivery of health care and child care. As a working mother, I need both, and I also know that both are extremely costly in this country. Every month I pay over $700 of my take-home paycheck for one child's care and my family's health care. That amount of money is probably equivalent to a good family income for much of America. Yet I have seen such countries as China and Cuba apparently manage to deliver more equitable health and child care; although it may not be the quality we expect. But I do not want to compare the United States to those countries. Other advanced industrialized countries in this world, for example, Western Europe and Japan, also seem to have done a better job of delivering those services in terms of quality and equitability than the United States.

I wonder if any of the panelists would like to help me understand why it seems so difficult for this country to at least approach some of the successes of those western advanced industrialized capitalist countries?

E. Cortés : I was always told that Bismarck developed a much more equitable and fair social insurance system, one which is much more progressive than anything we have ever seen in this country. Of course, he did the right thing initially, as most people do, for the wrong reason.

R. Valdez: In a recent lecture in my class at UCLA, we were talking about the basis on which the current U.S. health care system has been structured. On the medical care issue, what we have is the conflict in the United States of two basic social values in which the actual goals of those social values are the same. One viewpoint suggests that social and personal responsibility are best achieved through individual achievement and, therefore, individual achievement should be rewarded. One of the rewards that our society has to give is medical care.

The other viewpoint also believes, from a personal responsibility point of view, in individual achievement. But that viewpoint believes, in addition, that there are commodities in our society that should remain outside the reward system in order to provide everyone an equal chance in that competition for individual achievement. One of those commodities is education and the other, I would suggest, is medical care.

This constant conflict runs through the course of the history of the United States and its development of social institutions. We see a constant pull back and forth between these viewpoints in the system that we currently have.

R. Reischauer: I can answer the question posed a little while ago, which was how does Japan do such a wonderful job with health care and child care. With day care, it does a wonderful job by having mothers stay home. The fact is that the women's participation rate in the labor force, particularly women with young children, is very low in Japan. So I would not hold them up as a model society that has answered the question of child care.

E. Cortés: How do they do in health care?

R. Reischauer: Better than the United States, but that does not say much, because most of the industrialized world, with the exception of South Africa, does a better job in this area than the United States.

Just one note on Bismarck, since we are going back in history here. He has a much better reputation now than he did then. He set up a wonderful retirement system that everybody looks at as the great-grandfather of our Social Security system. He had a retirement age of 65, but, the fact is, only 5 percent of the population lived to be that age and to collect from it.

Manuel del Valle, Attorney: I am moving away from German history to some American history. Ms. Burbridge made a comment that seems to imply that there is somehow less employment discrimination today, looking at the statistics. My personal experience, having spent a year chronicling employment discrimination on the basis of national origin, is precisely the converse of that. In point of fact, employment discrimination, as well as illegal discrimination in the area of sex, is increasing across the board by race and national origin. What the Supreme Court has done is merely increase the burden of proof of plaintiffs so that plaintiffs will no longer bring suits they cannot afford to litigate. A suit that once cost $10,000, which was an astronomical sum once upon a time in the 1970s, today would easily run about $100,000. The court has reallocated burdens and costs. But I wonder what you meant when you commented that employment discrimination somehow appears to be less.

L. Burbridge: What I was referring to was the growth in inequality and the extent to which you can focus on employment discrimination as a causal factor of increasing inequality. I would never deny that employment discrimination is a very important factor in terms of the existence of overall inequality. Whether or not it has increased is hard to say. Certainly the enforcement of civil rights has not been what it has been in the past. Discrimination may very well have increased, because enforcement has been much less rigorous than in the past, particularly in the complete unwillingness of the federal government to take on class action suits. I think it is more difficult to argue that increasing inequality, as opposed to the overall level of equality, is due to employment discrimination in its very limited, narrow sense of the definition.

M. del Valle: When you look at inequality, what is it that you are really talking about? What is it that you are including and excluding? For example, Mr. Valdez easily speaks about public health "utilities" and residence as a basis for health coverage without also indicating whether undocumented workers are covered by these proposals. When we talk about inequality in numbers, we talk about the percentage of whites in the areas, but we are leaving out a definitional framework. Are we including those who under various statutes would not be covered? What do you mean when you say "inequality?" Are you talking about the Hispanics in New York who are undocumented and working but not getting benefits, and so on?

L. Burbridge: That is a legitimate point. I was talking about those who are in the income distribution statistics in the first place. When you are talking about undocumented workers, they are not even counted in any of statistics that are available. From a researcher's point of view, it becomes a very difficult problem to deal with, because you cannot measure their presence. You cannot grapple with the problem. Clearly, that is an issue that is very significant, particularly in light of the recent immigration reform law.

Celestino Mendez, American G.I. Forum: My question is, how do we make socialized services more acceptable to our society? The panelists have tended to say this is one way that we are going to solve some of our short-term problems.

E. Cortés: The problem is nobody here wants to touch that question. Evidently, socialized services are two of the words that you do not use in polite company. Obviously, there is not a very strong inclination on the part of those who have power in this country to do the right things for the right reason. Maybe we could convince those in power that they ought to do the right thing for the wrong reason, which is probably the way most policies happen anyway. Maybe at some point people who are poor, who do not have choices, will begin to get more power and begin to make the Michael Dukakises and the George Bushes begin to pay more attention to them.

Right now, unfortunately, they are not getting attention because of the way presidential campaigns are run, which I find extremely abhorrent and distasteful. The whole marketing approach to politics has taken over. There is a lack of real public debate taking place. There is an old bumper sticker that says,"I don't vote because it only encourages them."

But most of us are going to vote. In fact, that's part of my profession, to get people to vote. Unfortunately, by voting we will continue to encourage lack of attention to real issues. So there is an irony and sadness about all of this. Hopefully some of us who are here will begin to devise more innovative ways to bring these questions to the attention of those people who have the power to make changes.

TOP (Left to right): *Ricardo Romo (back to camera), Frank Bonilla, Edwin Melendez, Margaret Simms, Leobardo Estrada*. BOTTOM LEFT: *Ricardo Romo*. BOTTOM RIGHT: *Edwin Melendez*

PART V

Economic and Community Development Policies

PART V

Introduction

Ricardo Romo: First, let me say that this session focuses on jobs and the changing occupational structure. We will talk about consumption, productivity, international cooperation, shifts in our spending priorities, and competitiveness. In the 1990s we are going to continue to examine and refute the old myths regarding Latinos in the United States, but the realities are going to be that Hispanics or Latinos are already the fastest-growing population in the country and soon will be approaching the size of the black population.

The reality today, which will be even more prevalent and evident to us in the nineties, is that the majority is going to be a minority population. The most recent example can be seen in Dallas, Texas. At the present time, over 50 percent of the public school students in Dallas are black and brown students. This pattern is occurring more and more frequently in various cities across the country, and we will see more of that demographic shift in the 1990s.

The debate in the next decade will not be just about jobs, but about job security; not only about steady work, but about comparable worth. It will be about the need for more job training and a guaranteed income for those who cannot work.

I would like to introduce the next speaker. Dr. Frank Bonilla is presently Thomas Hunter Professor of Sociology at the City University of New York and is the director of the Center for Puerto Rican Studies at Hunter College. He is executive director of the Inter-University Program (IUP). Dr. Bonilla is on various committees and is always very, very supportive of projects to bring Latino issues to the forefront.

Cooperation and Competition for Jobs and the Renewal of Community in a Global Economy

Frank Bonilla: I chose my title to bring forth elements that I think are present today and were absent when the Kerner, Katzenbach, and Eisenhower Commissions' diagnoses and prescriptions were formulated.

The first of these elements is the growing pertinence of the global setting in fixing parameters for U.S. economic development. Within this global perspective arises the centrality of cooperation. Thus, along with its competitive capability, the United States has a constructive role not only in promoting its own economic growth but also in helping the rest of the world economy in ways not conceived of in the past.

The second element has to do with access to jobs and the adequacy of incomes as foundations for the economic security of individuals and families. Access to jobs and adequate income are also the foundations for that sense of community and social integration necessary to hold the nation together.

A third tension, present today and absent twenty years ago in the United States, concerns enlarged democracy in participation, that is, democracy and participation not just as political values but as the foundation for renewed economic growth. Unless there is a renewal of faith in the democratic system and in genuine participation at all levels, in fact, economic recovery will prove to be very difficult.

Fourth is the present reality of the withdrawal of the federal government and federal leadership, which stood in the forefront of the reforms that the earlier commissions proposed. The federal commitment is no longer there, and, as a result, we are seeing a new configuration of state and local powers, in combination with private sector and community organizations, trying to fill this role. These groups are clearly quite successful in many settings, but this shift of powers must be closely examined in terms of its viability as a long-term basis for filling the role that the federal government played in the past. These new configurations of powers are creating and implementing policy in a stopgap way.

There is a fifth element that is different from the decade of the Great Society and our present situation in the cities. In the 1960s there were research efforts, advisory bodies, and technical consultation in the preparation of the several commission reports. Herbert Stein, whom some of you may know, is certainly a person who has carefully chronicled the advice that economists have provided to presidents over the last forty-five years. He has remarked that the Employment Act of 1946, which established the President's Council of Economic Advisors and the Congressional Joint Economic Committee, was supposed to bring economic science into the political process. In his view, what it succeeded in doing was bringing politics into economics.

In the late 1960s, the commission reports were never challenged on the basis of politicizing the policy process. That is, the seriousness, the competence, and good will of the people involved were never challenged. Today, we routinely find a skepticism regarding technical advice. Stein himself, in *Presidential Economics*, has said: "Economists do not know enough even to say with much confidence and precision what the effects of different economic policies would be. Even if one is able to describe what effects are desired, he cannot be sure of the prescription of policy that would yield those effects. . . . Even if it were possible to identify the policy that would be best or probably best from the standpoint of most of the persons concerned, it might not be possible to get that policy adopted" (New York: Simon and Schuster, 1984, p. 323).

This prevailing sense of gridlock and questioning and a loss of faith in the disciplines and the whole process of policy formation is a serious element of the present that has a new aura to it. That aura relates to another reality, which suggests that, as the diagnoses of the nation's economic ills increasingly focus on issues of productivity and competitiveness, the advisors in science and technology enter the picture in completely new ways. This is occurring at a time when the credibility of science advisors, along with that of individuals involved in social policy, also begins to crumble. Today we hear authoritative voices, such as Theodore Hesburgh, Edward Teller, Jerome Wiesner, and others, who testify about the difficulties, the impasses, and the shortfalls in bringing scientific knowledge to bear on national policymaking. They complain about the low esteem into which policy advising has fallen in the post-Eisenhower period. This low esteem of science advising has now come to affect not only the contributions of science to the nation's initiatives in defense and space but also the areas of international negotiations over technology and trade, environmental protection, and scientific cooperation.

This signals a concern pertinent to our discussion. That is, the falling from status and influence of national scientists interests us directly because it reflects a common challenge facing all of the disciplines concerned with social policy. Distinctions continue to be made between "hard" and "soft" policy advice, that is, advice given by true experts and politically seasoned individuals, which usually comes on request and is given privately, versus unsolicited and publicly delivered recommendations, such as those we are making here, that are presumed to be driven by ideology or special interest.

One aspect of this shift in the way scientists see their role is a readiness on their part to deal more directly with an adversarial dimension. Furthermore, the legitimation of public, nonexpert participation in the policy process along with the acknowledgment that scientific experts need to win public acceptance for their recommendations are points in the foreground of policy debates for the first time.

The stunning contributions that science and technology have made to U.S. defense and space programs have been substantially sustained by an extraordinary macroeconomic and fiscal environment. As these conditions have altered, scientists are called upon to guide the technological revitalization of the national economy. This shift of scientific concern from production for military defense and command of space toward a focus on competitiveness in production to meet social needs, within a new global framework of interdependence, could prove to be a historic watershed in the management of social change in all societies. The Soviet Union might even help by showing that some of its innovations contain workable approaches to dilemmas concerning work and sharing in consumption that are being confronted by both socialist and capitalist planners. One of the central issues present for both competitive market societies and centrally planned societies is the problem of the effective and productive use of human resources. Both types of regimes are facing similar kinds of problems.

The presumption that it is the scientist and engineers—the people who create and harness new technologies—who are now best equipped to guide the nation back to economic leadership flows directly from the premise that it is slackness in productivity and competitiveness that casts a deep shadow on the nation's future. The United States, in this view, is simply no longer first with the newest or the best. How do we account for this fall from grace? What can we do about it?

The answers that come from the circle of nationally recognized scientists and engineers, and the economists who enjoy their confidence, are frankly skeptical. I quote briefly from a piece by Raymond Vernon, addressing a 1986 forum on world technologies and national sovereignty that was sponsored by the National Academy of Engineering. He says: "Upon identifying the main issues, one is propelled to a basic conclusion: Given the nature of the issues, better data and closer analysis are unlikely to have more than a marginal effect on the behavior of the U.S. government and other governments. The problems are too large and too conjectural, and the domestic and international mechanisms for action too feeble, to generate more than a marginal impact."

Now, these constraints on policy weigh most heavily on the issue of inequality that concerns us most, that is, the problem of moving toward creative international agreements that lead the United States toward economic and leadership recovery without, as Vernon himself puts it, "beggaring other countries," without building our recovery on the impoverishment of others.

Next comes the problem of countering internal trends toward economic and ethnic polarization. Vernon's conclusion is that, in present circumstances, there is realistically room for only a few principled interventions: (1) working at the margin to prop up the educational system; (2) promoting a few promising technological spin-offs that may bolster new production; and (3) providing ample freedom and incentives to managers and investors that may have similar effects.

Today, this repertory of limited interventions appears repeatedly in the commentary and analysis from scientific circles and in the scientific journals. The July 1988 issue of *Science*, for example, featured the theme of economic competitiveness. According to one of the analyses in that issue, the great strength of U.S. technological advance, despite its narrow concentration on nuclear weapons, aerospace, and electronics via a small number of very high cost projects, has been the high mobility of factors of production. The United States has flexible capital, labor, and technical resources. This is also true of the institutions, such as the academic research laboratories, that undergird these initiatives. Thus, the United States, as a paradigmatic shifter of technical capabilities to new products and sectors, should continue to build on this flexibility. This position translates into investment in human capital, further deregulation, decentralization of the private sector, and added incentives to business. Thus, there are many plausible rationales that sustain this very standpat, limited intervention alternative.

The basic point here is that the illusions linger that competitiveness got us to the top and can restore the United States to command of the world economy, as long as we build on the leverage provided by technological advantage. Despite passing references to the growing problems of inequality within and among nations and the urgency of arresting a decline in the real incomes of U.S. workers, there is little social or ethical content in the emerging debate within the framework of productivity, competitiveness, and the place of the United States in the world economy.

The most authoritative and resolute break with this minimalist strategy for economic recovery, and one that has been cautiously advanced in the platforms of both national parties, turns out to be the program of the candidate who decided not to run. The Cuomo Commission's Report on Trade and Competitiveness presents several alternative strategies. Although the Cuomo report is couched in the same rhetoric of postwar U.S. ascendancy, that report at least acknowledges some of the major dilemmas the nation confronts in dealing with the realities of declining power. These realities bear directly on the issues of social integration at several levels: the transnational; the internal articulation of regional, state, and local initiatives; and workplace democracy.

What the Cuomo Commission is saying is that the new global interdependence, in Cuomo's own words, calls for "responsible internationalism." Loss of dominance does not mean fewer, but more, opportunities for creative leadership. Conditions are ripe in the international sphere for unprecedented successes in learning to share. The Cuomo Commission reports that it is at the state and local levels that "the American tradition of positive government is alive and well." The commission report goes into a great amount of detail pointing out the ways in which state and local governments have shown initiative and creativity in ways that the federal government has not.

And, most pertinent for our discussion, the third arena for creative collaboration and cooperation that the Cuomo report highlights is in the realm of employer-worker relations and collective efforts. Again, chiefly local initiatives have been responsible for rebuilding local infrastructures, especially in education. Local initiatives have introduced many aspects of sharing in decisions and participation in gains and profits through ownership and management by workers. Collaborative arrangements have resulted in local governments, firms, labor unions, and community groups structuring ways of defining production goals, managing the work site, and making major decisions about investments.

Even in the Cuomo report there are great silences and reticences about the major problems facing U.S. cities. Nonetheless, the Cuomo Commission recommendations represent the only opening within the official structure for the revitalization of a national movement toward full employment. The shifting fortunes of this idea have begun to be tracked and brought into public view in recent work by Bertram Gross and Stanley Moses.

For several years the Black Legislative Caucuses have spearheaded a move in the U.S. Congress that culminated in 1988 when Congress introduced the Economic Bill of Rights Act and the Quality of Life Action Act. Both of these bills were endorsed by the National Democratic Committee, just as the Cuomo Commission completed its work in the fall of 1987. Neither the action of the National Committee nor the initiatives of the black legislators and the many white cosponsors in the Congress are mentioned in the Cuomo report. It is important, however, to understand that this is a movement that now includes not just those legislators but also major church groups, labor unions, and community organizations around the country.

There may seem to be a contradiction in low employment rates in many areas around the country and the continued demand for full-employment policy. With unemployment hovering nationally around 5.5 percent and well below that in numerous key states and cities, some suggest that full employment is not a distant dream but an accomplished fact. Ironically, what commands attention and preoccupation in the business and financial pages of the press are the slight gains in the cost of labor as millions of jobs are said to go begging, and an "overheating" economy is said to threaten new inflation.

But today's "full employment" comes with more people than ever outside the work force and with millions intermittently in and out of work, as spells of unemployment become more frequent and more prolonged. A smaller proportion than ever of those who are jobless are covered by unemployment insurance. Millions are involuntarily in part-time jobs or working full-time for poverty wages. The political need to couple rights to jobs with job quality and minimal income for those within and outside the work force is thus compelled not by ideology but by harsh economic pressures.

What the proposed full-employment legislation and parallel initiatives by unions, churches, and voluntary associations bring most sharply into focus is the range of side conditions now necessary to give genuine social content to any formula for U.S. economic recovery. The new initiatives must be more than a replay of New Deal and Great Society stratagems, because the problems today are rooted in a fundamentally transformed global economic and political context.

Generally, there are five points of reference that no set of recommendations concerning the future of work and the reconstruction of the economy in the United States can afford to treat tangentially, especially with regard to African Americans and Latinos. These points are the following:

1. The assertion of economic rights to jobs and adequate income. Few Americans know that an Economic Bill of Rights was placed before the Congress in July of 1987 or that its guiding principles were articulated in 1944 by President Franklin D. Roosevelt in a State of the Union Message. This "unfinished constitutional business" must be resumed to bring these rights within the realm of law, political accountability, and adequate implementation. A powerful ethical foundation and an organizing impetus for advancing this agenda of full employment have been provided by the report of the National Conference of Catholic Bishops published in 1986 and titled *Economic Justice for All*. The organizing at the grass-roots level inspired by this pastoral is just one example of the forces now gathering strength for full-employment goals.

2. A foreign policy integrating shared economic objectives and collaborative strategies for improving living standards and reducing inequality within and among nations. H.R. 1398, the Quality of Life Action Act, states this goal succinctly: "It shall be the policy of the federal government to cooperate with the governments of other countries and with the United Nations in helping develop an international community based on rising living standards, particularly for those people with the lowest levels of income, wealth, access to public facilities, free trade union organization, and political power." The basic principle in this act is that as the capability of nations to single-handedly guarantee economic security to their own citizens wanes, human rights, jobs, and incomes must be projected to an international level.

3. A rearticulation of sovereignties. This refers to the question of how local initiatives are to be coordinated with federal and state economic undertakings.

4. The democratization of economic policymaking and work in both the private and public sectors. We must come forward with designs for democratizing private sector employment. If this is to make a difference, there must be a parallel process of democratization of economic policymaking and of public sector employment.

5. Breaking down the legacy of racial, ethnic, and gender inequality. If the United States really were on a track of rebuilding a full-employment economy, we should not have to worry about the disadvantaged situation of particular groups. However, it is now well established that no matter how ambitious a scheme or how evenhandedly the scheme is administered, implementation of full-employment policies would leave most of the players in approximately the same position in which they entered the game. Most would remain with the unequal endowments with which they began. The fact that affirmative action legislation and enforcement have been at a standstill in the 1980s means that the U.S. government must reinvent a new affirmative apparatus with respect to equal opportunity for women, African Americans, and Latinos.

R. Romo: Dr. Edwin Melendez is one of the few Latinos with a Ph.D. in economics. There are probably not more than five or six Latino economists in the whole country. Thus, we are privileged to have his participation. He is an assistant professor of economics at the Massachusetts Institute of Technology (MIT). He has worked in various areas, including research on Latinos in the labor market, wage inequality, female labor supply, and employment policies.

Toward a Good Job Strategy for Latino Workers*

Edwin Melendez: Frank Bonilla's presentation focused on the structural or macro level of jobs, job strategies, and public policies regarding employment. I will address employment policies and the integration of jobs and employment opportunities at the local level.

As we worked on this presentation, Governor Dukakis had a substantial lead in the polls, and no one suspected that the author of the Job Training Partnership Act (JTPA) was going to be nominated as the vice-presidential candidate for the Republican party. I doubt that the JTPA will be changed in any substantial way, and, in that context, local reform seems to have greater meaning.

I will make three basic arguments. The first is that the issue of employment and training, despite the lack of discussion in the presidential race, has become one of the most important public policy issues. Second, the current employment and training programs mostly associated with the JTPA funding and policies are inadequate. And, finally, there are positive policies that can be implemented at the local level. I will discuss some of these possible strategies.

I would propose that we pursue a good-job strategy as a policy goal. As long as we pursue a policy of employment and training programs that focus on placing people in low-wage jobs, the issue of employment opportunities will continue to rise to the forefront of public policy. At least three factors are important in explaining why job policies and employment and training issues continue to come to the forefront of public policy.

The first one, and Frank Bonilla talked about this, is the issue of international competitiveness and the U.S. position in the global economy. On that factor, public policy analysts are convinced that our loss of competitiveness has to do with the decline in the quality of the labor force in this country. Therefore, there is an important policy discussion about how we can improve the quality of labor. The second factor is the polarization of jobs and wages in this country. In general, throughout the sixties and seventies, the share of low-wage jobs in the labor force declined, but it increased during the late seventies and eighties. Furthermore, a change in the distribution of high- and low-wage jobs has adversely and disproportionately affected Latinos and blacks in the United States. Finally, the recent welfare reforms are intended to channel workers to low-wage labor markets.

---

* The paper on which this presentation is based will be published by the John F. Kennedy School of Government in the *Journal of Hispanic Policy*, vol. 4 (April 1990).

The public policy dilemma seems to be whether to shift the focus to long-term employment and training programs or to continue to emphasize short-term employment and training goals, with the main objective of the latter being to provide a supply of low-wage labor to secondary labor markets. This policy debate is extremely important to Latinos for three reasons: (1) Latinos are overrepresented in secondary labor markets and comprise a good share of the low-wage workers; (2) Latinos are an important and an increasing proportion of the workers in this country; and (3) the changes introduced in the last eight years in the employment and training system have disproportionately affected Latino workers. These factors together have increased the barriers that Latinos face when they come to labor markets.

During the Reagan administration, the main employment and training program has been the Job Training Partnership Act (JTPA), which was a substitute for Comprehensive Employment and Training Act (CETA). CETA, in the later years of the Carter administration, was under heavy attack for numerous reasons. The public sector employment program of CETA received heavy criticism for federal monies going to subsidize jobs at the local level that would have been created anyway. Other CETA programs were criticized for selecting job-ready applicants for the program and for having a small impact on participants' skills.

The increasing criticism of CETA allowed the Reagan administration, in the worst recession of the postwar period, to cut funding for employment and training programs. It represented the first time in the postwar period that a major employment and training program was not enacted to combat rising unemployment. Rather, the Reagan administration eliminated public sector employment and cut funding for programs such as youth employment and summer job programs that were having a positive impact on youth unemployment.

As if that were not enough, the Reagan administration introduced reforms that made it more difficult for those participants in need of longer-term services to participate in job training programs. JTPA instituted new regulations to minimize cost per participant, maximize placements at the local level, and eliminate participant stipends. Under these provisions service providers selected the more-job-ready applicants for the programs in order to have higher performance evaluations.

There is some evidence that these changes affected Latinos more than blacks and whites. If we look at Chicago and New York City, where there are large concentrations of Puerto Ricans, Latino participation in JTPA declined more than that of any of the other groups. The cuts in stipends were one factor for this decline, but a substantial reduction in the support for programs such as English as a second language and other classroom training programs that targeted populations in need for longer periods of service was a more influential factor contributing to the decline in Latino participation.

In this context, what can we do at the local level? As long as we do not change employment and training policies to provide long-term services, these programs are going to be highly ineffective for Latinos. They will continue to circulate low-wage workers from one dead-end job to another. To remove these barriers and to improve employment, we have to address not only increasing the human capital of these workers in terms of education and skill levels but also the demand-side barriers created by discrimination.

Four basic reforms should be supported. The first is to increase the funding of JTPA. It is difficult at the current level of funding to provide more than token service to a very small proportion of the population. Some analysts have suggested, at least in the short run, to double the present funding of JTPA to about $11 million or $12 million, with a portion of this increase going to public sector employment.

The second reform would be to link employment and training programs to economic development programs. The separation between economic development strategies and employment and training programs is not only unwarranted but also a waste of public resources promoting economic development. Human capital improvement is an important part of any economic development program. In cities with substantial economic resources, such as New York and Chicago, it is unfortunate that economic development projects are not used more often to promote equal employment opportunity. For example, such projects should include stricter employment targets for disadvantaged workers.

The third reform is to integrate more employment and training programs into the educational system, to mainstream educational programs in such a way that employment and training programs are not perceived as second-chance institutions for those who cannot attend college. Negative images affect not only those who participate in the programs but also the expectations of the programs' success.

Finally, community-based organizations (CBOs) should have greater participation in JTPA programs. JTPA has affected in a very negative way the CBOs' involvement in job training. Most CBOs do not like to get involved with JTPA. Not only do CBOs believe that the program is not providing meaningful services, but they also believe that it is providing short-term solutions to a very complicated problem and cannot make any meaningful difference. Overall, the role of CBOs in the JTPA has changed. Now the private sector has more to say in job training than do CBOs. Moreover, the ideological direction of JTPA seems to be to satisfy private sector needs at the expense of good jobs for the community.

Until we promote a good-job strategy at the local level as well as at the federal level, as opposed to just circulating workers among low-wage temporary positions, the creation of jobs for disadvantaged workers is going to continue to be a problem in public policy.

R. Romo: Margaret Simms is commenting on a paper prepared by Bernard Anderson, who is not here today. Dr. Simms is also an economist and is deputy director of research at the Joint Center for Political Studies. She was formerly the director of the minorities and social policy program at the Urban Institute, and editor of the *Review of Black Political Economy.*

Economic and Community Development Policy: Issues and Challenge for a New Administration

Margaret Simms: Bernard Anderson sent me this paper with a note that said I could summarize it and add any comments that I might like. I was tempted to say everything and not distinguish between Bernie's thoughts and mine. Then I could deny espousing anything that was attacked during the question-and-answer period. However, it is difficult for me to keep my opinions to myself, so I am not sure I can make it through this presentation without making distinctions between Bernie's thoughts and mine.

In preparing for the conference, I read the report summaries of the Kerner Commission, the Eisenhower Commission, and the Katzenbach Commission, and I was very much struck by how far we have come and how little things have changed. Of particular interest, in the context of the present discussion, is material in the Kerner Commission report that revolved around employment and family. I would like to read a few quotes to contrast the Kerner report with the information provided in the Anderson paper.

In discussing racial differences in employment and income, the Kerner Commission stated, "Yet despite continuing economic growth and declining national unemployment rates, the unemployment rate for Negroes in 1967 was double that for Whites." The report goes on to discuss family disintegration by stating, "Men who are chronically unemployed or employed in the lowest status jobs are often unable or unwilling to remain with their families." In discussing the welfare system, the report says, "Our present system of public welfare is designed to save money instead of people, and tragically ends up doing neither."

The Kerner report contrasts with the evidence presented in the Anderson paper. In looking at overall economic expansion and its role in increasing employment, Dr. Anderson points out that, in August 1988, the proportion of the working-age population in the labor force had reached a record 66.3 percent at the same time that the unemployment rate stood at 5.6 percent, half the unemployment rate in the nadir of the 1981-82 recession.

During the economic expansion since 1982, black workers have experienced noteworthy gains in employment and reductions in unemployment. Their employment has risen by about 2.6 million since November of 1982, with employment increases among adult males and females being approximately equal. These gains were significantly larger in relative terms than those for other workers. Indeed, black workers comprise 10.6 percent of the civilian labor force, but blacks in the labor force obtained 16.3 percent of the jobs created during the expansion. Nonetheless, Dr. Anderson notes, "Even after six years of continuous economic growth, the black unemployment rate remains at more than twice the unemployment rate of white workers (with a ratio over two and a half times that of white workers)." That rate is actually higher than it was twenty years ago. In other words, things have changed, but, in many ways, things remain the same.

Among youth, a group that is of particular concern as we look at the future, there is good news and bad news. This group is noteworthy because the Kerner Commission identified black males between the ages of fifteen and twenty-four as those most likely to be involved in crime and riots. There are fewer youth than there were in the 1960s and that should mean a decline in crime. Even among blacks, the youth population has declined by approximately 100,000 during this decade. However, because black population growth is falling more slowly in terms of absolute numbers, blacks are becoming a larger proportion of the youth population and, therefore, the youth labor market. Dr. Anderson notes that, in 1987 alone, employment increased among black youth almost as much as it did during the five-year period from 1975 to 1980. Most of that job expansion was in the private sector, which is promising, because during the 1975-1980 period the gains were attributable to youth employment programs. However, even with this optimistic note, unemployment differentials remain quite severe between white and black youth, with about half of all white teens having jobs compared to only about a fourth of black teens.

Those of us who live in the inner city note, perhaps, that there is some decreasing fear of crime, because rather than purse snatching, people are involved in selling drugs. The decline in muggings is overshadowed, however, at least in Washington and perhaps in other big cities, by the nightly drug-related murders among black youth. Thus, we can hardly take much encouragement from this economic change.

Previous discussion at this conference has revolved around the changing economy and the extent to which those changes have played a role in redefining the economic opportunities that are available. Much has been made of the changing economic structure within the U.S. economy, particularly the decline in manufacturing employment opportunities, which has changed the structure of wage opportunities for those with less than a high school education. Decreasing opportunities are also often linked to the higher concentration of poverty within the inner city. It has been noted that this concentration has increased among blacks more than among whites, and that 34 percent of the black poor live in the low-income areas of the fifty largest cities in this country. Thus, when we talk about poverty, we are talking about cities and, in some sense, a few cities.

The high rates of poverty among children are particularly acute. Recent figures from 1987 show that the growth in the poverty rate among blacks is particularly high among children. Now, this is heavily tied to family structure. While the Kerner Commission report looked at unemployment and underemployment as factors in family disintegration, today the problem is more one of a lack of family formation. During this decade much of the growth in female-headed families among blacks has been due not to divorce but to births among never-married mothers. The fathers of those families are not participating in the legitimate labor market, if one can judge by the statistics on both employment and income for black males under the age of thirty.

The question then becomes, what kinds of policies do we need in order to change the structure of economic opportunity within cities? Here, several suggestions can be made, and they reinforce some of the factors that Edwin Melendez pointed out. That is, the way we have structured employment and training programs during this decade does not provide opportunities for those who are most in need of them. The training periods are too short, and the emphasis on job placement tends to cream the applicant pool and does not make distinctions among the types of jobs, even though performance standards are tied to minimum wage rates. Very little actual training is provided, and the lack of stipends during the training period tends to make these job training programs an unattractive option for youth from low-income families.

The proposals put forth in the Anderson paper revolve almost exclusively around changes in the employment and training system as a way of promoting economic opportunity. He suggests an enriched work experience program that involves the private sector and points to what is called in Philadelphia the "five percent solution." This approach requires or promotes incentives for the private sector to hire one economically disadvantaged youth for every twenty new employees. Mr. Anderson suggests an increase of about a third in the current expenditure on youth programs, which would amount to about $400 million.

He suggests retargeting funds to take account of joblessness, basic skill levels, and the availability of jobs rather than putting the emphasis exclusively on family income. Anderson's plan would target support services, particularly English-as-a-second-language programs, which would improve the benefits for Hispanics and others who have problems with the English language. He also proposes improved child care, which is an important factor for young mothers. Evaluations of existing employment and training programs show that the least benefit seems to accrue to young mothers, and it is difficult to separate their failure to benefit from these programs from their child care responsibilities.

Anderson suggests transferring funds from in-school programs to out-of-school programs, with the assumption that school budgets could be expanded to pick up the in-school and transitional programs that are currently funded under employment and training. This transfer would free more money for concentration on out-of-school youth.

However, national economic expansion in the United States seems to be leaving people behind, and it is also leaving neighborhoods and cities behind. The question then becomes, is it possible to bring jobs to people? The policy perspectives presented in this country seem to focus on moving people to jobs instead of trying to find ways to move jobs to people. This dilemma suggests not just jobs programs but also economic development programs. This might mean promoting the location of existing firms in areas with low job opportunities or the creation of new firms in those areas. Certainly, such programs as Urban Development Action Grants (UDAG) did put more emphasis on trying to get large companies to stay in high-unemployment areas or to move into certain areas within central cities.

In addition to these efforts, perhaps we should examine initiatives that would supply more business opportunities for members of minority groups. There has been evidence in the past ten years that business opportunities, where available, are taken advantage of by blacks and Hispanics. More important, blacks and Hispanics are moving away from the traditional community-oriented company into nontraditional, technologically advanced industries that provide not only the opportunity for greater profits but also the opportunity for more employment of other members of their respective communities. Certainly, in the last ten years, little has been done at the national level to provide the right incentives for business development. Specifically, this support might involve capital availability, support for business set-asides, and the promotion of markets for minority firms.

R. Romo: Our commentator, Dr. Leo Estrada, is an associate professor in the School of Architecture and Urban Planning at UCLA. He is also a member of the IUP/SSRC Committee for Public Policy Research on

Contemporary Hispanic Issues. For several years he has been one of the principal Hispanic advisors to the U.S. Census.

Policy Analysis

Leobardo Estrada: We have two papers that deal with very complex issues. Community development sounds simple in terminology but, in fact, it encompasses a number of levels of issues. We generally work with some basic assumptions, and I should begin by identifying the basic premise that I work from: while I know no persons who would stand up and say they are against community development, in practice it is clear that there is support for only very limited forms of community development and only half-hearted support for that minimal development by the administrations and local governments with whom most of us have contact.

It is quite clear that the limited nature of community development and the limited support for it have to do with the fact that community development can be threatening. If community development is done well, it empowers neighborhoods. Economic stability brought about by good steady jobs can bring a strong sense of community to the people with those jobs. It creates a will to fight. It gives the people a vested interest that they then begin to exert. They begin to make demands. It is this sort of power that local governments want to maintain at a limited level.

If one wants to read some interesting history about community development, one should read the legislation surrounding the development of Community Action Programs, particularly the Green Amendment, which was an effort to dilute a program that was successful in fighting city hall. Thus, what we are talking about, first of all, are very limited views of what community development could possibly be, because we have allowed ourselves over the years to constrain the concept of true community development in a considerable way.

Community development is about solutions to poverty at the collective level. Community development is trying to deal with poor people in a geographic spatial area, such as a neighborhood, a ghetto, a slum, or a barrio. Today there are new communities, like Chinatowns and Little Saigons, that fit into the same mold. Most of the work done in community development, and I think it was clear in the presentations, generally revolves around job development and job creation. This is a typical way to approach the concept of economic community development. Community development takes the form, therefore, of either trying to prepare people and give them better skills for the jobs that exist elsewhere or attracting business into the area through efforts like enterprise zones or tax incentives for businesses that hire local residents. In theory, if you do either one of those things, money begins to circulate in that community. Entrepreneurship begins to grow, and the multiplier effects make the quality of life in that neighborhood better.

The federal government is not new to the idea of community development and has been very proactive in some ways. In recent history, just within the last fifteen years, the federal government has had a significant impact through Community Action Programs, urban renewal efforts, the community development corporations, CETA, summer youth employment programs, and the Job Training Partnership Act (JTPA), the most recent major program. Revenue sharing, UDAG funds, and block grant funds, as well, can be considered part of the package of federal efforts to improve communities.

If one looks at the results of these programs, one would expect that things would be better in the barrios or ghettos of our cities. In fact, conditions have not improved. What does exist in the cities is an interesting mix of issues. Places like Miami, Florida, or Bayonne, New Jersey, or Lawrence, Massachusetts, have undergone tremendous changes that are visible to anyone who knows these areas. However, there are still places like the South Bronx in New York, the Second Ward in El Paso, and areas of East Hartford, Connecticut, and Chelsea, Massachusetts. Thus, it is clear that there are places that have changed and others that have not, and most of the changes seem to be quite haphazard: you cannot pinpoint a program that worked in all locations.

It actually appears that gentrification and the recent arrival of newcomers in an area have had more effect in terms of community development than any planned program. Gentrification is a particularly important process because it has, in fact, improved areas of our cities tremendously. But gentrification is a haphazard system, almost a passive one, and, more important, one that has created a great deal of displacement. We cannot allow our neighborhoods to gentrify, to just wait for speculation or land value increases, as a way of transforming them.

Over the past few years, the changes in strategies for economic development have revolved around five factors, particularly for Latino communities. The first factor is an interesting imbalance that has occurred in the last few years. Latino community leaders seem to be shifting more responsibility for job creation to the private sector and away from the federal government, the state government, or the local government. They put their faith in the private sector as the key element and critical actor in creating better jobs. The second factor is job training. Latino leaders believe that job training is critical. This fits the general value traditionally vested in education, particularly for unskilled and displaced workers. The concept that training and the educational process are important for Latinos is key, and Latino leaders have emphasized and focused on that principle. The third factor would be youth jobs, and I separate youth jobs from job training because youth are particularly affected by the changes in our cities. The fourth factor that has been important for Latinos in urban areas has been job counseling, job referrals, and other employment assistance programs. Finally, a fifth factor that Latinos have identified as helping neighborhoods attain better economic situations is entrepreneurship.

These five strategies are those that, in general, Latinos have chosen to improve life in the cities. Each of these strategies, in fact, would improve certain situations in the cities, but it is difficult to find all of these working together in the same place. However, there is hope for the future of our neighborhoods because of some of the issues discussed here today. As Frank Bonilla has indicated, the United States is, in fact, in a period of economic global interdependence, and, as a result, numerous changes and transitions are occurring.

Two weeks ago, the conservative magazine *Business Week* published an extensive segment on the changing global economy. The authors of that piece concluded, not unlike the conclusions heard in earlier discussions, that the future of our cities lies in the role of minorities, women, and the elderly in the future economy. It is clear that this issue has finally penetrated the consciousness of the business sector in a strong way.

The second process that suggests an encouraging future is that the United States is preoccupied with being competitive. Our leaders are preoccupied with the fact that the United States may fall from number one to number two, and there are sectors in which this has already happened and other sectors in which it may soon occur.

We must take advantage of this preoccupation. A real hope lies in the ability to manipulate this preoccupation as an opportunity to argue that the decline of the United States as a world power is something that can be avoided, if certain actions are taken that benefit Latino and black communities. This approach can be taken because Latino and black communities cannot afford to remain in the present circumstances—exploited by the U.S. employers, exploited by Japanese employers or other foreign firms. This represents a "change of masters" concept.

Latino and black leaders must be very persuasive and force the recognition of the vital role that minorities are going to play in the labor force. If, in fact, people believe that the decline in our competitiveness is due to the decline in the quality of our labor force, then certainly we can argue for numerous ways to improve the labor force now and in the near future.

In conclusion, it is important to understand where we stand in the whole arena of economic development. We are trying to improve Latino and black neighborhoods, but we are stalled at the moment because this nation does not want to politically empower our neighborhoods, and the programs that currently exist are flawed. To bring about significant changes, we must think about packaging a mix and match of innovative programs.

It is critical to realize—this was strongly suggested in the Anderson paper—that jobs are not enough. We are proposing the creation of a social service infrastructure that has within it elements of child care, basic skills training, job counseling, better schools, adult vocational education, Graduate Equivalency Degree possibilities, English-as-a-second-language training, health, welfare, and community colleges all playing a role in the community development process. It is clear that community development is not just jobs. It has to be more than jobs. All of these areas interact with one another.

We must, of course, live with JTPA, at least for the moment. As flawed as it is, we have to utilize the pieces of the act that work and try to use them constructively, possibly by finding ways to link jobs to the subregional economy. Perhaps what may be the most important thing that occurs in the near future is a move away from the concept of a national economy to the concept of subregional economies. It is clear that this way of thinking has already begun. The future trend will be job development and job creation and will be in terms of interrelationships at a subregional level rather than the national level.

In this symposium we are speaking to the next administration. I would like to conclude by saying that what we need is leadership that will facilitate this innovative packaging of programs. We must move the existing programs off the shelf and into our neighborhoods. It is clear also that some existing programs need modification. JTPA has already been noted several times and suggestions have been made for modifications. JTPA is one example of a program for which slight modifications can remedy some of its major flaws.

It is more important to realize that not only the private sector but also local governments and state governments are true beneficiaries of economic development. As low-income neighborhoods improve, the tax base goes up, local governments benefit, and so do the state governments. The concept of user fees within the concept of community development is also acceptable if people in fact do benefit from the process. But these propositions have to be built upon the national preoccupation with loss of preeminent position in the world economy. Unless we manipulate that issue, we will be caught in the process in which economic development is seen only as an empowerment issue, which is a level at which it will not receive adequate attention.

Finally, the context of this discussion has been based on the last eight years of sustained economic growth. The growth has not been substantial, but it has been sustained. None of these proposals will make sense under a process of recession. We have a vested interest in maintaining some form of sustained economic growth, because without that growth the core issues of job creation and job development as the focus of economic development, along with that infrastructure that we discussed, will not work and will not be viable.

Discussion

R. Romo: We have seen the progress that is possible in conditions of sustained economic growth. It is also possible to make progress in a weak economy. In the case of Texas, despite the fact that there has been a recession, some of the factors you mentioned, particularly through the private sector, have created some growth in numbers of jobs. For example, in San Antonio, the attraction of Sea World created several thousand jobs in a very depressed economy. Likewise, building on assistance from the federal government, which included a $100 million congressional contribution, state and local governments and institutions have laid the foundation for Sematech in Austin, which is expected to stimulate the state and local economies.

Josephine Segura, Hispanic Women's Network of Texas: My question is to Dr. Melendez. Reviewing twenty years of the Manpower Development Training Act, CETA, and now the Job Training Partnership Act, which of these training programs do you feel has best addressed job training programs for Hispanics in the metropolitan areas?

E. Melendez: That is a difficult question because, in part, when some of the more effective programs were implemented, Latinos were not as large a population in the major cities. Latinos were present in some places, such as Los Angeles, Chicago, New York, and San Antonio, but the growing Latino immigrant population presents a new problem that our cities have not faced for some time. In the Southwest, New York, Chicago, and some other major cities, we have had a large concentration of Hispanics. Recently, however, we have faced the challenge of incorporating new immigrants, a large proportion of which are Hispanics, and incorporating those left behind in the recent economic expansion of the seventies. Few of those programs have had significant impact with respect to the Hispanic communities. However, long-term programs are clearly a solution.

Look at the impact of classroom training and English-language programs for example, at the local level, like ET Choices in Massachusetts, in which a decent portion of participants are Latinas on welfare. It becomes obvious that what is needed are long-term interventions. That is, you cannot provide a mother on welfare, a teenage mother with a couple of kids, with a good job unless you invest significantly in her human capital development. That means providing child care subsidies, housing subsidies, and so on, as well as education and training. We must also convince the private sector, where most jobs are, to open jobs for people who have great difficulties in being employed because of their social circumstances. Just living in a ghetto is a strike against you when you have to find transportation and so on. There have been some successful programs, but most of them are long term.

J. Segura: Under the Manpower Development Training Act (MDTA), there were long-term job training programs and many of the jobs were created in the public sector. The intent was to provide jobs. There were programs that provided six months to eighteen months of job experience for individuals. Then when CETA was enacted, that legislation was much more comprehensive. CETA included educational training in classrooms, training allowances, and larger stipends. It was not only job training but a comprehensive approach including child care and support services. In addition, there was a coordinated approach among those entities that were implementing these job training programs.

Now in JTPA the government has eliminated the comprehensive approach, the support services, the child care, and the allowances. These provisions are in place, and we are back to twenty-five years ago, before MDTA. My concern is that the proposals presented place the emphasis and responsibility in the private sector. Is the private sector going to be responsive to the underlying reasons why people are impoverished and in the position of being unemployed? Or will employers revert to racial discrimination? Having worked in all of those programs, under all three of those acts, it is my personal opinion that CETA addressed a greater range of problems in a more comprehensive way to assist people out of poverty.

M. Simms: Could I add that one of the problems with JTPA, in addition to the way the incentives and performance standards were set up, was the failure of the federal government to provide guidance when the program was first implemented. The government failed to point out some of the available options, such as the possibility of providing support services and stipends with a certain limit. The 5 percent limit was not taken advantage of in most jurisdictions. Under JTPA it was also possible to set up alternative performance standards. However, without guidance and assurance that alternative standards would not jeopardize a program, there was no incentive for the service delivery areas to step out and try something new and innovative. Thus, one of the factors to be considered in evaluating JTPA, in addition to the fact that JTPA also had less money, was the kind of national support for the structure and the degree to which service delivery areas could undertake new or different and daring initiatives.

William Diaz, Ford Foundation: I would like to pursue this question about the effectiveness of the JTPA and CETA programs. One of the problems in talking about the effectiveness of those programs and numerous other social programs for Hispanics is that only recently have Hispanics been included in the research determining program impacts or the evaluations of demonstration programs, such as those run by public-private ventures in Philadelphia and Manpower Demonstration Research Corporation of New York. The inclusion of Latinos in the data analysis is beginning now, and we hope that, over time, it will provide a better sense of what program effectiveness means for Latinos.

This omission is a very real problem. One area of concern is a panel study of income dynamics. Much of the recent welfare debate has revolved around analyses of the Panel Study on Income Dynamics from the University of Michigan, and yet this data set has a miniscule Hispanic cohort. Thus, analysts cannot tell over time what is happening to Hispanics economically or socially in the same way that they can identify trends for low-income whites and low-income blacks. The issue of data—and we have all become data conscious in the last decade or two—is an important one for the next administration to ponder and develop.

Clara Rodriguez, Fordham University: I would like the panelists to comment on the workfare legislation or the welfare reform.

F. Bonilla: It is interesting, but I am not sure to what extent the legislation will actually bring about reform. Since there is considerable latitude in the legislation in terms of localities defining the actual structure and configuration of the work, the nature of the jobs that people will be prepared for, the type of training they will receive, and the kinds of working conditions and wages they will encounter, the variance in local welfare standards will remain. Whatever consequence may occur in terms of evening up those standards as a result of the new legislation, there will continue to be considerable differences and a variety of ways for local factors to affect actual outcomes.

There is an earlier Cuomo report for New York State on social welfare that explicitly stated that, in order to motivate people to leave welfare and take real jobs, the jobs offered to a person through welfare must be less attractive than the poorest private sector job. Offering poor jobs seems to be a peculiar way of motivating people to move into demanding positions from a sheltered space. This raises several issues regarding the extent to which a program can, in fact, motivate people to leave welfare. In most programs, there is not enough incentive to formulate goals nor a realistic foundation for people to rebuild their lives on their own.

M. Simms: There is less innovation in the reforms than is touted. Certain features are less favorable than the reform supporters had hoped. As Lynn Burbridge pointed out earlier, there is a tremendous variety among the states in terms of what they provide, and the reform legislation does not discourage that. In fact, the legislation may encourage wider gaps, because, clearly, in most cases the ability to provide any kind of comprehensive program is going to require the addition of substantial state and local money. Certainly, the modification in the Unemployed Parent extension is going to limit its value because of the time restriction. The workfare component, of course, may be viewed as being counterproductive instead of promoting movement into regular employment.

R. Romo: Could I ask a question about the Philadelphia Plan, the 5 percent proposal? How does the government assure that the jobs provided are not dead-end jobs? In essence, if there are twenty jobs, and one should be offered to a disadvantaged minority, how do you assure that that one position is not a dead-end job or a menial job?

M. Simms: The Philadelphia Plan is a fairly new program and I am not sure exactly how it works. In any of these compacts, such as the Boston Compact, the employer defines the terms that are involved. However, some would argue that the first job that most females have is not the job that is going to start them on a career ladder. The most important thing is to provide that initial work experience within the private sector because many people look more favorably at private sector jobs. Some view job training programs as programs for those who cannot succeed in the private sector. Thus, if someone has a private sector job on her résumé, somehow that is proof that that individual has the work ethic necessary to move on to a job with a career ladder and more training.

Rodolfo de la Garza, University of Texas at Austin: In some ways it is really not useful to think of Latinos as a national population, but rather to think of Latinos within certain states. Thus, it seems that, given the distribution of Latinos, there should be a great opportunity for local and state innovation, especially if a Republican administration remains in office. In California there is senate legislation focusing on the role of Hispanics in the future. Texas has been able to pass some legislation on health care for migrants. That legislation developed, not because of the federal government but because of initiatives at the local and state level.

E. Melendez: Even if we do not want to accept that the Reagan administration has succeeded in some areas, the Republican administration certainly did succeed in reforming the relationship between the federal, state, and local governments. Basically, because they cut federal funding there is less opportunity for federal intervention or influence.

That trend is going to be very difficult to reverse. Therefore, I do not think we should expect major changes or new leadership in federal policies that will have any positive impact on the Latino community in particular. And, therefore, it becomes more important, more essential, to develop local- and state-level strategies. I am not saying that federal policies are not important. I am saying that under present conditions we are less able to implement policy changes at the federal level.

Truthfully, several interesting experiments are underway linking employment and training to state economic development policies. These programs are perhaps more effective than the previous federal programs. In a short period of time it is difficult to say definitively, but perhaps Latinos can have more influence through state and local policies, particularly at the community level. Perhaps we should reorganize our troops, so to speak, and try this approach of intervention to solve our community problems in a more effective way. The struggle has shifted from federal-level policies to local- and state-level policies. And, indeed, because Latinos have more political power at the regional level, we are more able to influence policy at that level. Perhaps one day we may even have influence in the formulation and administration of those policies. This possibility contributes to the imperative of supporting employment and training policies at the local and state levels.

R. de la Garza: What that may mean is that the presence of a Republican administration and its policy of decentralization may, in fact, maximize the political strength of Latinos because of the population's regional concentration. For example, if people in South Dakota voted on job training or welfare reform measures, they may not want to provide for southern Texas. If the decisions are moved to the state level, where Texas

Latinos are much more numerically important, that is a strategic advantage.

F. Bonilla: Jane Jacobs said recently that "nations are now lethal environments for regions and cities." It is clear that regional initiatives represent a major part of the action that will most directly affect the lives of Latinos. One of the conclusions from the Cuomo Commission report was that, in fact, we might more usefully be turning our energies to state and local levels rather than preparing suggestions for the next president.

Again, federal policies are extremely important and whatever regional mobilizations occur, whatever ways we engage the political economy of the local regions, must keep that federal and international perspective in view. Latinos are in a way uniquely situated to give some content to the idea that there can be a foreign policy that is economically informed and links people and regional interests within the United States directly to other countries with which they have natural connections. And, of course, this brings us to another issue that has not been mentioned: the question of the different regional concentrations of Latinos and the different political realities of the major groups, such as Cubans, Mexicans, and Puerto Ricans. We have everything from a bilateral process of adjustment and accommodation between the United States and Mexico in which Mexicans inside the United States could play a very positive role, to a situation in Puerto Rico where national legislation applies automatically without any mediation or actual adaptation to the island situation. The Cuban case is even more complex with the strains and threats involved in the U.S. relationship with Cuba.

What is occurring, in fact, is that the regional factor has taken on greater and greater importance, and that change enhances Latino ability to make a contribution and to actually engage in the system rather than pull away from it.

Henry Cisneros

PART VI

Changing Cities:
A Success Strategy

Changing Cities: A Success Strategy
Henry Cisneros

Discussion

PART VI

Changing Cities: A Success Strategy

Henry Cisneros: I noted from the outset, from the invitation to participate, that this was not just a conference on cities. There are many
conferences on cities, but this one had a particular slant and orientation,
and that was toward the role of minorities and the evolution of minorities
themselves within cities. This is a very important focus for a conference
such as this for a number of reasons.

First of all, minority populations are growing in America's cities and,
in some sense, it will be impossible to address the questions of social
justice in our society except through urban policies, because the largest
number of minorities in our population will live in cities. Second, as cities
grow and develop, as they create new economic momentum and new
economic engines, there is the potential to create some sense of a new
democracy within our cities to harness that economic momentum and
make it work for those who are outside the economic mainstream.
Finally, I have discovered over the years that some of the most practical
problems that any policymaker confronts are confronted by those who
govern America's cities. We have a duality about the responsibility. On
the one hand, those who live or work in cities have to keep one foot in the
city hall office, where one encounters the petitioners, those who have
particular problems. On the other hand, one also walks past those who
are sleeping on the sidewalk. It is impossible to ignore the realities of life
in our society, the underside, if you will, of American life. Those who live
and work in the cities maneuver within the level of government that is
most directly attached to the concerns of the American people. To be sure,
what is being decided in the Congress on strategic defense initiatives or
social security matters is important. And what is decided in the state
house about highway financing or university funding or public education is important. But what can be more important in a direct sense than

to know that one's decisions impact every member of that community immediately that night, that day?

For example, to know that if one of you is in your home and your spouse or another one of your loved ones suddenly turns ashen gray and falls on the floor, there is the capability to have an emergency medical team there within minutes. Or, if in the middle of the night, you suddenly hear a crashing of glass in the back room and you know with certainty that someone is coming into the house at that moment with no proper intentions but to steal property or to hurt you, to know that there is police response at the other end of a dispatching system, two or three or five minutes away, that can literally save a life. Or to know as you send children off to school in the morning on sidewalks, across city streets, that the traffic flow is regulated so that their lives are not in danger. What can be more important than going to work in the morning in a revitalized downtown district where retailing is strong because the city government was able to stimulate and encourage business, or to go to an industrial park where new jobs have been created because the city government was involved in the process of attracting technological jobs or light manufacturing?

It is in the cities of America where we see the fabric of life in our country in all its real dimensions. Over 80 percent of the American people live in urban areas, and those urban areas are the windows through which the rest of the world looks at American society. Visitors come to our country, not to see shopping malls or suburban subdivisions, but to find the real character of the American people on the streetscape of our nation's cities and towns.

It is in the cities that we will find a cure for cancer, in the medical center of some great American city. New forms of art are developed in the galleries found in America's cities. New forms of architecture change the skyline of America's cities and town. When business experiments with innovations such as the paperless office or the completely electronically functioning office, this occurs in America's cities. When we find innovations in music, they happen in the great halls and amphitheaters of our nation's cities. When we find the American people experimenting with new approaches to governments or more effective ways to govern ourselves, it is likely to be in a neighborhood movement that is thriving so strongly in our country's cities. And when the immigrant story plays itself out one more time, with people arriving on these shores attempting to climb the ladder of upward mobility, we find those immigrants first in the staging areas and the older neighborhoods of our country's cities.

It is clear what our cities mean to our country, historically and today. They are the focal point of all the essential dynamics of the American story, a story of striving and of hope juxtaposed against the pathologies and cycle of despair that are too frequently a part of the American story. Our cities mean hope. How else is it possible to describe the story of immigrants who once came to Ellis Island in New York, wide-eyed, awestruck, in near terror, clutching all their worldly possessions—the same story playing itself out tonight in Nogales, Arizona, or El Paso, Texas, as immigrants arrive, perhaps not through the same legal channels but nevertheless trying to make their way to a city where they can work.

Our cities mean striving. The same sense of rebirth that has allowed Savannah to evolve from a slave trading center to its role today as a historic asset is played out in San Jose, California, on the other end of the continent, in a totally different way. In San Jose, this sense of striving is acted out as new age pioneers have created a technological complex, arguably the greatest concentration of technological might in the world, concentrated in cities located in the area south of San Francisco.

That same sense of striving is the only explanation for the repeated efforts of tired, grimy, western Pennsylvania's coal and steel cities to transform themselves. Look at Pittsburgh, for example, which *Rand-McNally* magazine ranked as the most livable city in America. Pittsburgh has transformed itself over the course of about twenty years from a city where people literally took extra shirts to work in the white-collar downtown area because the grime of soot in the air would make those shirts dark by mid-afternoon and persons had extraordinarily high levels of respiratory diseases to a city today with a glittering downtown. The city's efforts to emphasize a technological and small business program have completely transformed the aging Pittsburgh industrial center to one of America's most livable places. That same sense of striving is evident in Fort Wayne, Indiana, a city that rebounded and transformed its economy after the loss of International Harvester. That striving is present in Los Angeles, as it becomes America's first truly pluralistic city. In Los Angeles, a majority of the population is so diverse that there is no longer a dominant population group.

The American city is the point of convergence of all those hopes and all those ambitions that we must not lose, even as the evidence mounts that there are continuing difficulties, such as needle-littered junkie havens where people experiment with the new alchemy of death. I have walked into shooting galleries where the police say, "Mayor, make sure that the soles on your shoes are thick, because where we are going the needles, the abandoned needles, are so thickly scattered on the floor that you will get hepatitis just from walking through the place if they penetrate your shoes."

Our cities have problems: epidemic teenage pregnancies—literally, children having children—elderly people waiting in fear in cold tenements, afraid to leave the barred existence behind which they live, even to get their Social Security check from their front step; men trying to hide tears from their sons as they sit on the edge of their bed contemplating the loss of a lifetime job during the sweeping transformation of the American economy. It is a complex and sad duality, the hopes and despairs in the crucible of the American city. But our cities are where the American story plays itself out, the real human drama of America, the drama that all of those who care about our society must acknowledge.

Nonetheless, our cities are our best hope for making our democratic processes work. The cities are our best hope for integrating the races. The cities are our best hope for making the ideals of American society come to fruition—"One nation under God, indivisible, with liberty and justice for all." Yet our cities are at a fork in the road. Down one road is the American city as an urban reservation, home to a structured permanent underclass, drugs and lawlessness, neighborhoods in decline, capital stocks eroding, tax bases declining, infrastructure in obsolescence, schools in crisis, abandonment by Washington—a story of economic bankruptcy and spiritual exhaustion.

But, fortunately, there is another road. We can view the cities as the engines of a new and revitalized democracy; as a laboratory for experimentation with emerging citizens' organizations that can end the sense of apathy and anomie; as neighborhood groups participating in that process of creating jobs in practical relationships with big business; as a place for harnessing the service economy and making it work for those who have labored without skills and must find a place in the new American economy; as a means of educating young people for this new democracy; as incubators of small business and a place for reinvestment in housing; in effect, as a place where it is still possible to hold out a hand of respect, to hold out hope, dignity, and an end to polarization.

In order for this to happen, the cities must begin by acknowledging that they are not fixed institutions, somehow prepared to respond to all the changes that are sweeping our world. Cities, like every other institution in America, must understand change and relate to it: a change that is massive in scale and touches every dimension of our lives; a change that is rapid in pace, so rapid that what we hear in this evening's newscast may have a different slant on it by the time we hear it repeated in tomorrow morning's radio broadcast; and a change that, ironically, is permanent. This is to say, change is a constant relentless feature of our world. Cities, perhaps more than any other institution in America, are touched by change.

Let me just describe two or three of the changes that will go right to the heart of America's cities and will require in many instances a redefinition of the very concept of what a city is and a redefinition by those who manage it of what their responsibilities and priorities must be.

Clearly one of those changes that is sweeping across America and is at the heart of this symposium is the dramatic demographic shift that will change the very composition of our population and the complexion of American life. It is not an accident that the mayor of Philadelphia, Wilson Gould, is black; or that the mayor of Baltimore, Kurt Schmoke, is black; or that the mayor of Atlanta, Andrew Young, is black; or that the mayor of Los Angeles, Tom Bradley, is black. Nor is it an accident that the mayor of Miami, Javier Suárez, is Hispanic; or that the mayor of Denver, Federico Peña, is Hispanic; or that women manage coalitions in such cities as Houston, where Kathy Whitmire has won four terms; or that Annette Strauss governs as mayor of Dallas; or that Maureen O'Conner is mayor of San Diego.

Those are not accidents. They are reflective of new population realities, new demographic mixes in our cities that make it certain that we will see increasing numbers of minority and nontraditional persons come to leadership in America's cities because the population that elects them will be minorities and nontraditional persons in the years to come.

While we have grown accustomed over the last twenty years to seeing the black mayor of a northern or a southern city, and we will increasingly grow accustomed to seeing Hispanics in such positions all across the country, that is not the whole story. It is no longer a story of just some concentrated dense central city juxtaposed against its suburbs, as in the case of Denver, for example, or Cleveland or other such cities. The fact is that what we are witnessing and what we are about to experience is a massive demographic change that may indeed be the biggest story in America in the next century.

Recently I was asked to go to California to respond to a study at the California state library system, which is the overarching entity and resource center for over twelve hundred libraries in California. The study, which is the only one of its kind that I have seen done by any governmental agency, basically asks this question: What do we have to do governmentally in the year 2000 to respond in a way that is different from how we are responding today to the reality of demographic change?

What the library system discovered, after having the Rand Corporation do the analysis, is the following: California, not some central city, but the state of California, the massive empire of twenty-seven million people that it is, will in the year 2000 be fully 48 percent Hispanic, Asian, and black. The county of San Francisco—not the city, but the county of San Francisco—will be 65 percent minority, with the Asian population the largest minority. Los Angeles County—not the city but the county, including some of the suburbs—will be 60 percent minority, with the largest minority being Hispanic. Even Orange County, the center of traditional politics and population in the national image, will be 40 percent minority, with the largest group being Hispanic. And that change sweeps across rural areas as well—the Imperial Valley, for example, will become fully 73 percent minority, with the largest concentration of population being Hispanic.

The most stunning statistic was not what will happen in particularly central cities, but the following statistic: the Rand Corporation concluded that in the year 2000, 92 percent of the people of California will live in a county that is at least 30 percent minority. Thirty percent minority is a significant population grouping and can have a notable influence in the population. It is visible, and the signs of minority participation in a community of 30 percent are significant. Once again, 92 percent of the people of California will live in a county that is at least 30 percent minority. Furthermore, those demographics will sweep across the whole country.

In Texas, the majority of the children under the sixth-grade level in the Houston central city school district, the massive Houston Independent School District, are today Hispanic and black. In Dallas, a city often considered a traditional population center, the majority of the children under the fourth-grade level in the Dallas school system today are Hispanic and black. Within a very few short years, the majority will be Hispanic alone in both Houston and Dallas, with the black population increasing that number and taking those central city younger age group percentages to the 70 to 75 percent range. As that population cohort moves through their life cycle, their presence will change the futures of places such as Dallas and Houston as well as the state of Texas, places that are not thought of as being on the pioneering edge of demographic change.

Clearly, this demographic change will continue and sweep across all dimensions of American life. The implications are significant in political processes, in leadership development, and in many other areas. There are those who are afraid of this change. I submit to you that there is nothing to be afraid of if we meet one condition: if we continue to train and educate those of minority extraction for full participation in the society.

Prime Minister Nakashoni of Japan, a few years ago, was roundly and appropriately criticized for a statement that he made. He said that America would not be able to compete with the Japanese or any of the other northern industrialized nations in the next century because, as a polyglot nation, America had too many Hispanics and blacks. He could have changed his statement only slightly and have been correct: America will not be able to compete with Japan or the other industrialized nations if this country decides to leave its large population of blacks and Hispanics undereducated, underproductive, and operating and living at the margins of the society. No country can compete in the present world competition—a competition in which a slight change in the ratio of the dollar to the yen signaled in Tokyo overnight manifests itself in London on the stock market and by noon alters massive capital flows within the United States—if that country has a poorly educated work force. No country living in such a competitive world can afford to carry ten or fifteen or twenty million people in a permanent underclass. It is simply a question of rationality and logic.

The question of how we deal with this large and emerging demographic change and how we deal with this question of an underclass is no longer an issue of civil rights; it is no longer a question of Christian compassion or a question of national or constitutional ideals. It is a question of national survival, because it is not possible for us to compete head-on with other industrialized countries if we allow ten or fifteen or twenty million people to live in a structured, inescapable underclass.

Matching the demographic trend in the changing ethnic composition of our population is another trend that Ben Wattenberg chronicled in his recent book *The Birth Dearth*, which investigates the lower birth rates in traditional American populations. As traditional populations grow smaller in the working-age years and larger in the years that require income support, and as minority populations grow at the bottom of the population cohort, a very explosive picture emerges. We have a scenario in which older persons say, "No more social spending, no more bond issues. Let's hold up on tax increases. Taxes have gotten out of hand and are threatening my income security. I can't afford it." There will be many instances where legitimate concerns about personal income security are juxtaposed against populations that are saying, "No, our best days are yet ahead. We need more schools and more social spending."

This problem has been confronted directly in San Antonio, where retiree populations who wanted to index city spending to the cost of living presented a spending cap proposal virtually making it impossible to do any capital spending. In San Antonio, the city council must bring large projects on the budget line in the year they are ready to be constructed; as a result, policymakers may encounter amounts in the budget beyond the cost of living for a particular year as they attempt to accommodate projects that were planned several years ahead of time. This proposition was defeated with minority population and growth advocates. But the fact of the matter is that cost reduction propositions, such as Proposition 13 in California, the proposition in Massachusetts, and spending cap restrictions in San Antonio, will become much more a dimension of our reality. This situation is one of the dimensions of change that will characterize the world in which cities must operate.

Implementing policies in the city is further complicated by a second dimension of change, and that is the transformation of our country's economy. The economic issue is not a partisan question, nor is it a question of what a government might have been able to do. It is not an issue of maliciousness in government. It represents the dynamics, the forces unleashed by world economic change, and the transformation of our country's economy from manufacturing to services.

The reality is that, as recently as 1950, approximately 60 percent of the American people worked in some relationship to the manufacturing process, the manufacturing of goods and products. Today about 17 percent of Americans work in manufacturing. The largest number of jobs are now in information processing and services, and we have lost literally hundreds of thousands of jobs in manufacturing.

The first issue that economists were concerned about was, would there be enough jobs in the new economy? Well, it is clear there will be jobs, a substantial number of jobs emerging in these new areas. But the new question is, what will they pay, and will they pay enough to sustain our middle class as we know it? We have lost hundreds of thousands of jobs paying thirteen, fourteen, and fifteen dollars an hour and replaced them with hundreds of thousands of jobs paying five, six, and seven dollars an hour. It is, therefore, not an accident that we are seeing polarization of our society along income lines. In 1985, income distribution data presented to the Joint Economic Committee showed that the top one-fifth of Americans—the top 20 percent—earned fully 43 percent of the national income, the largest percentage earned by the top 20 percent since the end of World War II. The bottom 20 percent, the bottom one-fifth, earned 4.7 percent of the national income, the smallest percentage earned in twenty-five years.

Now, I do not attribute that to malicious government. It might be that some of that polarization could have been abated if the safety net had been stronger, if the reductions in social spending and education and other fundamental needs over the last few years had been prevented, but fundamentally the dramatic differences in income are due to the forces and dynamics unleashed in this massive economic transformation. These patterns will continue and, I suspect, there is very little that government could have done. Certainly, a government that believed in targeting our resources to keep old industries alive or targeting research to support the sunrise industries that would allow us to compete head-on with the Japanese, the Koreans, and others, instead of allowing their products to inundate us, a government that believed in a more aggressive trading policy and a trading state instead of the emphasis on defense spending, might have been able to influence these numbers. But the fact of the matter is that these trends are inherent in the economic dynamics that we live with, and no institution has been more hurt by those economic dynamics than the cities.

Detroit, which once had 40 percent of its people in manufacturing, today has approximately 25 percent of its work force in manufacturing. Dallas, a city in which fully 30 percent of the work force engaged in manufacturing in the 1930s, presently has less than 20 percent of its workers employed in the manufacturing process. This phenomenon goes on and on across America's cities. One feels emotional pain for our country to see the U.S. Steel Works in Gary, Indiana, that used to employ sixteen thousand people, utterly and completely abandoned, and the surrounding neighborhoods of nice stock construction, of brick homes, once viable neighborhoods, completely abandoned and burned out. In Gary, Indiana, in Youngstown, Ohio, one can see miles, literally mile after mile, of abandoned industrial plants. These industries were the reasons this country was able to gain its prominence in the world, not only economically but also strategically. These industries were what Franklin Roosevelt referred to as the arsenal of democracy, able to churn out airplanes and tanks and automobiles and put millions of Americans to work. These industries that kept Americans at work through the fifties and sixties are now in decline. No institution is more affected by these economic realities than the cities.

Finally, another overarching dynamic macrotrend that is having considerable impact on our cities today is the political trend toward decentralization. We have experienced decentralization steadily since 1968, when Richard Nixon become president and began to talk in terms of returning power to the people. Decentralization has been a constant theme in American politics since and has accelerated in the last several years under the Reagan administration. Political decentralization, however, has not meant more money for state and local programs. When I became mayor in 1980, the total dollars coming to cities for urban programs was about 69 billion. Last year's federal budget, in terms of direct aid to cities, was about $17 billion, a dramatic decline in the amount of money that comes to cities. Elimination of revenue sharing, reductions in the Job Training Partnership Act funding, reductions in the amount of money coming in community development block grants, repeated attempts to eliminate the Urban Development Act Grants (UDAG) program, and many, many other reductions have short changed our cities.

We have seen tax cuts in Washington that have essentially benefited those with the highest income and have resulted in an aggregate decrease in the tax burden generated by Washington. Frankly, these cuts and this decentralization trend just push responsibilities further down the system, so that states have to wrestle with higher tax requirements and local governments, school districts, and cities have to make up the difference in instance after instance. It is clear that tax reduction and decentralization are popular politics, and I do not expect these patterns to change. I cannot imagine that whoever is elected president in 1988, Governor Dukakis or Vice President Bush, is going to enforce dramatic returns to the Great Society era of large-scale governmental programs—not with $100 billion deficits to be inherited by the next president, not with tough negotiations with the Soviets on new arms control measures, and not with the requirement to continue to produce certain weapons systems. We cannot expect large-scale governmental programs.

The point I am emphasizing here is that another feature of the decision-making environment for cities for the next few years will be the continuation of local initiatives, local tax capability, and local fiscal innovation to deal with this environment. It is in this environment that I have tried to cite several dimensions of change. I would like to perhaps capsulize my remarks on change as it affects the cities by just summarizing some material from the Governors' Council on Science and Technology that related to the dimensions of change in Texas. The cities are affected by this new world, and any city that tries to carve out its future without being attentive to these realities is going to be swimming against the tide.

The Governors' Council on Science and Technology made the following conclusions about the old Texas and the new Texas, but these insights apply to any state. In the old economy there was little foreign competition. In the new economy there will be very heavy global interrelationships. In the old economy it was possible to depend on natural resource development. That is clearly a Texas theme—oil and gas and agriculture. In the new economy investment must be in technology and in human capital. In the old economy we could anticipate stable markets. In the new economy we must anticipate very vulnerable markets for our most basic products. In the old economy Texas was dominant and basically able to manage its economics internally. In the new economy there will be heavy competition among the states. In the old economy Texas and other states depended upon a production economy. The new economy is services oriented with a premium on knowledge and information. In the old economy states were able to look, in the last resort, to the federal government for job creation initiatives and for critical governmental spending. In the new economy it will be the initiative of the states or the localities to deal with job creation or those job opportunities will not be there.

In the past it was possible to accept a minimally skilled work force. Today's preconditions for competition are an adaptable and technically proficient work force. In the past we could tolerate weak educational systems. Today it is imperative that we have the strongest educational systems possible. In the past we lived with basically traditional populations in dominance, in charge of the political dialogue. Today's diverse population groups require schooling in citizenship, governance, and problem solving that involves consensus building to work with the differences and the realities of diversity. What, then, is the cities' response to these dimensions of change?

Clearly, one dimension of the response is defensive. That is, city governments must stop the hemorrhaging in terms of the loss of federal supports and the attack on municipal prerogatives. In every session of the Congress, new mandates are passed by congressional representatives who have a constituency to please but no money with which to do it. They simply say, "We are going to clean the streams and rivers, and the states and cities are going to pay for it. We are going to provide new levels of workers' compensation, and the cities are going to do it. We are going to provide new levels of social security, and the cities are going to do it." So one dimension of defense is to stop the attack on municipal prerogatives and authorities and on municipal budgets and to continue to try to get as many revenues as possible through the most efficient mechanism that exists—the federal income tax mechanism. That was the concept behind revenue sharing when it was first proposed by Walter Heller in the 1960s and then passed by the Nixon administration in the early 1970s. Richard Nathan of Princeton University was on the staff of Elliott Richardson and the Domestic Council at various points in that administration and was responsible in part for the thinking about urban problems that allowed a program like revenue sharing to come into existence.

But the fact is that mayors are too frequently cast in the posture of being only defensive. It is the traditional picture of the mayor to go to Washington with hands out saying, "We want more money," and, asked for a solution to urban problems to say, "Well, if Washington would only fork out more dollars . . ." It is a caricature, but unfortunately, without a concerted and strategic municipal response, forged in community after community, it is the posture into which mayors too frequently fall.

The focus should be instead on an urban offensive, not defensive strategies but offensive strategies, operating from the belief that cities can indeed be masters of their own destinies. Now, this sounds like a strange concept because it is a common view to think that cities are just tossed about like driftwood on the stormy seas of change. I may have even suggested that in my remarks heretofore. But the truth of the matter is that I am a firm believer in the idea that cities do have significant, not complete, but significant mastery over their own destinies. I know this because I have seen it with my own eyes. I have seen it in Baltimore, where one of the best public servants in the country, Don Shafer—he is called the Mayor of Maryland, although he is actually the governor of Maryland—performs as governor in much the same way he did as mayor of Baltimore. He has been able to take a dying, old, industrial port city and change its direction and sense of itself by investing in the inner harbor, by investing in the neighborhoods, by rebuilding the educational base. Baltimore is still plagued with immense difficulties, such as drugs and poor educational performance, but offensive leadership has created a real sense of possibilities in a place like Baltimore.

The man who I think is the current best mayor in the country is Bill Hudnut, the present mayor of Indianapolis. He took a city that was called "Indian No Place" by its own citizens just a few years ago and gave it a sense of direction and mission. Focusing on amateur athletics, on the biosciences and technology, on rebuilding the downtown through the construction of hotels, the Hoosier Dome, and the convention complex, Hudnut has literally taken a city and defined for it a new place in the American structure of cities. He has done that by simply asserting new roles.

It is fashionable, I suppose, to dismiss something like amateur athletics as a city-building device, but the mayor of Indianapolis literally decided that, if conventions bring people and, therefore, money to a city, amateur athletics could do the same. Amateur athletics has the added advantage of bringing to a city headquarters operations and major or special events that create opportunities for the citizens themselves. For example, if you can imagine the Pan American games, an amateur track and field international competition normally played in "Hispanic cities" of this hemisphere, such as Caracas, Bogotá, São Paulo, or Mexico City, being played in 1987 in the Hispanic city of Indianapolis, Indiana, that is exactly what occurred. The city simply willed this competition into existence, building the facilities and, as a result, attracting the headquarters of many amateur athletic institutions. What follows is that the quality of life is notably improved in Indianapolis by many, many other organizations.

Atlanta is another case of offensive efforts willing into existence a role for a city. This idea of Atlanta as a regional center was started first by Mayor Ivan Allen and pursued by subsequent mayors, including Mayor Maynard Jackson, the first black mayor of a major city in the South, elected in the 1970s. These efforts built upon the brilliant efforts by Andrew Young, who uses international contacts he made as former representative to the United Nations, to build the international capability of Atlanta. These efforts have transformed the economic momentum to create opportunities for the majority black population of the central city of Atlanta.

I could continue with instance after instance. But enough examples. The point is that cities can be masters of their own destinies if they have about them a sense of strategy, a sense of target. Some cities are going to be victims of the changes I have described. They will not understand or have the unity of purpose or the political will to point themselves in a direction or to invest in a manner that creates opportunities. Other cities will prosper. The difference between those cities that fail and those that prosper, those that are victims and those that are successful, is that those that are going to be successful have some vision, some plan to follow. This must be a plan that is more than next week's zoning case or next week's reorganization of an internal department of the city. A successful vision asks the bigger picture questions, such as, what is the role of Atlanta in the national system of American cities in the year 2000? In the year 2010? What is the obligation of Youngstown to invest in its new industrial plant as it tries to wean itself from its older industries? What is the possibility of Akron to define new industries? For example, Akron, Ohio, is attempting to work with the rubber companies, recognizing that rubber is in decline but that synthetic chemicals are in emergence. Akron leaders are thus attempting to transform the economy of Akron around that new industrial base.

I am very proud that San Antonio has been able to follow this model, beginning in 1983 with a process we call Target 90. We have spent the last seven years redefining San Antonio from the sleepy city on the banks of the San Antonio River, whose pace was about the same as that meandering river, to a city today that has built on the base of resources that exist and added new economic engines for its future.

The real questions that municipal leaders need to ask themselves in this environment are: Should we continue what we are doing? What are our strengths? How can we build on those strengths? It is not imperative to follow a recipe book of things that were popularized in the popular press. To build a downtown mall or to pursue high technology may not work in every place. The options depend on the particular strengths of that place.

Thus, the role of cities will be to be proactive, not reactive, to understand new economic realities and to learn a new language. The old language that said, "We'll do just fine because we have cheap jobs and cheap labor and cheap water and cheap electricity," is no longer good enough. There is a whole new language in American cities. Investment in education at all levels, including the best primary and secondary education and the expansion of curriculum in institutions of higher education, is essential. Investment in research, including the creation of industrial and research parks, and attracting foreign investment as befits a global economy are other topics of concern for cities. Creating export capabilities in small business includes not just smokestack chasing to attract business from elsewhere, but developing the capabilities of indigenous businesses through small business incubators, specialized strategies in purchasing and development, venture capital, and working with banks. Other offensive strategies include convention centers, downtown revitalization, historic preservation, new air routes, world trade, marketing, and projecting and creating an identity for the city.

Now, you may ask, what does all of this have to do with minority development in our society? Well, there are two fundamental principles. One is that a precondition for minority upward mobility is economic prosperity and growth. It is virtually impossible to create the conditions in which minorities can climb the ladder of mobility without economic growth as a precondition. Whether it be national growth or regional growth or urban growth, economic growth is a precondition. This is evident from several national aggregate statistics. In 1947, 33 percent of the American people lived under poverty. By 1960 that number had declined to 22 percent. By 1973 that number had declined to 11 percent. All this occurred in a period when national GNP growth was about 4.4 percent per year, an average of 3.8 over the period but in some years stronger than 4 percent. After 1973 there was essentially a stabilization in the poverty rate, until recent years when it has grown. I think the latest statistics show the percentage of people living in poverty at approximately 15 percent. The percentage of people living in poverty has been climbing the last several years, during a period when America's GNP has been less than 2 percent.

Thus, I am saying that economic growth is an essential precondition for creating minority upward mobility and lifting people out of poverty. The best poverty program is a prosperous economy that can produce jobs. Clearly, there is a massive role for government in alleviating poverty and helping to create the jobs. Nonetheless, as a precondition to everything else, there must be a growth-oriented economy.

The same is true in local urban settings. It is not possible for a mayor, no matter how sincere, how energetic, or how able to devote twenty hours a day and sleep for four, to create poverty programs capable of dealing with every person standing on every street corner, or every person standing in an empty lot, or every person looking for a job, without first creating the overarching conditions of growth.

In San Antonio I have tried to reduce this to a simple cliché, and it has become a cliché because I repeat it so often. Our objectives are two-fisted. The first fist is that which says we are going to build economic prosperity, whatever it takes. We will go anywhere, talk to anyone, do anything, consider anything that is prudent and will not put us in jail, to create jobs. We will be the best at what it takes—licenses, permits, fees, zoning, traffic, security, personnel matters, new sites, tax abatements—you name it. Our efforts to create jobs will be the best. As a result there has been a certain amount of general economic growth. I don't want to brag on San Antonio, but of the major cities in Texas there was only one that did not lose jobs in 1986, 1987, and 1988, only one that did not actually have a decline in its job production. That was San Antonio. There was only one that suffered not one single month of gross product decline but stayed positive through every single month of the Texas recession of 1986, 1987, and 1988. And that is the first fist—economic prosperity.

The second fist, however, must hit with equal intensity. That is to say, the reason we are doing this is not to line pockets of developers or realtors but to create the conditions in which jobs can reach those who have been outside the economic mainstream. That means we need to locate some of those new plants in central city areas. We need to create innovative relationships to train people using our Job Training Partnership Act money. We need to make our education and schools a way to create the skills that will allow people to develop their own lives. It means that we need to leverage business to support central city housing and literacy programs and other kinds of city building and human resource development strategies.

The last several days I have heard that two new industries will be coming to San Antonio, and in both instances they will be going into facilities in the western sector of San Antonio, in the Edgewood School District, a school district with one of the lowest tax bases in the entire state. Again, the strategy is one of building facilities speculatively with city funds, so that when we do attract industry they cannot say there is not a place for them to go.

So the first principle that I want to define as a success variable for cities in this era is a sense of targeting and mission matched with a responsibility to harness economic growth and make it work for those who have been outside the economic mainstream. A second principle that will characterize the successful cities, those that can manage this environment of change, is the concept of inclusiveness. Cities that will be successful will understand that they must bring people together.

William Ochee, a professor at UCLA, wrote two important books. The first was called *Theory Z*, in which he tried to build on Japanese quality methods applied to American industry. The second, a book called *The M Form Society*, says, essentially, that in America today there are few people who alone can make things happen, but there are many people who alone can keep things from happening. Change in mechanisms of authority have made those in authority less capable of simply saying, "Do it because I said so," which is good. The other factor is just the sheer challenge of diversity. With diversity, with difference, with different ideologies and philosophies, comes a more difficult environment for producing results. This is a simple fact, and there are mathematical models that describe the complexity of the process. The role of the municipal leader in this setting is not just to be a project planner but to be a consensus builder. It is to keep an attitude that allows for constant search for that little sliver of daylight that constitutes the middle ground, that little sliver of daylight through which to provide a solution to a situation that appears to be total confrontation and obstruction. As a mayor of a major city, I spend the greatest amount of my time not necessarily getting things done, but keeping bad things from happening.

I was asked the other day, "What would you say to your successor in San Antonio about skills to think about?" I replied that San Antonio is a city that is 53 percent Hispanic and 8 percent black, figures that make the city over 60 percent minority. Yet it is a city in which economic power continues to be concentrated in the traditional white population. This division creates an effective veto, one community against another, requiring that any progress be a result of agreement and consensus. Thus, the greatest skill is bringing people together. A leader must also be willing to concentrate on keeping the flash points from flashing and just spending whatever hours it takes to keep the momentum going forward and the negativism to a minimum. This consensus building is a major responsibility. The public officials in this era will spend more time on consensus building, cooperation, and constant, patient, exhausting dialogue than anything else, but these are the essential skills for this environment.

Finally, some of the themes that will characterize successful cities are a commitment to action, a commitment to results, a commitment to finding ways to get things done, no matter what combinations of factions, blurring of the lines between what is Republican and what is Democratic, what is liberal and what is conservative. Successful cities will find a new matrix, a new matrix of pragmatic results-oriented project management where it is possible to produce not only projects but also a larger sense of momentum. My own experience in San Antonio is that when you are able to do that, many people who have been negative before contribute positively, and there is a real sense of participation by minority persons.

Let me quickly highlight a few specifics, because I am very proud of some of the things that have happened that relate to the minority agenda in San Antonio. First, the creation of a small business strategy in San Antonio has become a small business incubator in which seventy-five new companies have been formed creating about 250 jobs. Small businesses are critical to a minority strategy. If you gave me as a mayor the choice between 500 new jobs in a plant or 500 people who were each allowed to start a small business, it would not even be a close call. To be able to start a small business means control over your own time, assets that are bankable, assets to pass on to your children, and participation as a citizen in the community with a sense of mastery over one's own destiny and self-reliance. It is important to create that sense of entrepreneurship in minority communities. So I am very proud of San Antonio's small business strategy.

Second, we just passed in San Antonio the most progressive minority purchasing policy in Texas. This policy provides for 32 percent of all discretionary contracts by the city to be minority contractors: architects, consultants, accountants, lawyers, consulting engineers, et cetera. There were no goals before and our performance was very low. For the first year, 32 percent is a good strong goal that probably can be attained and ought to be. Also, San Antonio now requires that 25 percent of all construction contracts over $200,000 will go to subcontractors who are minority. There are ways to work around the very tough Texas laws on this question, and we think we have found a way that will work.

A third strategy is investment in literacy. Literacy centers have been built as part of libraries and as part of the public school systems with investments in computer programming with the capability to focus on literacy.

Fourth is creation of a housing trust fund. This fund will focus on downtown high-rise housing as well as housing in the neighborhoods that surround the city and is designed to create a central city constituency and support for the retailing and the other activities that we hope will once again populate our downtown.

Fifth is continued investment in education. We have just formed in San Antonio what we call the San Antonio Education Partnership. We selected the eight poorest-performing schools in San Antonio, based on SAT scores and dropout rates, and said to the high school students, "If you, the senior class of 1989 and every class that comes behind you in these schools, can perform at a B average, 80 percent grade ratio, and attend school 95 percent of the time, you will have a guaranteed four-year financial package to go to college; and/or if you cannot go to college for whatever reason, then we will offer access to the career-oriented jobs that one hundred San Antonio businesses have agreed to create via this San Antonio Education Partnership."

The job is complex, but I continue to believe that the cities are the best places to uphold the American ideals, those ideals that I described earlier. Our ideals are fundamentally so basic that we teach them to children when they first come to school, even before they know the meaning of the words: "One nation under God, indivisible, with liberty and justice for all."

One nation. Not Sunbelt versus Rustbelt, not burned-out cities set against prosperous suburbs, not urban reservations of a permanent underclass juxtaposed against islands of privilege; one nation.

Under God. A God who can see even into the junkie havens, the shooting galleries; even into the dimly lit tenements where the senior citizens wait, cold and afraid; even into the gang hangouts or the home of the abused child or the battered spouse. A God who can see into the home of the unemployed manufacturing worker rendered obsolete at age fifty. One nation under God.

Indivisible. Not divided into black and white or rent asunder by polarization of selfishness or hate or battling over a shrinking pie. One nation under God, indivisible.

With liberty and justice for all. Not just for those that come from the right neighborhoods, who have the right color of skin, the right color of hair or eyes, the right accent or last name, the right schools or origins. One nation under God, indivisible, with liberty and justice for all.

The American city has been the integrating mechanism, has been the engine of our national economy, and it must not be allowed to die. Our nation's cities are part and parcel of the American ideal, the American optimism, the American quest for self-determination, and they must continue to be.

To support America's cities is to be in a position to support the aspirations of those minority populations that are the focus of this conference. Any strategy to support America's minority populations and disadvantaged populations in the years to come must begin by focusing on the condition of the cities in all their dimensions.

I close my remarks to you today with the same sense of optimism with which I have tried to cite the possibilities that confront our cities, in quoting a senator who was shot in Los Angeles twenty years ago this last summer and who was attorney general in the administration of the great President Lyndon B. Johnson, Senator Robert Kennedy. In a book of his speeches I found these remarks, and I have taken them to be a philosophy of life. My staff framed them for me some years ago, and they sit on my desk. This is what he said: "The future may be beyond our vision, but it is not entirely beyond our control. It is the shaping impulse of America, that it is not fate, nor is it chance, nor is it the irreversible tides of history that determine our destinies. Rather, it is reason, and it is principle, and it is the work of our own hands." He went on to say, "There is pride in that, even arrogance, but there is also truth and experience; and in any event, it is the only way we can live."

What will improve our cities? It is not fate; it is not chance; it is not a random toss of the dice; it is not an inevitability generated by these dynamics of change that I have described. In the final analysis, it is reason, our powers of logic, our preparation, the kind of reasoning that goes on in institutions such as this, principles, the guidance of our Creator, our own strength of character and, in the final analysis, the work of our own hands.

That is what generations of Americans before us have believed. That was the fuel that spurred Lyndon Johnson through the difficult years of the Depression and through those years of his presidency. That is the American ideal, a sense of optimism and self-determination. We find it in so many ways in America's cities today. Where we find it, we must fuel it and encourage it. And I would be presumptuous enough to suggest that that is really what this conference is about.

Discussion

From the floor: I would like to ask you to elaborate on the comment you made about the conference on libraries in California that you recently addressed because, if there is an institution that has adapted itself to the changing realities of society, it is that old library institution. We continue to think of the library as a fuddy-duddy institution, but, in fact, it has changed remarkably.

For example, one can get just about any video needed today, except for X-rated videos, in the local library, and that seems to be a way to change. But libraries also function as child care centers these days, as you well know. I wonder if you can talk a bit about what is happening to libraries generally, what the future is for libraries in California, and how other institutions, such as the library, can be revitalized.

H. Cisneros: That is an excellent question, and it really is the kind of thing I want to work on. One of the things that I want to do after this term is over is to write. I will tell you that, being a mayor, there is almost no time to think beyond immediate obligations. To try to take information that you hear generally and that you can regurgitate in a speech and to look two or three levels below it, to have time to sit down and give some attention to it, is not what you can do while serving in a position such as mayor, where your next obligation is to be at a ribbon cutting at a business at 7:30 in the morning looking as if it is the best day of your life. So between ribbon cuttings and solving intergovernmental problems and personality disputes between council members and zoning cases that go on for three hours and such, I look for the opportunity to write. One of the things that I want to do is to sit down and write about changing institutions, because I really do believe that one of the big challenges for the country is managing the demographic changes that will be occurring in the future. There is a lot to be written on that topic.

There is one page in a Rand Corporation study on libraries that is a good simple attempt to discuss this subject. What that report does is describe the implications of demographic change in certain characteristic areas, and then the authors suggest what those changes mean for the library. For example, if there are large minority populations that do not speak English, obviously this requires the adaptation of collections to provide materials for those persons. If there are populations that are poor and seeking jobs, one of the functions of the library can be to serve as a clearinghouse for job-related information—job preparation, job training, and certain kinds of information about where to go and who to see to get plugged into the job market. The Rand report talks about the role of a library in providing early childhood education, particularly in a bilingual environment; about marketing the library to a population whose ethic has not been reading or education, to very poor populations who may not appreciate the library, and to those for whom the majority of the materials are unavailable because they cannot get there. Thus, the challenge becomes how to market the library to people who are not culturally or traditionally readers.

Implications for other dimensions of the society are immense. This same kind of study needs to be for other institutions as well. Libraries are important institutions, although I would not rank them in the top five of the governmental institutions that ought to be thinking about these questions. Job-training centers, the schools, city departments related to police and fire and other emergency services—all have responsibilities in these areas that go beyond the obvious. Small business development must relate to these demographic realities, as well as economic development activities. Housing departments involved in housing development and home ownership incentives and other such policies must address demographic changes. One could go down a whole list of governmental functions that interface with the public and do the same kind of analysis; it is warranted and useful.

From the floor: I have a question that relates to your experience as an elected official. A disturbing trend across the nation's cities is the high segregation of cities, with a concentration of minorities in the inner cities and a concentration of whites on the outside of those inner cities, in the suburban settings. This segregation has an important impact on the quality of education for minorities, since minorities make up a significant portion of the students in those inner city schools. Do you think that there is a political will at the local level among the elected officials to implement some type of metropolitan or regional desegregation plan comprising both its communities and its schools, particularly in a city such as San Antonio, which has numerous independent school districts?

H. Cisneros: There is no question that we are experiencing a concentration of minority populations and poor people in particular school districts, although I think that this pattern of movement into the suburbs and concentration of minority students in urban school districts in Texas is more fluid and less rigid than we find in other places. For example, the wealthier and, therefore, probably better school districts in Dallas— Plano/Richardson, for example—or in San Antonio—Northeast /North Side—have a larger percentage of Hispanic students in comparison to the percentage of black students found in the suburbs of the North, but there is a serious segregation problem in San Antonio.

The issue is probably not overall consolidation. There is little suggestion that that is going to solve the problem. Indeed, I have suggested consolidation in San Antonio, and even minority officials oppose it on the grounds of loss of local control over a minority school district, such as Edgewood or South San or Southwest or Harlendale or San Antonio. They are not interested in consolidating with the North Side, and, as a result, losing their decisionmaking position.

The answer probably lies more along the lines of the educational suit now being considered by the state, which includes mechanisms that rely on a formula for equitable financing, and possibly some magnet school concepts that allow really good quality education to be available to every student from every school district.

We now have a high-technology high school operating at the San Antonio College that students from every school district can attend. We have a health careers high school operating at the medical center, and students come from all over the metropolitan area to the health careers high school. We are now working on an arts magnet school downtown in a theater district to which young people would come from every part of the metropolitan area.

I suspect that in the short run, before we see explicit steps toward consolidation, we are going to see a series of these types of measures: formulas of equitable financing, financial support that is not dependent upon property tax base, magnet school approaches, and programs such as the one described here today in the San Antonio Education Partnership.

I believe we will see some consolidation, but it's more likely to be caused by economic realities and near bankruptcy of particular school districts than an overarching strategy. That has been my experience in actually suggesting consolidation to the school districts. Districts are not interested in consolidation. It is hard to persuade school board members and a constituency that has established a position of leadership to consolidate with another entity and lose their power and position in a larger setting.

From the floor: Mayor, would you describe the program that guaranteed a college education for students in several San Antonio high schools and how those packages are funded?

H. Cisneros: Yes. This is a program that is modeled after the Boston Compact and the Baltimore Commonwealth Agreement. Ours is a variation of those programs. There are four partners involved in the program: the schools, which have promised counselors and enhanced liaison within the schools; the colleges and universities, of which there are eight in San Antonio; the Chamber of Commerce, which has agreements with one hundred businesses; and the community organizations led by COPS (Communities Organized for Public Service), which are working with the parents in unique settings, such as parishes, churches, neighborhood groups, and Parent-Teacher Associations, to really energize the young people. I have chaired the group as it has come together and continue to serve as the chair of the working committee.

The promises are twofold: one, career-oriented jobs. In our case, one hundred businesses have promised preferential access to career-oriented jobs to youngsters who meet the partnership requirements. Second, the colleges and universities have each promised financial packages. In the case of the junior college, the plans they have promised are relatively inexpensive. Trinity and Saint Mary's University have provided more expensive packages.

In addition to these efforts, we are organizing massive fund raising within the community at large to supplement the financial packages that the colleges put together. At the present time, the college packages include partial loans, and we want to eliminate the loans and convert that four-year financial package to a full scholarship.

In other words, as soon as we find out how many young people are eligible—and we will know roughly how many are eligible at the end of the first grading period, although there are still students who will qualify—we will begin to match students with the school they want to attend of the eight colleges that are participating and begin to match each student with a financial package at that campus. I am responsible for raising the sum of money—I think it will be about $500,000 this first year—to offset the loan portion of each package with a grant, therefore assuring the student of a four-year scholarship not just a financial package but a scholarship to college. That is the goal.

Baltimore has raised about $4 million for an endowment, with a goal of $20 million in an endowment, which would spin off sufficient interest earnings to make that promise work year in and year out in perpetuity as a replacement for any loan funds. That is my goal in San Antonio, but we have just started the program.

The first year the program will pay as we go out of monies that we raise. Then I will begin to build an endowment that can generate interest for the long run. I acknowledge that this effort is not a panacea. Although our goals are to reduce the dropout rate, to increase performance on test scores, and to increase the number of students going to college, the program will have limited impact on all those goals. For example, when I stand before a senior class and talk about the dropout rate, I am talking to students who have already made it that far; therefore, the influence of the Education Partnership Program on the dropout rate is not going to be big.

As a result, we are going to do two things. The first is to establish the criteria for participation in this program back through the eleventh, the tenth, and the ninth grades. Beyond that, we are going to initiate the program in the middle schools and elementary schools and begin to talk about going to college. Young people can begin to sign contracts early on. The program will emphasize that they are signing up for a college scholarship if they will do minimal things along the way.

The highest dropout rate occurs between the eighth and the ninth grades, then it lessens. But students continue to drop out over the high school years. We are asking them to sign contracts early, even in the middle school, so that the program is setting the environment for attending college.

The role of the community organizations is key; although they do not bring money to the table, they bring people resources to talk to the students and the parents and the churches about participation in the program. This, obviously, has to be related to many, many other anti-dropout programs and other types of positive school programs.

In the Baltimore project, in two years of existence, 23 percent more students qualified for the program than in the preprogram class. In only two years, 23 percent more students achieved the B average and the 95 percent attendance rate, and 20 percent more went to college after two years than before the program. So, while it does not solve everything, such a program does help create an environment that changes the structure of incentives within the school. Our job is then to change whatever other dysfunctional things exist in those schools, to create a totally different school environment in those poorest-performance schools.

TOP (Left to right): *Joan Moore, Paul Peterson, Robert Reischauer*
BOTTOM: *Joan Moore, Raquel Rivera (SSRC staff)*

Financing New Initiatives in the Cities

PART VII

Introduction

Joan Moore: It is difficult to follow Mayor Cisneros, but one thing I can promise is that if yesterday was a day in which we raised issues that presidential candidates do not raise and do not discuss, today is certainly a day in which we will raise those issues. Our focus is, where is the money to finance new initiatives and programs coming from, and how is it going to be raised?

Paul Peterson is a professor of government at Harvard and was a scholar at the Brookings Institution prior to that for a number of years. He is currently the chair of the Social Science Research Council's Committee for Research on the Urban Underclass, which is a venture in which the IUP/SSRC Committee has considerable interest .

Professor Peterson has written a book currently in publication called *A Case for a National Welfare Standard*. He has edited another new book called *Can the Government Govern?* which provides some hint of what he is going to be talking about. He has had a very long and distinguished career. He has brought together numerous scholars and has edited books as well as written his own on urban issues. Several of his edited publications have been very useful to those of us interested in the urban political sphere.

A Budget Deficit Reduction Approach to Reducing Poverty

Paul Peterson: Poverty over the last ten years has not declined. It has actually increased, even though the state of the economy has gone down and then come back up to where, at the very least, poverty should be back down to where it was in 1978. But if you look at the statistics between 1978 and 1987, the poverty rate is two percentage points higher today than it was then.

The nature of poverty has changed, as well. It used to be that poverty was mainly a rural phenomenon. Today poverty is to be found disproportionately in our central cities. It used to be that the people who were poor were elderly. With the advances in Social Security, Medicare, and Medicaid, there has been a noticeable decline in poverty among the elderly and that trend has continued with further reductions even in the last ten years. Where the growth in poverty is occurring is among single-parent families, with the result that we have had a 5 percent increase in the poverty rate among children in the last ten years, a dramatic and striking statistic.

When we think of what Mayor Cisneros was saying about the next generation and its minority composition, and when we take into account the fact that the poverty rate in the United States is much higher than in European countries, much higher than in countries that are our competitors, and when we think that this problem is particularly concentrated among children uniquely in the United States (more so in the United States than in any other industrial country), we have to ask ourselves the question, don't we need to do something more than just the ordinary in order to address problems of this magnitude?

It is fashionable to say that the problems have to be addressed at the state and local levels because the resources are not going to be made available in Washington. Certainly, there are numerous things that can be done at the local level. The most urgent thing that needs to be done in our cities is to think very seriously about the problem of urban education. I was pleased to hear the mayor address that question not only in a general way but in a very concrete way. Much more creativity needs to be given to this issue. I am concerned that our large urban educational bureaucracies seem impervious to change. It is extraordinarily difficult to turn experimental programs and imaginative new ideas into systematic approaches within our central cities.

I am reminded of the phrase of a former commissioner of education in the state of Massachusetts, who once said, speaking about the Boston public school in an observation that is all too characteristic of urban schools in general, "The public school in this city is a wonderful place if you know what it is doing. It is providing a system of adult employment." Too much attention is being given to the needs of the adults in our public school system, especially in our central cities, and not enough attention is being given to the needs of the children in those schools. Exactly what to do about that problem escapes me, but I do think that that is one of the most urgent questions that need to be addressed by people who are thinking about the future of our cities.

I am pleased to say that the Rockefeller Foundation and the Russell Sage Foundation have given a very substantial sum of money to the Social Science Research Council to encourage new ideas and new ways of thinking about the problem of poverty in our central cities. A committee interested in persistent poverty is being formed there, and a postdoctoral program, a doctoral dissertation program, and an undergraduate training program are being established. The program is aimed particularly at minorities, not exclusively at the postdoctoral level, but the initiative is one that will try to encourage the scholarly community to take the questions of what is currently being called the underclass much more seriously than it did in the last twenty years. Professor Bill Wilson at the University of Chicago has done a lot to bring this issue back to the forefront, and Bob Reischauer is also doing work in this area.

Dick Nathan has argued that, in particular, we must look at our service delivery systems and ask what can be done about those systems to improve the context within which young people find themselves thinking about the future in our central cities. As important as these questions are, their answers must address financing. Certainly, if you look at welfare policy today and at what is happening at the state level, over the last fifteen, twenty years, we have had a major decline in what states are willing to pay the people who are in need of welfare assistance. We have experienced a decline of over 30 percent, which represents a dramatic change in the policies of state governments with respect to the needs of the poor, especially poor children.

The federal government set up a food stamp program that we all believe has immeasurably improved the position of those in poverty since 1960. However, this improvement happened for only a short period of time. Today food stamp benefits and cash benefits combined in the average state equal only what cash benefits amounted to in 1960, once the cost of living differences are accounted for. Really, all we have done is change the nature of the assistance to the poor. We now call it "food-stamp-plus-cash assistance." We have not really increased the spendable resources of our people who are in most need of governmental assistance.

So I wonder whether we can address the problems of concentrated poverty, of persistent poverty, if we leave the financing of this question to the state and local governments alone. That forces us to go back and look at the national picture. This is the topic we avoid these days, saying that, really, we cannot expect anything at the national level; the problem of deficits on the part of our national government makes it impossible to think of new and creative ideas with respect to the problems of our central cities.

Partly out of desperation at the current situation, I propose something that I think initially you will think is absolutely ridiculous and out of the question. However, I believe we really have to rethink some of the well-known positions that we have held for a long period of time. It is too late for the 1988 election, but it is time for liberals in this country, if there are any left—at least that admit to being called such—to embrace the concept of the balanced budget amendment to the Constitution. That was an idea that Paul Simon raised in his unsuccessful presidential campaign, but he was the one candidate who understood this particular issue correctly. The reasons for this are both substantive and political.

The problem of deficits in the United States was steadily disappearing in the fifties and sixties. The public debt of the United States federal government as a percentage of our gross national product declined dramatically from 122 percent of our GNP in 1946 to approximately 33 percent in 1981. What has happened in the last decade is that this figure has climbed back to over 50 percent. There is actually quite a dramatic change in the whole pattern. Problems of deficits were simply political propaganda during the fifties and sixties. During the eighties they are not. The deficits are a serious problem that is cutting into the saving rate of the nation and having an effect on international trade.

The major factor in the control of the national government affecting our international position in the last decade has been our deficit, because our deficit has had an effect on our dollar, and our dollar has had an effect on our ability to sell products abroad. Once foreigners became entrenched in the U.S. market after the dollar climbed to unprecedented highs, it has been very difficult to regain the ground lost by American business.

Thus, the deficits are substantively a very serious problem. The old clichés about needing deficits in times of recession no longer hold. When the stock market crashed in 1987, no one said the solution was more deficits. In fact, Congress and the president tried to reduce the deficits even more, while according to Keynesian theory, the government should have been talking about increased deficits.

The current policy is to turn over the management of the economy to the Federal Reserve. The person mainly responsible for the economic progress made in the last decade is Paul Volcker. He drove inflation out of the economy and managed to put the economy on a fairly even keel. In the future we will look to agencies in the federal government, such as the Federal Reserve, to manage our day-to-day economic situation. We do not need deficits to do that. From the point of view of substantive public policy, we want to eliminate deficits.

Now, who is responsible for the deficits? One of the arguments is that Congress is responsible. It is those spendthrift liberals in Congress who are responsible for the deficits. However, the facts disprove that accusation. Congress has not appropriated more money for public expenditures or cut taxes more than the amounts the president of the United States has requested. That was true in the days of Truman and of Eisenhower and Kennedy and Johnson and Nixon, and it has been true in the Reagan administration as well. Congress basically takes its cue from the president as to the level of macrospending, and Congress does not change that level very much. Thus, it is a presidential responsibility to come up with a balanced budget, and that is something presidents are discovering is not a very politically popular thing to do.

It must be admitted that Franklin Delano Roosevelt was the first president to discover how advantageous it is to run huge deficits. The only other president who ran deficits on a scale as large as those we have today was FDR. His excuse was, "Well, there is a recession." Ronald Reagan does not have such an excuse. His excuse is that if we have big deficits we can keep pressure on the expenditure side of the government and keep domestic spending down.

Spending did not go down in the 1980s. Spending by the federal government, as a percentage of the gross national product, went up in the 1980s. We spent more for defense, and we spent more for financing our deficit. We spent as much on Social Security as ever and even a little bit more for retirement programs. The only areas where there were major cuts were on the domestic side. After a steady increase in the seventies in social and domestic programs, we had in the 1980s a steady decline in expenditures on the domestic side, a steady decline in the kinds of programs that Mayor Cisneros was talking about. He is exactly right. General revenue sharing, block grant programs, and a host of other domestic programs were severely cut in the 1980s, precisely at the time that we began to allow huge deficits.

The strategy seems to have worked. The strategy of running huge deficits in order to eliminate social programs from the domestic agenda while calling for a balanced budget amendment to the Constitution has been a brilliant political strategy, and it has produced a control of the policy agenda that the conservatives have wanted for many, many years. The consequences have been that liberals have been blamed for the deficits, even though they are not responsible, and liberals have been unwilling to take a second look at this question of a balanced budget amendment. Liberals have been unwilling to say, "Okay. What if we had a balanced budget amendment? What would happen then? Would a balanced budget necessarily be to the disadvantage of those who are concerned about the problems of the cities and the problems of the poor?"

I submit to you that if we were to have a balanced budget, there would be only one way to get it. We could get a balanced budget only by compromising on our defense programs, on our tax policy, perhaps on our entitlement policies with respect to Social Security, and on some of the benefits received by people whose incomes are very high in the Social Security area.

It is not at all clear that the reduction in the deficit would be targeted for programs aimed at low-income people. In fact, the one thing that happened in the eighties is that, despite attempts by the Reagan administration to make cuts in entitlement programs aimed at the poor, such as the so-called safety net programs, those programs survived the eighties much better than did most of the other domestic government programs. This was mainly because "safety net programs" were a high priority on the part of Congress. This type of scenario is what I would expect if we went into a balanced budget context.

Once in a balanced budget context, there can be a reopening of issues as to what the government should be doing, where the government should be allocating its resources, and a renewed discussion of issues that are currently off the political and fiscal agenda. Until the liberals decide that they want to say, "Okay, we are as much for fiscal responsibility as the conservatives say they are," and put the budget deficit issue back at the center of the debate, we cannot really address the problem of financing the kinds of programs and concerns we have been talking about at this conference.

J. Moore: The next speaker is a distinguished economist at the Brookings Institution, Robert Reischauer, who is currently working on a book on the underclass. He has worked as deputy director for the Congressional Budget Office for a long period of time. He has been involved with budget issues at the federal level for about fifteen years.

Working within the Realities

Robert Reischauer: I am tempted to talk about city politics since my good friend Paul Peterson, who is a political scientist, talked about macroeconomics and budget matters. We have heard at this conference very compelling pleas for why we should devote more resources to education, training, human services, employment, health, income security, economic and community development, and the list goes on. It was a time to dream, to wish, to hope, to think about what might be.

With this session on financing new initiatives, we begin to come back down to earth and ask the very difficult questions that have to be answered: namely, how can the obstacles be surmounted to get these programs? How can we develop a political constituency to support efforts like these? How can we find the money to finance them? How can we implement them? For we should remember that this country has not had a particularly good track record for implementing the programs we are discussing.

The answers to these questions are difficult. They are the kinds of things that economists like myself, practitioners of the dismal science, are always asked to speak about. We never get to talk about the good, the nice, the expansive. The best way to begin this discussion is to review with you three relevant but somewhat discouraging facts of life that we must deal with.

The first is the realization that the 1980s have not been a good time for the types of social programs we are all concerned about. The political constituency for these programs is not strong. If we review what has happened to several of the city-oriented programs during the last eight years, the facts are discouraging. We had a general revenue sharing program in 1981, that distributed $4.5 billion. Today we do not have that program. It disappeared.

We had an Urban Development Action Grants (UDAG) program in 1981 that distributed in that year $675 million. This current fiscal year the same program will distribute about $200 million, and then it will disappear, for Congress did not reauthorize it. Funding for urban mass transit, another important program for cities, has fallen 28 percent in real terms over this period. Community development block grants are down 44 percent, after adjusting for inflation, over this seven-year period. It is not just brick and mortar programs, either. The other human capital programs that we discussed earlier are also affected. Job training, previously called the Comprehensive Employment and Training Act (CETA) and now the Job Training Partnership Act (JTPA), is down 56 percent in real terms over the last seven years. Chapter One for the disadvantaged, which is one of the programs people think has done moderately well over this period of retrenchment, is down 13 percent.

We have to face the reality that when push comes to shove, when deficit reduction is the order of the day, these programs have not made out very well. Now, many think that everything in the domestic budget has experienced cuts. But this is not the case. Allocations for space programs are up considerably, health research is up significantly, airports have received increased allocations. Some areas of the domestic budget have increased in real terms at a pretty good clip, 30 percent for the three programs I just mentioned. The belt tightening that is going on is not across the board. The American public is selecting which things are the most popular. And the social programs that we are concerned about and the "safety net programs" by and large have come out on the short end of the political stick.

The second fact we need to face is the obvious one, that the fiscal cupboard is bare. It is totally bare at the federal level. There may be a few crumbs floating around at the state and local levels. The federal budget deficit for the fiscal year that ended October 1 will be about $155 billion. That represents an increase from the previous year and will cause a little tizzy because the deficit is not continuing on a downward trend. The budget for the fiscal year of 1988 has an estimated deficit of $148 billion.

A new president is going to have to put together a budget for fiscal year 1990. That budget is going to require between $26 billion and $36 billion of cuts to meet the Gramm-Rudman budget reduction targets. Both of the candidates running for president have said they will stick with the Gramm-Rudman targets. Both of them have said they will not raise taxes. What is going to give? The answer is, some of the same programs that we have seen under so much pressure during the last eight years.

On the surface, things do not look bad at the state and local levels, but when one looks beneath the surface, there is very little wiggling room there either. State and local taxes have been bolstered in the last few years by two extraordinary things. The first is six years of uninterrupted economic growth. However, we must plan policy with the realization that we are at or close to a high point for local and state taxes. It will be nice if we can sustain this economic recovery, but history leads us to the conclusion that it cannot go on forever. Second, the state and local revenue figures look fairly healthy because of the windfall that was received from the Federal Tax Reform Act of 1986 and the misestimation by many state governments of how much effect that windfall would have on their fiscal situations. Of course, in a few areas, most notably New York, California, and Massachusetts, the state and local fiscal situation has turned sour.

Despite these two generally positive forces—economic recovery and fairly healthy state and local situations—the National Governors' Association's latest analysis of the year-end fund balances of state governments finds that the states have the lowest balances that they have had in the twelve years that the association has collected these kinds of data. That twelve-year period has included a terrible recession and some very difficult economic times. This suggests that the margin for error at the state level is not particularly high. It is also important to remember that the positive conditions that exist at the state level have been purchased by increased taxation. The average state and local tax burden in America has risen by 13 percent, or 1.2 percent of the GNP, over the 1981-1987 period. This trend suggests that there may not be much room to go without reigniting the taxpayer revolts of the mid-1970s.

The third fact of life that we must face is that the competition for new resources is going to be fierce. We are not the only group with lists of new initiatives. I am invited, on the average, to two meetings like this one each week in Washington, which is, of course, the hotbed of this kind of activity. People are meeting all over Washington, D.C., all over the country, developing agendas for the next president, and those agendas do not say, "We can do with less."

There are actually three types of competition for monies out there. First, there is the competition from the folks who said, "We have been battered, we have been bruised, we have been abused over the last seven years. Give us more." This group includes the environmentalists, the energy groups, the natural resources advocates, and the people favoring infrastructure investments.

Second, there is competition from the claimants who are the big boys on the block, the tough guys who have had their share but are hungry for more. This includes health research, space, and defense. They have done very well, but Congress provides more funds to these claimants each year. A new poll just appeared that showed that Americans are eager to increase funding for space. This competition is particularly difficult for the kinds of programs we support simply because the appropriation bills for space development are in the subcommittee that deals with many of the economic development and housing and urban development appropriations. What happened this year is instructive. The final decisions came down to choosing between UDAG and space. The Congress chose to build new cities in space, not rebuild cities on the ground. There is no indication that these kinds of pressures are going to be alleviated.

Many times when one thinks of room for budget cuts, one thinks of defense. We must keep in mind, however, that the defense budget in real terms peaked in 1985, and for the last four fiscal years it has decreased in real terms. In other words, the money provided has not kept pace with inflation. The defense budget is now about 10 percent below the level it was in 1985. This makes the politics of defense very difficult. This dilemma transforms doves into hawks, because every decision made to cut a dollar from defense no longer comes out of the big wad of unobligated funds that was previously swirling around in the Pentagon's bank account. Now it comes out of the assembly line of the Grumann factory on Long Island, which is in some member's district, which makes that representative think twice about cutting back on the F-14D or A-6.

These decisions are difficult ones. No one has indicated that Congress or the president would cut the defense budget below the amount necessary to keep pace with inflation. If we keep the defense budget at the level that would be required to keep pace with inflation, as a percentage of gross national product by the year 1993, the defense budget will be no higher than it was in 1981. It will be no higher than before the Reagan buildup. And in 1981, most Americans felt that we were spending an insufficient amount on defense. My sympathies in this area are very much like Paul Peterson's, but I think we have to realize that making these choices is a very big political challenge.

Third, several new priorities have been embraced by the political leaders and by the American people that are going to demand attention and compete with other social programs and community development efforts. These include child care, long-term care, and acid rain. Both presidential candidates have indicated that they are willing to spend billions of dollars on those programs, so the competition for funding will be fierce.

In light of these three facts of life, what can we do? What can we do to find funds? The answer here depends very much on what we are suggesting for policies. There is no simple answer. The answer might be one approach for education policy and a very different approach for economic development policy and still a different approach for community development.

Having said this, there is one answer, though, that cuts across all areas, and that is that it is clear that the old way, which is to walk up to the budget till and say, "Give me more of what's in there," won't work. The competition is too fierce. The public support for domestic social programs is too limited, and there is little money in the till.

What then are the options?

Here I will offer three suggestions to stimulate more creative thinking. They are not blueprints but, instead, are general approaches. The first is to think of ways in which we can create dedicated trust funds or dedicated funds can be created that provide a specific source of revenue for a specific set of programs. People do not realize how much of this type of funding already exists. It has not receive front-page news coverage in the 1980s. The government has cut back in numerous areas, but there are certain areas that it has expanded tremendously using this device, particularly in the environmental area. For example, in the last seven years the following trust programs have been enacted:

1. The Hazardous Substance Super Fund, in which oil, feedstocks, and chemicals are taxed for cleaning up the environment

2. The Reforestation Trust Fund, in which a new tax on imported plywood and lumber goes to reforestation

3. The Harbor Maintenance Trust Fund, in which the loading and unloading of boats in harbors is taxed, and the money is used specifically to dredge the harbors and encourage more ships to use them

4. A Leaking Underground Storage Tank, or LUST, tax (better than sin taxes, and no one should object to paying a LUST tax); companies with underground storage tanks have to pay a tax, which is then used to clean up the leaking storage tanks

5. The Oil Spill tax, similar to the LUST tax

6. The Natural Aquatic Resources Fund that taxes fishing tackle and gear; the funds are used to develop and preserve aquatic resources

There are numerous such mechanisms that could be applied to the kinds of programs you are concerned about, and attention should be paid to these possibilities. Jules Sugerman, the welfare commissioner in the state of Washington, has a very innovative and expansive plan of this sort for children's programs. Two other alternatives present possibilities. One is a small addition to the unemployment insurance tax, which could be used for an expansion of employment and training programs. Much of what JTPA is doing now, and which an expanded program would do, would, in fact, save corporations training costs. Collectivizing this effort and improving the distribution of training programs might make sense.

Another suggestion is to auction off the import quotas that the United States has established. Presently, we have quotas on cars, on steel, on textile, on foot wear, et cetera, that limit the number or amount of particular products that can be imported to the United States. What this basically allows the Japanese to do in the case of cars is to raise the price of the cars. The Japanese get excess profits because the U.S. government limits the supply of the product that can come in. New Zealand and Australia and a number of other countries with similar quotas have decided that they should benefit from the quotas. We could auction off the right to import cars into our country and use the proceeds from this auction to account for industrial relocation problems, for economic development, and for community development programs.

A second general approach is to come forward with packages. The initiatives that have worked in the last year have all been package proposals. For example, a catastrophic health insurance program will go into effect next year. That program was financed by a particular set of revenues that were attached to the bill. A welfare reform bill passed Congress two weeks ago. It contains a series of very specific revenue increases. Changes in the tax code are identified and tied to particular program expansions. The same thing can be done on the spending side. We should not shy away from admitting that there is a considerable amount of spending on domestic programs that do not involve high priority items.

Untargeted vocational education grants, untargeted elementary and secondary education grants, and untargeted Economic Development Administration grants are political sources of funds for human and community development programs. There is economic development money for which 80 percent of the country is eligible. Redirecting some existing funds toward the things we care more about makes sense.

A third general approach would be to create a new federalism by tying new federal monies to added effort at the state and local levels. New grants could be tied to the amount of added effort expended by state and local governments. Florida, for example, has a new system in which counties levy special sales taxes for the homeless and the underprivileged. A program that gave federal assistance to match local monies should encourage local initiatives in these areas.

Let me conclude with two observations. One is that there is a need to set priorities. We referred to the need for education, for health, for economic development, for training, for social services, for everything. If we ask for everything, we are going to get nothing. This is clear. What we have to do is be able to say A is more important than B. Ideally, we would like them all, but in these fiscal times we cannot get all, and some, in fact, are more important than others.

Second, a fundamental decision has to be made on whether it is best to pursue place-oriented policies or people-oriented policies. Conferences on the cities always end up focusing on place-oriented policies, such programs as Community Development Block grants or Urban Mass Transit grants that give money to particular localities or jurisdictions.

There are good political reasons for this, but there are also good reasons to suggest that a people-oriented policy is the right one for these times. People-oriented policies are very difficult for place-oriented politicians to support. We have a system in which politicians belong to a geographic piece of turf, but policy analysts and researchers do not. Public policy researchers, academicians, and constituents are highly mobile. In fact, success in America is usually associated with geographic mobility. But success for a politician is associated with one piece of turf. The only kind of geographic mobility that politicians engage in is leaving their hotel home in Texas and going to Washington, but they still have that home base, which they regard as sacrosanct.

Thus, we should stand back and consider whether, in this climate, in this time, we must sacrifice place-oriented policies and pursue people-oriented ones. People-oriented policies will have a broader appeal to the American middle class, to jurisdictions that inevitably do not receive targeted resources. People-oriented policies might be a way of breaking down the difficult institutional problems in the schools and elsewhere where some of our programs seem to be more focused on supporting and maintaining the providers of the services than on helping the client.

Discussion

P. Peterson: Bob has done a very fine job of describing the future that has been laid out for us by key decisions made in 1981. The entire political and policy landscape changed in 1981 with the 20 percent tax cut, which has left us with revenue flows to the federal government where one dollar out of every five spent is being borrowed. That policy has remained in place more or less, with some variation, since that point in time.

In the presidential campaign, George Bush is going explicitly back to the themes of the 1980 campaign, talking about increases in expenditures for defense and talking about tax cuts and the need for a balanced budget amendment. These themes are resonating with the American public very effectively. Now that this formula has been discovered, it is not going to go away. These themes set the context for a struggle for every dollar. The brilliance of the Reagan administration was that they were able to change the landscape. That is what is really required at this point in time, a way of rethinking. The entire way in which people are debating and formulating these issues must be altered once again.

Bob has done an excellent job of identifying the most likely context within which the questions of the cities are going to be debated. Now the challenge we face is how to change that context.

Marta Lopez-Garza, IUP/SSRC Postdoctoral Fellow: I have an overriding concern that has been addressed somewhat by the panelists but should be addressed more fully. That concern is, given the political and economic trajectory of both our state and federal governments, i.e., cutbacks in social services and health services, the English-only amendments, attacks on abortion rights, and the possible continuation of this agenda into the next administration, public policy researchers and action researchers, such as ourselves, are faced with a dilemma. On the one hand, we are creating progressive research and working in areas that we think are very important, focusing on people who have felt the impact of the last eight years. On the other hand, after doing the research, we have to reach out and discuss the results of our studies with government officials and policymakers who are limited in funds and, in fact, sometimes hostile to our progressive agenda.

It seems that we are putting sand in a pail that has a sieve at the bottom. No matter how much progressive research we do, we are seeing the suggested reforms and the progressive agenda we have had for the last fifteen or twenty years being eliminated and cut back. What is our new strategy? What do we do now?

P. Peterson: I think you are absolutely right. I am not convinced that the problem can be solved by saying, "All right, we can push this question at the state and local level." I think there are real limits to what can be achieved at that level. Bob is absolutely correct that there has been an increase in expenditures at the state level, and, in some ways, there has been a countertrend at the state level that has been helpful. Nonetheless, it has not begun to meet the needs, and I do not think it can.

R. Reischauer: Let me provide a glimmer of hope. Substantial proportions of the research on social service and community development programs have been devoted to trying to see whether these programs have an impact. From the early seventies to the early eighties the prevalent view was that government programs do not work. It is not surprising that public support for these programs has eroded.

The research done in the late seventies and the early eighties showed that the Women, Infants, and Children (WIC) Program had a very positive rate of return. Head Start also seems to be having a positive effect. The Chapter One program has also received positive evaluations. Certain portions of the Medicaid program made an impact. This research has influenced the expansion of these programs. For example the WIC Program is one of the fastest growing components of the federal budget.

It is also worth noting that the welfare reform bill went through Congress in an era of austerity. In that same era we did not pass a minimum wage increase, an initiative that would not have cost the government any money and one that had the approval of 70 percent of the population and both presidential candidates. Yet a welfare reform bill went through Congress. Modest to be sure, but legislation that will add $3 billion to welfare programs. In large measure, that success came about because of research done by people like yourselves. Much of it was done by Manpower Demonstration Research Corporation (MDRC). This demonstrates that research in these programs can make a difference. It is very important that this effort continue.

J. Moore: If you do research, as I have been doing, on stigmatized population groups—which few pay any attention to, or, if the media and policymakers do acknowledge the research, it is to sensationalize findings—it is extremely important to continue those research efforts for a variety of reasons. One is that such research represents a mode of interpretation from the communities to a broader audience. Research not only has an ostensible effect on policy, but it also has an effect on public interpretation and public perceptions. Sometimes the perceptions are not positive ones or effective ones. Nonetheless, after entering my field in the hope of having an impact on local situations and getting absolutely no place, I have found that I am having an impact because people have read my work and applied it to other situations. This demonstrates that the effect of doing research is not necessarily immediately that of bending the ear of particular people in political power at that time.

Bob Wrinkle, Pan American University: Dr. Reischauer, it seems to me that when you talk about people-oriented policies, implicit in that orientation could be a move to a vouchering system. I would like your perceptions concerning the order and type of policy areas in which vouchering would work. I am sympathetic to the use of vouchers in many ways because there are certain institutions in our society, such as inner city school systems, that are incapable of changing themselves.

Many of us live and work in institutions where the employees are the most important factor in making business decisions. I am interested in providing low-income, powerless people with choice, with power over what can be done in the educational system in several ways. A first step is to let people go to any school within their district. If that is not sufficient, a metropolitan approach across school districts, a Minnesota-type of plan for example, should be tried. Beyond that, think about vouchers. There are ways to protect a voucher system from discrimination. If there were not, I would not be sympathetic to a voucher system at all.

Housing is certainly an area where vouchers work effectively. Day care is another. There are some issues in society about which there are fundamental disagreements regarding the nature of government regulation. A good example of such an issue is child care. We are worried about providing resources to low-income families and then discovering that the child care that is supported is inadequate or viewed as inadequate. Thus, we put a series of regulations on low-income people that middle-class people would never tolerate. The end result is, basically, that we then do not provide any money at all for these programs. We are left with a choice: do we want to provide the money in perhaps a suboptimal way or not provide it at all in the right way?

Harry Pachon, National Association of Latino Elected and Appointed Officials: I think both of you have mentioned that the biggest cuts during the 1980s came not in the entitlement programs and the social domestic policy but in the so-called discretionary programs. In light of that, I have two questions. First, Mr. Peterson, if you suggest a balanced budget amendment, wouldn't that put pressure on the House Appropriations Committee to further cut discretionary spending?

The second question is that we hear rhetoric now, Mr. Reischauer, from one of the presidential candidates on the line item veto. Should minorities be strongly opposed to the line item veto because those programs that benefit minorities would be seriously affected?

P. Peterson: Well, in response to your first question, I think that a balanced budget amendment is the only way to get out of the situation that you have correctly identified. From 1981 to 1988, we have been in a context where we have said we cannot touch entitlement programs, and we have to keep defense spending almost level or increase it a bit. We have had a substantial increase in defense spending until 1985 and a leveling off or a slight cutting since then. Consequently, we are faced with the cost of financing the debt, which is climbing all the time. Therefore, the only way we can address this problem is by cutting discretionary programs.

However, Congress cannot cut discretionary programs enough to bring the budget into balance. What the Gramm-Rudman targets have done is to keep pushing the balanced budget off into the future. Every year the five-year deadline gets pushed back another year or so. What we now have in the current context is tremendous pressure on the discretionary programs. If we were saying we really have to address this problem, I do not see how the politicians could resolve the issue apart from a tax increase, apart from reducing the entitlement programs, or apart from cutting defense programs.

Then, I think, once we have addressed the problem, we could expect a positive context for people-oriented programs. Look at what happens at the state level where a balanced budget is required. They from time to time discover they are running surpluses. When officials work at trying to hit a balanced budget, they underestimate revenue flows because the economy does better than expected.

This also happens at the national level. It is not the case that the government always predicts an economic picture that is rosier than actually happens. However, when officials start aiming for a balanced budget, they will start running surpluses on occasion, and that will provide an opportunity for developing new initiatives and moving in new areas. A balanced budget amendment will not immediately allow for new opportunities. It is a way of changing the political agenda.

R. Reischauer: Let me confess that I have some sympathy for a line item veto. It would not make a significant difference in the budget situation. A line item veto would transfer more power to the executive branch and would cut down a bit on the rhetoric of who is to blame for deficits. However, I do not think we have to go as far as a line item veto.

There is a proposal in Congress for what is called "expanded recision authority." Right now we have a system of recisions in which the president can send a notice to Congress saying, "I want you to eliminate A and C in this spending bill." Under the current rules of the House and the Senate, Congress can ignore the president's request and never take action. There is a proposal by Senator Domenici, the ranking member of the Senate Budget Committee, and others that would change the rules of the House and the Senate. The change would require action when the president sends a recision message to Congress. There would have to be an up or down vote in a short period of time on that specific item. The recisions could not be lumped together into a big unwieldy package. This modification would bring 90 percent of the benefits of a line item veto with 2 percent of its costs. We might be better off as a nation as a result. The "expanded recision authority" does not have particular implications for cities' programs, for minorities' programs, for defense, or any areas in particular. It would allow some weeding out of special interest legislation.

P. Peterson: Let me add to the discussion on the line item veto. What has happened over the last twenty years is that one political party has put together a coalition that is well equipped to capture the presidency.

The other political party is well entrenched on Capitol Hill. In the House of Representatives, to be sure, the Democratic party has had a majority for a very long period of time, and the Senate also seems to be falling to the Democratic party. Now developing in Washington is a situation where each political party has a vested interest in strengthening the powers of a particular institution of government. The Republican party wants to do anything it can to strengthen the powers of the presidency. The Democratic party wants to do anything it can to strengthen the powers of Congress.

I am worried about what this does to produce an institutional stalemate in our country and an unwillingness to see that these institutions were created to be above political parties and above factions. I think it is a dangerous development. Moreover, in terms of the item veto, it is very unlikely that Congress will give power to the president in a context where the Democratic party is controlling Congress.

From the floor: I believe that the vast majority of Americans believe in and want a strong defense, but this goal is not necessarily achieved by throwing money into defense. As the president's budget advisor has said, "The Defense Department is a swamp of waste." Do either of you see any hope for more efficiency in defense procurement in the near future?

R. Reischauer: Unfortunately, there is no line item in the budget labeled "waste" or "fraud" or "abuse," and it is terribly difficult to root these things out. Often the waste, fraud, and abuse occurs, not through deliberate effort, but through inadvertence, through the workings of very complex bureaucracies. The experts that I have talked to about this problem do not expect to be looking at substantial reductions in procurement costs in the near future. We can, however, clean up the contracting system, which is a very difficult system.

The easy solutions, such as "Let's have competitive bidding" or "Let's not have the military folks who run the tanks or the airplanes define specifications for building those items," are unrealistic. There are not a large number of experts in our society who know how a tank should run who are not in the Defense Department. For example, we cannot pull the man out of a factory or the engineer off the street and ask, "What do you think? What should a battle tank be able to do as it rumbles through central Germany?" These are very specialized areas.

There will be modest reforms, but the reforms will generate savings that represent a million dollars here, a million dollars there. Those amounts are the equivalent of rounding error in Washington, D.C., and would not mean big money to devote to other priorities.

J. Moore: My question is also about productivity and waste management. The largest and the fasting growing items in state and local budgets are corrections budgets. That is true also in the federal budget. In fact, in New York State, Urban Development Act Grants (UDAG) money is used to build prisons. This is actually quite a progressive housing program for poor people at both the state and local levels.

When you speak of special funds, is there a way to advocate that percentages of those huge budget increases are diverted to front-line programs? Is there a way to divert some funding directly into the kinds of programs that would eliminate human need? I think we could make a case for that. I do not think you can say to people, "Go all the way back and fund infancy programs to prevent unemployment," but you certainly can make a case for funding job-training programs targeted to the same population.

P. Peterson: In terms of job-training programs, it is my belief that we need to focus our attention on the public schools. I believe the job-training programs that are now being developed by welfare departments are replicating the work of the public schools. And the welfare agencies are dealing with fewer resources, with people who are less professionally well trained, who work under poor working conditions, and whose careers have a shorter trajectory.

Rather than trying to build what I regard as racially segregated, separatist, class-segregated, stigmatized institutions to serve the poor, we need to try to use our mainstream institutions, our public schools, much more effectively to meet the needs of the poor. We have really gone off in a very strange way in order to, after the fact, deal with the problems of what some people call the underclass and other people call persistent poverty. Instead we should attack it through the largest, most well-funded, most mainstream institution in our society, the public schools.

R. Reischauer: Interestingly enough, in the evaluation studies of Head Start and Job Corps, one of the findings is that a major component of the savings that result from the investments in these programs is less criminal activity. Those findings have been used extensively on Capitol Hill to try to maintain funding for Job Corps and Head Start.

Celestino Mendez, American G.I. Forum: If we see defense and defense spending as a patriotic duty, why do we allow it to be so profit motivated?

R. Reischauer: There are a number of studies on the rates of return for defense industries versus other industries. I think that there is not a huge difference. It could be that this is the result of the way the books are kept and the accounting incentives that are available to the defense industry. Changing defense contracting procedures would not be high on my list of priorities. But I am not convinced that we would achieve more efficiency if we had a nonprofit sector building airplanes. We have tried to control the rates of return on the contracts over the years and have been relatively unsuccessful.

John Gilderbloom, University of Louisville: I cringed when you talked about housing vouchers as an ideal. Generally, the newest research is showing that housing vouchers have been a total failure. When Reagan took office, roughly 25 percent of the people who qualified for federal housing aid were getting help. The ratio in terms of military spending to housing was one to seven, for every seven dollars spent in military, one dollar spent in housing. Now Reagan has slashed the housing budget by over 80 percent, increased the military budget by 20 to 30 percent, depending on how you measure it, and the ration in terms of spending on military to housing is now forty-four to one.

Studies sponsored and funded by the Ford Foundation in such cities as Houston show that those who qualify for housing aid now represent only one out of every twenty persons in need. For Hispanics, these figures are one out of thirty; for blacks, one out of every twenty-five. The cost of vouchers is high. Presently we spend $7 billion in federal money on housing programs. In comparison, the cost of implementing a voucher system to effectively work would cost close to $140 billion.

Clearly, the subsidies need to be cut. The biggest housing subsidies right now go to the middle class and to the rich in the form of home ownership deductions. That costs approximately $48 billion at the present time. We spend eight to nine times more money on home owner tax deductions and subsidies for the middle class and the rich than we do for the poor. We should reduce those figures.

In addition to the liberal supply-side programs or the conservative demand-oriented housing vouchers, we have community-based housing programs. There are several such national housing program initiatives. For example, I am a member of the National Urban Coalition Task Force on Affordable Housing. This group is analyzing the possibility of using federal money to fund community organizations at the local level, such as churches, ethnic organizations, and nonprofits. There are hundreds of nonprofits now in New York, Boston, and Houston. Jim Robinson, who started Co-op Houston, is building over one thousand units of affordable housing, taking dilapidated old buildings and refurbishing them. This is a first in Houston. Now two or three other organizations are developing low-cost housing. In sum, what is needed is a third-stream housing program, to support the Ron Dellums bill, which allocates over $448 billion, the same amount that home owners get in terms of subsidies, for nonprofit community-based groups to develop housing for low-income families.

P. Peterson: If you are looking at housing policy, you are inevitably looking at a context where the middle class must participate in any program to make it politically feasible. In the Dukakis statement in the debates, when he was asked about low-income housing, he immediately turned that concern into housing policy in general, mainly aimed at the middle class. That is just the way politics moves in that area.

At the local level, it is difficult to encourage local governments to concentrate housing resources on programs for the poor. If we pursued an alternative to that, such as raising the welfare assistance program to the level of the poverty line, instead of one-half the poverty line, which is where it tends to be at the present time, that would mean a general increase in resources available to low-income people that they could use however they wanted. Certainly, one of their major priorities would be to use it to get better housing. Wouldn't that be a more efficacious way of targeting the monies that are needed for housing to the people who are most in need of it?

J. Gilderbloom: Our studies basically show that whenever you raise incomes you get corresponding exact increases in rents. If you raise incomes by ten percent for the poor, you get an exact 10 to 15 percent increase in rents. Landlords target rents, not according to supply and demand, but according to the resources of the individuals in their apartments. So that approach is absolutely a waste of money and is too costly.

R. Reischauer: A considerable literature emerged from the housing allowance experiments in the 1970s. That research does not support the notion that increased incomes were translated into higher rents. I believe that either vouchers or raising incomes is the best approach to resolving the housing problem for the poor, and raising incomes is a better policy. That direction is one less likely to be supported by the American people, but it is the way to go. I was comparing vouchers to Section 8, new construction, and the substantial rehabilitation efforts of the 1970s. Vouchers are certainly not the only way to go.

The efforts of community-based organizations at the state and local levels represent some of the most exciting and positive developments in the housing area, but there is a question of scale here. Community-based efforts are an important element and should certainly be supported, much more so than is presently the case. But do local groups have the capacity to solve this problem in and of themselves? No. In certain areas they will make an important difference. In other areas, they will not have an impact at all. The United States is a big nation with a big problem. A mix of policies is probably the correct emphasis.

Andrés Torres, Center for Puerto Rican Studies, Hunter College: I believe that the panelists this morning have pushed the flow of the discussion of the last two days beyond acceptable limits. From my point of view, I do not believe it is good for worthy advocates to concede so much and to simply try to manage better the very initiatives that have been introduced by conservatives in this decade.

Making appeals to minority communities to adopt these mechanisms and policies, which really, although presented here as neutral in terms of their effects, would vary under differing conditions, would simply reinforce the dominance and the inequality and the same problems that we had going into the eighties.

To have enlightened Democrats adopting and rationalizing these same ideas and proposals is not productive. It is, from your point of view, realistic politics. For Latinos and blacks who are doing research and political analysis, our conception of realistic politics is that we must organize at all levels in the terms of Barbara Jordan's recommendation: The price of having so many on the outside must be made much more explicit to the entire society.

One of the presidential candidates remarked that the United States can never maintain its leadership in the world as long as it has the continuing divisions and poverty that it is suffering today. We do not want to legitimize too much of the careful, analytical, apparently objective, discussion of practices and techniques that minimize racial and class divisions.

P. Peterson: We had the largest expansion of the welfare state during the period of 1945 to 1980, when we ran budgets essentially in balance. I do not think returning to that state is going to be a guarantee of inadequate attention to the problems of the poor.

Jimmy Snell, Travis County (Texas) Commissioner: I am with county government, and as we struggled to try to complete a budget yesterday, I noticed that the rural people are being left out of the county government. They are being left out of the state government, and they have been left out of the federal government. When are we going to do something about helping those who cannot help themselves? We have senior citizens, people on fixed income, and especially those who live in the rural areas who are not getting any help at all.

The rural citizens have been in transition for a long time but have not received any help at all. I just wonder, when will the federal government give the rural areas the help that they need? It is time for someone to look at the rural areas. I talk to representatives from Washington and there is always a promise that something is going to be done. General revenue sharing has been taking money away from the counties, yet everyone is pushing, saying, "Let the county, let the state, take care of its own." But nobody is doing anything. There are many services needed in the rural towns and cities.

In some of these rural areas people have no water; people do not have flushing toilets. These conditions are disgusting. We must deliver water to these people. These conditions are heartbreaking when you visit these areas. You see these people not getting services, and yet they are being raped by taxes by the county, the state, and the federal government.

R. Reischauer: I share your concern, but realistically I do not think American public policy is going to turn its attention to the poor in rural areas in the next few years. In fact, if anything the situation is likely to get worse. There are tremendous unmet needs in these rural areas, but indirectly the federal government does devote a considerable amount of resources to rural areas through farm price supports, Farmers' Home programs, rural electrification, and rural telephone services. These efforts are not sufficient. I am not arguing that for a minute, but these are some of the very programs that policymakers are talking about cutting back.

TOP: *David Dinkins*
BOTTOM LEFT: *Richard Nathan*
BOTTOM RIGHT: *Gonzalo Barrientos*

PART VIII

Administering New Initiatives

PART VIII

Introduction

Gonzalo Barrientos: I am the senator from this Fourteenth Senatorial District, which is Travis and Hays counties. It is a special honor for me to be part of the "Cities in Transition: Policies for the 1990s" symposium, because I was a community organizer for the National Urban League in 1965 and later a trainer for VISTA Peace Corps volunteers and a program officer for VISTA programs in Texas.

Our first lecture is by the Honorable David Dinkins, who is president of the Borough of Manhattan. [*Ed. note: Dinkins was elected mayor of New York in 1989.*] Mr. Dinkins is in the office some have called the second most powerful in New York City. He is a graduate of the Brooklyn Law School, practiced law from 1956 to 1975, received his bachelor's degree in mathematics from Howard University, and is a veteran of the United States Marine Corps. He is also on the board of directors of 100 Black Men, the March of Dimes, and the Association for a Better New York. He is a founder of the Black and Puerto Rican Legislative Caucus in New York State.

Elected Officials and Their Roles in Influencing Policies: The New York Perspective

David Dinkins: I was once in the state legislature for about half an hour. I was appointed to a one-year term in the assembly and then the assembly promptly reapportioned me out of my seat. I have a very healthy respect for members of state legislatures.

I feel at this point the need to tell you a story that I sometimes tell about Johnstown, Pennsylvania. There is a place called Johnstown, Pennsylvania, which actually exists, and back in the nineteenth century this area had a tremendous flood. A dam above the town gave way. The floods came down twenty, thirty feet high and washed away people, many of whom lost their lives. There were those who clung to a wooden railroad trestle, and they thought they might be saved. But somehow debris piled up around this trestle, and friction caused a fire, and they, too, perished. This was a tragedy of immense proportions. Nonetheless, there was a fellow who survived all this and lived to be 105. He died and went to heaven. In heaven he discovered that it was the custom that each new entrant got an opportunity to come forward and tell of a momentous event. He knew that when he told of this momentous event in his life, of how he had survived the mighty Johnstown flood, that he would be a celebrity in heaven. Ultimately, his turn came. He strode down the center aisle toward the rostrum confident that in seconds he would be a celebrity in heaven, for, after all, he had survived the mighty Johnstown flood. Well, as he walked down the aisle, an angel reached out and touched him on the shoulder and said, "I think you should know that Noah is in the audience."

The point is, surrounded as I am by such distinguished and learned academicians, I will not be so presumptuous as to lecture you, you who are experts on the state of urban America. As I listened to Mayor Cisneros's very fine presentation earlier today, I thought, "I can't see what I can offer." I will share with you, in all events, my experience as an elected official, in what is in many respects a very special city. Indeed, while America is home to many world-class urban centers, New York City is unique among our great municipalities. New York is complex and unlike any other city in this nation. Its population of more than 7.3 million persons is larger than that of forty states in this union.

The city's 1988-1989 budget of $26.2 billion is ten times greater than the next largest municipal budget in the country. Moreover, New York City includes five distinct boroughs, or counties, whose characteristics, population, and diversity qualify each as cities in their own right. Four of these boroughs are of sufficient size to rank among America's ten largest cities. Due to the nature of our city, the form of government in New York is equally unique. In addition to the mayor, who wields much of the executive power in a thirty-five-member city council elected from districts, there is an entity known as the Board of Estimate. The Board of Estimate consists of three city-wide officials: the mayor, the president of the city council, and the controller, each of whom is elected every four years city-wide. In addition, five borough presidents, elected borough-wide at the same time from each of the five boroughs, sit on the board. The Board of Estimate votes on major contracts, on land-use questions, and on franchises and has a voice in the budget. As a member of the Board of Estimate, as a borough president, I participate in the discussions and decisions related to these issues. It is from this position that I address the issues of this conference.

While I have described the manner in which New York City differs from other urban centers in its complexity and form of government, the issues we face are no different from those confronting every major urban center in the nation today: persistent poverty, a failing education system, unemployment, homelessness, and the growing chasm between the haves and have-nots. The status of blacks, Latinos, and other minorities in New York City is of especial concern.

Indeed, a conference convened earlier this year to assess progress in the twenty years since the Kerner Report concluded that our nation has, in fact, moved toward two separate societies, one white, one black and increasingly Hispanic. While we have not witnessed urban disorders of the type that gave rise to the appointment of the Kerner Commission, we are witnessing urban decay of no less dramatic or deadly consequence, conditions labeled by this commission on the cities as "quiet riots."

There is perhaps no better illustration of this tragic development than in our city of New York. There is no other city in this country, or perhaps in the world, where such extremes of wealth and poverty exist side by side. In New York, as in many major cities, it is the minority population that is concentrated on the poverty side of the equation. The problems facing blacks, Latinos, and other minorities in New York have remained virtually unchanged in the twenty years since the Kerner Commission issued its warning. Indeed, not only have we failed to cure the illness, we have allowed the disease to spread virtually unchecked.

Perhaps most insidious is the growth of racial intolerance and the development of an atmosphere wherein racism and racial discrimination have once again become acceptable. There is no better example of this phenomenon than the Yonkers desegregation battle. For the council members of a major city in the northeastern United States to defy the laws and face bankruptcy rather than allow integration in selected communities of their city is frighteningly reminiscent of the Deep South of the 1950s.

Howard Beach is yet another indication of the extent to which racial relations have degenerated. Who would have thought that we would have in the late 1980s a lynch mob in New York City, the bastion of liberal thought? Racism and racist violence did not begin or end with Howard Beach. Reports of bias-related violence have doubled since 1986. Moreover, racism continues to plague our public institutions and agencies.

Police brutality, the issue underlying the urban disorders of the sixties, has never been decisively rooted out. It has again come to the fore in New

York City with the deaths of Michael Stewart, Eleanor Bumpers, Nicholas Bartlett, Yvonne Smallwood, and Juan Rodriguez. Indeed, the police department is not the only agency infected by the cancer of racism. In late 1987 it was revealed that the New York City transit police had knowingly arrested at least fifty people, mostly black and Latino men, on false charges.

While police brutality and racially motivated violence represent racism in its most naked and vile form, there are other less violent but equally despicable forms of racism. Racial discrimination is manifested in 1,001 more subtle but no less devastating ways. Deaths that occur as a result of poverty and the lack of opportunity rarely capture the same sensational media attention as does a brutal act of racial violence. Yet, these deaths are no less tragic.

How often do we hear about the twenty-nine out of every one thousand babies born in Harlem who die before their first birthday? Or the twelve and one-half per one thousand born in El Barrio who fail to live a full year? These rates are nearly twice those of the silk-stocking district of Manhattan. How often do we hear about the fact that blacks and Latinos account for over two-thirds of the poor in New York City? And how often do we hear about the fact that 95 percent of all families living in welfare hotels are black or Latino?

Ironically, despite these conditions, the minority population in New York City continues to grow. Indeed, the population of our city is now 46 percent white and 54 percent black, Latino, and Asian. As in many cities, however, the structure of municipal politics and government has been slow to respond to the changing reality of a black and Latino majority. I am the only black member of the Board of Estimate; there was only one in 1968. There is only one Latino member of the board; there was only one in 1968. For an eight-year period commencing in January of 1978, there were no blacks, nor were there any Latinos, on our Board of Estimate. Keep in mind who the Board of Estimate is and what it does.

There are only nine minority members on a thirty-five-member city council; there were five out of thirty-six in 1968. No minority holds or has ever held city-wide office in the city of New York. I might add that there are sixteen city-wide elective offices in the city of New York. They include five borough presidents, five district attorneys, and six surrogates—six, because there are two in Manhattan. Of those sixteen elected positions, never in the history of the state of New York has there ever been an Asian elected to public office. Some have been appointed, not enough, but not a single one has ever been elected. I had the privilege of supporting a very fine young woman, Dorothy Chin-Brandt, who ran successfully for the civil court. She had all the qualifications, you know, Harvard, all of that good stuff. (I went to Howard, and if you say it quickly it sounds like

Harvard.) Moreover, Dorothy Chin-Brandt is a very fine lawyer and legal scholar. However, in New York we have a panel that serves as a screening system. The first time she ran, Dorothy Chin-Brandt cleared the panel, ran in the primary, and lost by a very small margin, some one hundred votes, give or take. The next year the panel did not approve her candidacy.

I supported her anyway and was criticized by some of my liberal progressive friends who suggested that I had violated procedures by not supporting only those who came out of the panel. She went on to win, and she now graces the bench and is doing a very wonderful job.

It is important, I believe, that we have the election of more progressive minorities to office. This must be a central component of any strategy to correct the ills plaguing the urban centers of America today. In my own experience, the mere presence of minorities on the Board of Estimate has changed the context of the debate over urban issues. How many of you have ever entered a room and perceived that the conversation changed when you came in? Or felt that you had better not leave because then they will have the "real meeting"? I believe that my mere presence—not that I am taller or smarter or swifter than anyone else—but just the mere presence of a black on the board has made a difference. Fred Ferrer and I among the eight members of the Board of Estimate do make a difference. It makes a difference, for example, when you are seated with the mayor and others to discuss the budget in intense negotiations, to be able to say with conviction, "I refuse to participate in a budget that will not reflect my presence after it has been adopted," and they understand what you mean. It does make a difference.

Furthermore, because of the presence of a Latino and a black, issues that might not otherwise be addressed are placed on the agenda. For example, such issues as infant mortality rates in Harlem and El Barrio, such issues as whether the city should contract with firms that do business with South Africa, such issues as set-asides for minority- and women-owned businesses are issues that might never be discussed without Latinos and blacks on the board.

Indeed, while I technically have only one vote on this Board of Estimate, it is not quite the custom, but often the case, that if a matter is peculiar to a given borough, the attitude of that borough president carries far greater weight than that single vote. So it does make a difference. While I have only that one vote and very little executive authority, as it were, in a more practical sense as borough president, I can wield power or influence the direction of public policy beyond the formal boundaries of the office.

On issues that come before the Board of Estimate, such as issues of housing and commercial development, zoning and the disposition of publicly owned land, my seat on the board enables me to intervene and modify city policy and program initiatives. I would like to share with you some of the strategies and approaches that I have utilized to influence public policy in New York City on key urban issues. Perhaps one of the most difficult of these issues is that of economic and community development. By difficult, I mean the effort to ensure that the benefits of development are shared by all sectors of our city.

We have a situation in New York in which we had a so-called fiscal crisis in the mid-seventies, and New York was on the brink of bankruptcy. There were some folks in the country who said, "Good for you, smart New Yorkers." There were others who were more understanding. In all events, we emerged from that crisis and, in fact, have experienced something of an economic boom. But not all have benefited from that boom, and that is the point.

In Manhattan, for example, development is concentrated in the midtown and financial districts of our borough, while communities like Harlem and El Barrio on the Lower East Side continue to suffer from urban decay and blight. On the national level, Ronald Reagan's administration's gutting of small minority business development programs and virulent opposition to affirmative action have hurt both neighborhood economic stability and minority employment prospects. In addition to large-scale employment and job-training programs, locally based business enterprises are essential to the long-term viability of black and Latino communities. Presently, just 2 percent of American businesses are black owned, less than that for Latinos. Although most minority-owned businesses have few employees, they hire minority workers at a much higher rate than do white-owned businesses. But minority-owned businesses serve a purpose beyond providing jobs. They create an independent economic base in the communities, contributing to neighborhood stability and cohesion. As such, the value of these businesses extends beyond the financial gains made by business owners.

In New York City, we in our office have supported programs to assist the development of minority-owned businesses, including set-aside programs. Members of my staff also helped to develop legislation known as "first source," which requires companies contracting with the city to turn first to disadvantaged city residents when hiring workers. I should hasten to say that "first source" is not presently the law. We merely have the legislation and have not yet been able to get it out of committee. The difficulty of this process says something, also, about the number of minorities in the legislature, which is nine out of thirty-five, no one of whom is a majority leader. This lack of representation creates a situation that does not give us great power in that body.

In addition, I have sought to use my vote on the Board of Estimate to encourage the city to implement both affirmative action and comprehensive neighborhood development programs. A city initiative known as the Construction Management Program provides an example. Since assuming office in 1986, I have consistently urged the mayor to develop a comprehensive plan for the rehabilitation of the New York stock of city-owned buildings. For instance, in Harlem, that section of Manhattan where most of the minority community resides, approximately 60 percent of the property is owned by the city. That property is mostly buildings that have been taken for nonpayment of taxes. Last year the first major redevelopment proposal, one to rehabilitate over nine hundred apartments in vacant buildings in the heart of Harlem, came before the Board of Estimate. Naturally, the city administration assumed that I would be delighted. The project is in Harlem. It is dedicated entirely to low- and moderate-income and homeless families. It involves revitalizing the majority of abandoned buildings in the immediate neighborhood.

While I was generally supportive of the project, I strongly believed that the city was missing an opportunity to comprehensively address the housing, employment, and economic development needs of the community. The redevelopment of nearly one thousand units of housing generates hundreds of jobs in the construction trades and potentially lucrative contracts for supplies and services. Harlem has the highest poverty and unemployment rates in the borough, and its residents occupy the most-deteriorated housing. In my view, it made sense to link the Construction Management Program to specific benefits for the residents of that community.

After several rounds of tough negotiations, we were able to extract an agreement that targets 40 percent of the apartments created to current Harlem residents. They get a preference. Additionally, 35 percent of the jobs generated in revitalizing the building are set aside for minorities and women. There are specific goals for awarding contracts to small minority- and women-owned businesses. All construction firms involved in the project are directed to patronize local businesses to the greatest extent possible. We are monitoring this as well as we can.

The package of concessions negotiated for the Construction Management Program set a precedent for integrating housing and construction with jobs and economic opportunities and for reserving some portion of both for residents and businesses in the surrounding community. This agreement was won in a city with a mayor who, as some of you surely know, vehemently opposes quotas or set-asides based on race. Even after the agreement was announced, the mayor and I stood side by side in the Blue Room, which is where ceremonies are held in New York City Hall, and as we stood side by side, the mayor put his arm around my shoulder and said, "See, and we got it done without quotas." And I said, "Mr.

Mayor, if it walks like a duck and quacks, you may call it what you wish."
Ed Koch is vehemently opposed to quotas and set-asides based on
economically oppressed areas, and he argues, "Well, after all, most of the
people are minorities who live in those areas," but to him that is not the
same thing as quotas.

Indeed, there was a case that went to the Supreme Court of the United
States regarding Local 28 of sheetmetal workers. There had been fifteen
or twenty years of proven discrimination by this union. You had to be in
the family to work your way up through the union. The apprentice
programs were limited to family members of a union member. When the
case got to the Supreme Court, and the case was to be argued jointly on
behalf of the city and the state, the solicitor general for the state, who was
from the attorney general's office, happened to be a black fellow named
Peter Sherwood. When this case was about to be heard, the mayor called
the corporation counsel's office and insisted that language be inserted in
the brief that stated that, whatever solution or remedy the Court offered,
that he opposed quotas as a remedy to this proven discrimination. Thus,
you can understand the difficulty of achieving these goals and objectives
for minorities in New York City.

Those of us in a minority community believe that quotas are not a
ceiling to exclude people and deny opportunities but represent instead a
ground on which to build. The mayor and I do not see eye to eye on that,
and we have had many polite but firm public discussions about the issue.
He believes very deeply in his position, and I disagree just as deeply.

On other matters of policy, my influence is less direct and less tied to the
specific duties of office. Nonetheless, occasionally we have been able to
influence policy in these areas as well. The issue of housing is an example.
In New York City the vast majority of people rent rather than own their
homes. Affordable available apartments are increasingly hard to come
by. Our rental vacancy rate is just over 2 percent, with fewer apartments
available at the lower end of the rent scale. Over 20 percent of both black
and Latino renters live in what is considered substandard housing. An
amazing 25 percent of households spend more than 40 percent of their
income on rent alone. Moreover, the New York City Housing Authority,
which is public housing, recently estimated that at least 20 percent of its
apartments are home to not one but two families. When privately owned
housing is included, there may be more than 100,000 families living
doubled-up, which obviously means that some of those folks are homeless in the sense that they do not have homes of their own.

The most severe symptom of the low-income housing crisis is the
growing homeless population. An astounding 28,000 people in New
York City are housed in homeless shelters; 12,000 of them are children.
Over half of them are under age five. The children, as a matter of fact, are

the single largest-growing segment of the homeless. Housing advocates estimate that there are as many as 30,000 additional homeless individuals outside the shelter system, because the official figures are always those persons who have presented themselves to the city seeking shelter. Those folks who decide that they would prefer to sleep on grates or in the park or wherever are not included among the official homeless figures.

The homeless population is not monolithic. The prevailing myth about the homeless—and I use the word myth with deliberation—is that the majority of homeless people are mentally ill or alcoholics. This myth flies in the face of reality. Over 5,000 families with more than 12,000 children are homeless. These children are not alcoholics, nor are they mentally ill. They may grow up to be if we do not do something about the problem. Those of you from the New York region are familiar with the sight of youngsters in the area of Herald Square, near Macy's, running around at midnight. Children not waist-high are hustling, trying to beg money for wiping windows or whatever. That is no way for children to grow up.

Rather than assisting the homeless, the policies of the Koch administration only seem to exacerbate the problem. The majority of homeless families are housed in the notorious welfare hotels—squalid, unsafe buildings where as many as four hundred families live, many cramped into single rooms. Most of these hotels are located in business neighborhoods that are unsuitable for raising children. There are few, if any, recreational facilities and an absence of schools and other familiar institutions that bind people and communities together.

For the privilege of housing homeless families in these deplorable conditions, the city of New York pays hotel owners, in some instances, as much as $1,500 a month. Indeed, in some cases the city pays much, much more. The rate is based on a per day, per person basis. Thus, it is not difficult to perceive of forty dollars a day, forty-five dollars a day, and then five dollars, six dollars, seven dollars, or eight dollars for each additional person. This results in some astronomical amounts. The weird aspect is that some of these people are there because they are on welfare and they get a housing allowance, but it is insufficient to pay the rent where they live. What they do is to use money meant for other necessities to pay the rent, on occasion. Then, when these other necessities become a higher priority, they do not pay the rent. Eventually, they get evicted. When they get evicted, the same city that was paying a housing allowance of $327 a month for a family of four, then pays approximately a fourth of something in the neighborhood of $1,500 to place the family in the hotels—a fourth of this amount from the state and the rest from the federal government. It makes no sense, because at the same time, the city owns in excess of fifty thousand units of housing in abandoned buildings, seized in tax foreclosure actions. These buildings are primarily located in black and Latino neighborhoods, the very neighborhoods from which the majority of homeless families enter the shelter system.

In late 1986, I appointed twenty experts in housing development and social service delivery to a task force and charged them with developing new approaches to solving the homeless family problem. The central finding of that report was that poverty and lack of affordable housing, rather than mental illness, substance abuse, or dysfunctional families, are the underlying causes of family homelessness. That task force recommended that the city should focus its efforts not on the expansion of an already unwieldy shelter system but on the provision of low-income housing and on increasing the ability of poor families to pay for this housing. With regard to transitional shelters, the task force called for the development of small-scale facilities that provide private accommodations for each family. The task force also substantiated the cost effectiveness of rehabilitating city-owned properties for use as apartment-style transitional housing. Moreover, housing rehabilitated in this way can eventually be converted to permanent use, thus contributing to the neighborhood revitalization. This plan removes the blight and provides some decent shelter at the same time.

The Task Force on Housing for Homeless Families accomplished two things. First, its diversity helped to build consensus in the broader community for the recommendations of the final report. Second, the prestige and professional reputation of the task force members lent weight to the efforts of our office to effect changes in policy. I was no longer merely a borough president with some ideas on the homeless. I was an elected official who had drawn on some of the best minds outside government to assist in the formulation of public proposals. Though its impact was not immediately felt, the report contributed substantially to changing the nature of the debate on public policy toward the homeless and laid the groundwork for intervention at critical moments. For example, when a major shelter initiative was up for a vote of the Board of Estimate, we were able to negotiate a compromise in which the mayor agreed to rehabilitate an additional one thousand apartments in city-owned buildings and to cease housing families in five hotels in Manhattan.

Later in the year, a proposal to open a city-operated shelter in a former school building came before the board. We opposed the plan from its inception, not because of opposition to transitional housing, but because the plan called for the creation of a barracks-style facility for families. With the support of community leaders and local elected officials, we were able to persuade my colleagues on the Board of Estimate to vote against the project as an expensive and inhumane way to house homeless families. The proposal was soundly defeated.

I believe that the report on homeless families and the consensus that formed around the administration's negligence with regard to city-owned buildings are partly responsible for the mayor's recent announcement of a plan to rehabilitate all vacant city-owned buildings within the next three years. In addition, he has pledged to close all welfare hotels within the next two years. Credit should also be given to Congressman Charles Rangel of New York and Congressman Bill Green, a Republican of New York, who convened a legislative hearing in Manhattan because New York City uses federal monies that are designed for emergency and temporary shelter to house the homeless in welfare hotels. The federal regulations say that you may use this money only for temporary stays, which is defined as thirty days. The average stay in a welfare hotel is thirteen months.

Thus, the city was faced with a dilemma, but Charlie Rangel and his colleagues were able to suggest to the city that they would support a moratorium on the enforcement of this regulation, which had not heretofore been enforced. However, this action required a plan to get rid of those welfare hotels. And we think that the work of our task force contributed to this effort. The Task Force on Housing for Homeless Families successfully accomplished what it was charged to do: to develop new approaches to solving the problem of family homelessness, which is such a serious problem in New York.

The concept of advisory bodies in the form of task forces evolved from our belief that effective public policy is a dynamic process that requires the input of those outside government, whether they be experts in a particular field or community residents. Such consultation enables those of us in public office to build working alliances on programs and consensus on important issues.

In addition to the task force on homelessness, we have appointed task forces on education, substance abuse, child welfare, youth, the elderly, and the disabled. Time does not permit me to share in detail the work and impact of these advisory bodies or to provide examples of the ways in which our office has attempted to influence public policy through their efforts. Let me just add that, in addition to the initiatives we have launched on issues relating to the work of our task forces, we have used our power to propose budget priorities, to earmark portions of resources for specific projects within Manhattan, such as expanded prenatal care for pregnant women in Harlem. We have also sought to use the annual budget negotiations to press for increased funding for critical social programs and capital projects. Finally, we have attempted to establish and support innovative models of service delivery, community housing improvement, and leadership development.

Our experience in New York City is unique only in the scale of urban problems and the complexities of local politics and government. The problems themselves—housing, employment, economic development, education, health, and racial polarization—are identical to those found in most major American cities. While I recognize the fact that urban problems have intensified since the Kerner Report, I refuse to believe that these problems are not solvable. Such a view would only deepen the despair of those communities we seek to help and intensify the cynicism among policymakers charged with improving and overseeing the conditions in these communities. I continue to believe that, unless the spirit is crushed, every child will want to learn. Unless the spirit is crushed, every adult will want to work and lead a productive life. People genuinely deserve better, and it is the job of public officials to pursue lasting solutions to the problems plaguing our urban centers.

If the nature of urban problems is clear, the solutions to these problems are, for the most part, equally clear. What is needed is a national commitment to end urban decay and blight, to quell the quiet riots destroying our cities and our future. The federal government must again assume its responsibility to produce low-income housing. We know now that this is the only way that such housing is likely to be produced on the massive scale needed. Cuts in college grant programs for poor students must be restored. We know now that these grants were primarily responsible for the short-lived spurt in black college attendance in the 1960s and 1970s. Early childhood education programs must be expanded. We know now that the Head Start Program improves the SAT scores of minority students twelve years later. We know that job training and retraining for workers displaced by the decline of American manufacturing is necessary if black and Latino men and women are to survive in the work force. We know that child care is an essential benefit for the majority of women who must work to support their families. We know that tremendous gaps continue to exist in the access to quality health care and that universal health insurance, with an emphasis on preventive care, is essential.

On the local level, the implementation of progressive policy will require an educated and mobilized electorate, with the cohesion to elect progressive candidates, minority and white, to office. Some might argue that the hardening of the underclass would preclude political organization. I say, to the contrary, that the deepening of racial and class polarization makes political consolidation all the more critical. The stellar success of the Jackson campaign this year is proof enough of this point.

What is required on both the national and local levels is political leadership unwilling to settle for the status quo; leadership that has the will to find solutions we know exist; leadership that will focus on the lingering social inequities at the root of urban decay; leadership that can heal rather than deepen wounds; leadership compassionate enough to understand and address the needs of every American—black, white, brown, rich or poor, male or female. Let us work together to forge the type of coalition necessary to empower leadership of this caliber.

As a coalition of blacks, Latinos, labor, and all progressive sectors of this nation, we can and must win the battle. In the words of Dr. Martin Luther King, Jr.: "This is no time to engage in the luxury of cooling off or to take the tranquilizing drug of gradualism. Now is the time to make real the promises of democracy. Now is the time to rise from the dark and desolate valley of segregation, to the sunlit path of racial justice. Now is the time to lift our nation from the quicksands of racial injustice to the solid rock of brotherhood. Now is the time to make justice a reality for all God's children."

G. Barrientos: Thank you, David Dinkins. It is interesting to note that the New York budget is some $26 billion. Our state of Texas budget is about $33 billion. So we can see the immensity of people and money there, the problems that must be solved, and the goals that must be reached.

Our second speaker is Dr. Richard Nathan, from the Woodrow Wilson School of Public and International Affairs at Princeton University. Dr. Nathan received his Ph.D. from Harvard in 1966 and has served at the Woodrow Wilson School as a teacher, researcher, and public official. He is currently the director of the Princeton Urban Regional Research Center. Before coming to Princeton, Dr. Nathan was the Senior Fellow in the Governmental Studies Program at the Brookings Institution in Washington, D.C. He has also served as the deputy undersecretary of the United States Department of Health, Education, and Welfare in Washington.

The Institutional Dimension of Change

Richard Nathan: I was on the staff of the Kerner Commission, so I have some memories of the turbulence and drama of that period. I want to begin by telling an anecdote that Mr. Dinkins will appreciate, since he presented such an eloquent and grim picture of the problems as he sees them from the New York vantage point.

I was sitting in my office at the Brookings Institution one day as a junior person there, and the phone rang. The person on the other end of the line said, "This is John Lindsay, Dick. They are out to get me." In those days, John Lindsay was Republican. He was the mayor of New York and he had just been named as the vice-chair of the Kerner Commission. And he said, "I am at the White House, and I need you to help." I did not know Lindsay well, but I am a Republican, too. It was a curious set of circumstances, which a month or so later led to my becoming the director of program research of the National Commission on Civil Disorders. I wrote, in fact, some of the sections of the report that have been discussed.

In the recent period, there have been quite a few meetings like this one to discuss the Kerner Commission Report twenty years later and how we now think about the things that were in that report. The report, as you remember, was a famous and influential public document because of this line right at the beginning: "This is our basic conclusion: Our nation is moving towards two societies, one Black, one White, separate and unequal." That sentence called attention to the problem of racism as the core problem of urban society in America. The report was widely discussed and had a dramatic impact.

Now, twenty years later, as we gather at the LBJ Library to discuss urban conditions and what they mean for blacks and Latinos in American society, how should we reflect on that central theme point of the Kerner Commission Report? I have heard many people today speak about something that I think needs to be mentioned in this context. I refer to the increasingly mentioned diagnosis of urban problems as problems of the "underclass," the concentration in the cities of minority poor in areas where multiple problems have become spatially more concentrated and more severe. The census data show this. Mr. Dinkins talked about it. William Wilson, Isabel Sawhill, Ronald Mincy, and Erol Ricketts have written about it. Many experts in urban affairs are trying to measure this increased concentration spatially, the geography of multiproblem families and multiproblem areas in the city.

Professor Wilson focuses on role models. One of the things we do not give ourselves credit for is the success of the civil rights revolution. Its success is not complete and not satisfactory for many of us, but quite dramatic nonetheless. It has offered opportunities for mobile, educated, and motivated members of minority groups to move out of segregated areas. What Dr. Wilson argues is that the underclass problem is a problem made more difficult by the fact that the role models of an earlier day, such as teachers and sales people, civil servants and postmen, do not live in these urban areas in which drugs, crime, and welfare dependency have become so highly concentrated.

I submit that, in thinking about the cities in the 1980s and in thinking about strategies for the next administration, this is a change from twenty years ago when the Kerner Commission wrote that famous line. What is involved is that there has been a bifurcation within the minority communities in the country. Better off, upwardly mobile people have left distressed inner-city areas, and those areas have become worse in terms of the problems of the inner city. The distressed urban areas are more concentrated. They are smaller, but their problems are more intense. That change has a big effect on the job we have to do to deal with these conditions. The change also exacerbates and underlies the politics of urban policy in that the programs required are expensive, and the problem is more localized, which makes it politically harder to mobilize support to devote resources to these conditions. Indeed, we have seen a decline in society's commitment to programs focused on these most severe urban problems.

One thing in terms of solutions and directions that is particularly important to me is the institutional dimension of government, which is frequently left out of the equation. People from policy institutes, with all their ideas about new problems, are constantly thinking of new things to do, but they do not give sufficient attention to how to do them. Social scientists and researchers—and that is my business—need to give more attention to institutions and institutional change and to improving the capacity of government to deal with the most difficult problems, particularly inner-city problems.

I recently completed *Social Science in Governments*, a book about what social scientists can contribute and what we have learned, using welfare policy as an example. My advice, however, is that one should not devote one's life to writing books. I went to a meeting recently where somebody was asked, "Do you know such and such a book?" And they responded, "Yes, but not personally." It is not easy to disseminate ideas, so I want to mention these ideas that are important to me because you may be in that group of people who know the book, but not personally.

The point that intrigues me is the need to give more attention in policymaking to what works. Robert Reischauer and others have mentioned the research of the Manpower Demonstration Research Corporation (MDRC). I am involved in the work of the corporation based in New York City. Over one hundred people in MDRC have been doing demonstration studies now for fifteen years to study what works to deal with the hardest problems of the disadvantaged, of underclass groups. Those studies have been rigorous social science studies using random assignments to see if a program makes a difference and to test it against the highest standards.

MDRC recently conducted studies in eight states of the welfare employment programs with 35,000 people assigned randomly to treatment groups and control groups to see what worked. The short answer is that the job approach to help welfare recipients, particularly female welfare family heads, makes a difference—not a huge difference, but a consistent, positive difference that endures. Training, child care, and education, as a way to meet the needs of people trapped in long-term welfare dependency, has promise, particularly for women. That MDRC research, I am happy to say, was cited frequently in the discussion about this new $3.3 billion welfare bill that was just passed.

The *New Yorker* magazine once wrote an article about a conference of mayors meeting on revenue sharing saying, "The mayors like revenue sharing or whatever else it is that the federal government is calling money this year." This welfare bill provides a substantial amount of money in a period of austerity and great concern about the country's budget dilemma. The legislation devotes $3.3 billion to job-training, education, and child-care programs by state governments. Other funds are available on an open-ended basis for so-called transitional child-care and Medicaid benefits. Senator Daniel Patrick Moynihan (D-NY) wrote this part of the legislation and should be praised for it. It will allow the states to devote more resources to these programs. Senator Moynihan and others cited MDRC research that showed that this type of approach works and that we are headed in the right direction.

I regret to tell you that, in my view, the present conservative period in this society is not going to end in 1989. The retrenchment and skepticism about government that we are living with in this period was not invented by Ronald Reagan or patented by Republicans. It began under President Carter in 1978. We have had ten years of considerable unease, and I would say restraint, to put it carefully, in the area of domestic programs. While I would like to tell you differently, history tells me, and the 1988 election certainly gives a lot of hints of this, that the next period is not going to be one of a Great Society or anything similar to Nixon's New Federalism. In a sense, I would say to you, we have time to develop our institutional capacity.

The welfare demonstrations were pilot tests of what works. Now the new law in effect says the whole country should make institutional changes to change welfare systems to stress jobs and job preparation. Instead of being payment systems, these systems emphasize training and child care. Welfare workers, it is hoped, will speak and act in different ways. I do not have to tell a sophisticated audience like this that changing welfare bureaucracies across this land—so that they do their job differently and emphasize their role in a different way—is a tremendous challenge.

Experts on research and government need to give more attention to challenges like this one for changing institutions. Three institutional areas are critical to the urban agenda today. These areas are where the big money is and where the big groups and agencies are in domestic policy.

The school system is one of these areas. The schools, urban schools, are probably the most serious areas in the failure of social programs. The welfare system is the second area. There is a movement now to try to change welfare systems. I recently had the privilege of interviewing the person who is the head of the Massachusetts ET Choices Program. It is impressive the way the welfare system has changed in Massachusetts. I was in a waiting room in a welfare agency in that state, and the employment workers came in, and they said to everybody, "We have hot jobs for you. You can get this benefit. You can get child care, and we will help you with transportation. The job pays seven dollars an hour." They will not provide any job to any welfare family head that pays under six dollars an hour. Massachusetts has changed the behavior of that bureaucracy. It took them six years, and it has not been easy. I am not sure how much they have changed it, but I am impressed with what they have done.

Other states, such as Michigan, California, and New Jersey, are trying to do this too. But California and New Jersey have county welfare systems, state-supervised county-administered welfare. It is very difficult to change the behavior of counties if you are a state official. Especially in regard to implementation of policies, making the institutional side of government work better is difficult. We must put more of our political, intellectual, and social science resources to work to understand and focus on implementation processes.

MDRC is doing an evaluation study of the so-called GAIN welfare employment program in California. A survey MDRC uses asks, "Do you think the welfare system has changed? Do you think the state is trying to do anything different? Do you believe that the services promised can really be delivered?" It also asks the welfare recipients, "Is welfare different?" to try to understand, to measure, and to reach this institutional challenge.

I said there were three institutions critical to the urban agenda, and I have only mentioned two. The three institutions are the school system, the welfare system, and the corrections system. I always try to get close to and look at the issues I care about, so lately I have been visiting prisons. Somebody mentioned that the biggest pressure point in state and local spending now is prisons. You have only to turn on your TV to know that we have overcrowded prisons right here in Texas. We have to develop strategies, as many states have, to take young offenders with particularly high risks of recidivism and put them in intensive training programs to prepare them for moving into the mainstream of society when they get out of prison. Programs have to be designed to select the people for whom such interventions are likely to make a difference and to test and understand how to implement those interventions. Some prison systems are beginning this approach.

My advice is that, as experts and as people interested in social policy, we must not neglect the institutional dimension—the "what works?" "How can we change institutions?" To repeat the theme I mentioned before, and I wish it were not true, we have time to use our energy for this, because big money from Washington is not going to be unleashed no matter which party is in power or who is president next year. However, I want to end on a hopeful note. As I was listening to Mayor Cisneros, I was thinking, "This is encouraging." Will Rogers once said, speaking, I am sure, of intellectuals, not politicians, "Things will get better despite our efforts to improve them." There is one way in which things may get better, despite our efforts to improve them. We desperately need workers in this society. We know the labor force is contracting, and the demand for labor is increasing. All across the country we are hearing of school reform and community economic development operations: the Boston Compact, the Baltimore Commonwealth Program, the program in San Antonio, where business is deciding that they need to find ways to train and to help the schools train people, because those businesses are going to need workers. In numerous quiet ways, the welfare system is also pointing more toward work skills, and the schools, as I just said, are adopting strategies based on the assumption that it is a social bargain to invest in educational success. Businesses and policymakers are saying, "You get a B average, you attend class 95 percent of the time, and we will pay for your college education." The welfare employment programs are a bargain, too: individuals are required to participate, but if they participate, they receive training, education, child care, and Medicaid, which are valuable benefits.

Overall, there is a change in philosophy linked to at least one somewhat hopeful note. All around the country, in the cities and in the states, new programs are being developed involving mutual obligations. We should study those programs and think about them in terms of how they work and how they change institutions and save some of the people caught in the underclass. We are not going to save all the people who are stuck in these worst areas—in Bushwick, in Harlem, in Detroit, in Newark, in Camden. People living in these areas tell me things are tougher now than twenty years ago, and I believe that is true. So we have to be realistic. In sum, I have one main message, and that is, give more attention and thought to institutions and demand that administrations build confidence in those institutions. Then the public will be willing to support social programs in the long run. It is a conservative message. Remember, I told you I am a Republican.

G. Barrientos: You know, Dr. Nathan, we have approximately 39,000 people in our Texas prisons. Of the 39,000, approximately 91 percent of them never finished high school. So we have a lot of work to do to develop recommendations to strengthen our schools, our welfare programs, and our prison rehabilitation programs.

Discussion

From the floor: Dr. Nathan, you also mentioned that there is a need for social science research to be channeled into actual policy. Through all these important topics, essentially no one has said anything about the topic of women. I think there are at least two of us, if not more, who are very concerned with women as an issue. I encourage you, Mr. Dinkins, in your efforts to promote policy on women as one resolution to many problems, such as homelessness.

D. Dinkins: That is why, when we appointed the task force to look at homelessness, we had to make a judgment about whether or not to look first at singles, who are the bag women and men that you see around the streets, or at families. A certain percentage of single homeless people, 25 to 50 percent, depending on whose figures you take, are persons who perhaps have some mental disability. More often than not, they have been released too soon from mental institutions and did not get the necessary supportive care that the state of New York promised at the time.

The other homeless are families, and families means women and children. It is not just that we are concerned with discrimination against women in the work place. Our office has fought for pay equity. We recognize that when a woman goes to the store to buy a loaf of bread, she is not permitted to pay sixty-two cents on the dollar. She has to pay a whole dollar like everybody else, and we have been supportive of pay-equity efforts. I am the first male member of the Manhattan Women's Political Caucus. I have been involved in women's issues, and I agree with you that policies addressing the needs of women will address other problems as well. Moreover, I have a daughter.

R. Nathan: I believe that Paul Peterson was correct this morning when he said that you should use conservative ideas and a conservative time to get what you want. An important note regarding this issue of homelessness and single women is that our demography and our social patterns have changed. Families do not form; people do not take responsibility for their children. The change in family patterns has changed our attitudes toward responsibility for others. The concept of family that all the politicians like to use as a theme ought to be tied to the talk about the need for responses to deal with social problems such as homelessness.

From the floor: I was so glad, Mr. Dinkins, that you brought up Asians, even if only in passing, because I think Asians have been a forgotten group as we discuss the cities. I would like to speak to my colleagues, mostly the Hispanic and black scholars who are working on city issues and inner-city issues. We may have to pay an academic as well as a social price if we forget the Asian Americans in the cities. They are not as monolithic as has been portrayed.

Mr. Dinkins, you mentioned in the portrait of Manhattan the bipolar character, the extremities of wealth and poverty. Then you concentrated on the poverty aspect, on the homeless, and on the poor. I want you to address that other side, also, the extreme wealth. Anyone who has lived in or visited Manhattan has noticed the affluence. There surely must be a connection between the extreme wealth of Manhattan and that extreme poverty.

And to Dr. Nathan, I was struck when you mentioned the three institutions that must be changed in the cities: the school, the welfare, and the criminal justice systems. What those three institutions have in common is that they are heavily populated by the poor and minorities, and they heavily serve those groups. My questions are: What about those who have created the extreme wealth in those cities? Why don't we reform the banking and financial systems and the other institutions that have created the elite side of the picture in the cities? Don't those institutions need reforming if, indeed, they are part of the problem that we are facing? Why must it be the problems of the minorities and the problems of the poor that must be reformed? What about those who are the cause of the source of our misery and our oppression?

D. Dinkins: With respect to the affluent, there is a connection. There have been programs in New York that have benefited the wealthy. Real estate development is an easy target, which to some degree has profited at the expense of those who are less affluent. There is now a move away from those kinds of development policies by many of us. But I think, also, that there are ways to involve those with money and those who are doing well in commerce in concern for the problems of the poor. One is to argue that most of the things we speak about are, in addition to being humane and proper and moral, cost effective. The examples that I frequently cite are infant mortality, correctional institutions, and housing. A child that is born with low birth weight could stay in a hospital more than twenty weeks. In New York that costs about $1,000 a day. Nutrition, education, and prenatal care costs $600 to $800 per mother. If that mother goes to the clinic and is rudely treated and has to wait a long time, she is not coming back. It costs us a great deal more money for having failed to spend a few dollars in the first place.

In our correctional institutions, a tremendous percentage of the people incarcerated are there for some drug-related crime. Yet, in New York many of the addicts who seek treatment are told, "We have no vacancies; there is not a slot for you." A drug-free program costs about $15,000 a year. Incarceration at Ryker's Island, which is a municipal correctional facility, costs in excess of $43,000 per inmate per year.

The housing situation is obvious. There are also other areas in which the cost of prevention is less than the cost of dealing with the consequences. I believe that it is possible to turn to our fiscally conservative friends and say, "This is cheaper. It is wiser to do this. You will benefit by this twenty years later, but I am also talking about tomorrow." Yes, there is that connection between the affluent and the poor in that sense.

In New York, where tourism is worth approximately $7 billion a year, it is my contention that if Johnny Carson is making fun of New York on the "Tonight Show" and saying "You can't leave your hotel, or somebody is going to get you," then this is bad for business. If we have homeless people sleeping all over the place, this is bad for business. If someone is about to take a trip to New York, and they have the impression that their visit will be unpleasant, they will say, "What the hell, why don't I go to London?" Because, today, you can fly to London more cheaply than you can travel from New York to Chicago. People will react that way. I think it is in our interest to promote tourism in the same way that I think we need to clean up the environment. We need to make sure our streets are cleaner, and on and on and on. We do not have a Boston Compact nor are we doing what some others are doing, but New York City and the business people are beginning to recognize that it is in their interest to educate people. A good example of this awakening is the Liberty Scholarship Program. Some people are involved because of a desire to help others, but they also recognize it is in their business interest to do better.

Juan Barrero, University of California, Santa Barbara: Dr. Nathan, I think your message came through very clearly, and there are merits to your proposals. Indeed, I think your approach is so meritorious that we should consider the possibility of extending it to defense spending.

R. Nathan: I have no problem with that. Your point is a good one.

Cordelia Reimers, Hunter College in New York: Dr. Nathan, in talking about the change in welfare institutions, you did not mention one aspect of institutional change that is being talked about quite a bit and experimented with in Wisconsin, that is, the initiative to replace the traditional means by which fathers' support is channeled to children.

We all know that both levels of awards—those given by courts for child support in the case of divorce and the collection thereafter—are a scandal. I am wondering if you have any thoughts about how that institutional change might work to assure that fathers of children are also responsible for their continuing support, even if the marriage does not last or never was contracted in the first place.

R. Nathan: I believe that child support enforcement is something that we should do and that helps legitimize and build support for welfare. It is morally right. Enhancement of child support was a strong theme in the provisions in the bill passed by Congress in 1988. The Reagan administration has had a major program to push in that direction. Additionally, the states have been working on it.

There are two research areas that I would mention in connection with child support. One is in Wisconsin. That state has had a demonstration-and-research program to improve their child support collection mechanism. I think other states have done similar things, but Wisconsin has worked particularly hard in this area. There is a consensus emerging that it is right to do that.

There is another plan also discussed in Wisconsin that is going to be tested in New York, which is called "assured child support." That plan says, if the state does not collect child support through rigorous enforcement, then the government should provide that amount of money for the child. That is a new way to support poor families. David Ellwood, in a book called *Poor Support,* with which I disagree but which I recommend to everyone, discusses making this so-called assured child support system a new form of welfare reform in the nineties. At one point, that was a component of Senator Moynihan's bill.

The ideas of child support enforcement and developing a new form of government assistance for poor families by making up the difference between the amount owed and amount collected are being widely discussed among experts in welfare policy. The research community and government researchers have been involved in gathering better knowledge of what this entails. For example, there is a request for proposals to conduct the New York "assured child support" demonstration research. Such a plan is a long way off in the future, and I have some doubts about it, but it is definitely something that Latino and black researchers interested in public policy ought to know about and, indeed, may want to read about and research. The strongest and the most convincing statement—although, again, I have some doubts about it—is David Ellwood's book.

He is a professor at Harvard, a labor economist, and a brilliant expert in this field.

Mary de Ferrier, Hispanic Women's Network of Texas: This conference is called "Cities in Transition," and I came here with a sense of hope that we were in transition from something that is very pathologically ill about this country to some sense of growth or change, a future direction for the 1990s. But throughout the discussion there has been no reference to accountability. Who has been responsible for the demise of blacks and Hispanics and women and children?

We have seen graphs that show increases in gross national product and inclines in national debts. No one has said, "Where was Ronald Reagan when these issues were being dealt with in the Congress?" It seems that we talk in generalities. It has to do with changing the moral fabric of the presidency and changing the moral fabric of the Supreme Court justices. But who has the power to make those changes? In my perspective, for the last eight years we have suffered at the hands of President Reagan, and none of us has talked about how he is responsible for our demise, our continued difficulties.

So when I think of cities in transition, I think that we are in transition from major depression to psychosis. We are in transition from hope to rage. As conferences like this occur throughout the nation, as we heard earlier, where do we go from here, and who will carry that moral responsibility?

The people who have attended this conference, white, black, brown, Asian, represent the healthy component of this nation. But people must be frank about the situation, deal openly with these problems, and quit hiding the fact that after eight years our country is sicker than it was in 1980.

Juan Flores, University of Colorado, Boulder: Richard Nathan made two points. One was somewhat blaming the victim with the remark about families not forming, without taking into account the whole social structure that forces people into those kinds of situations.

The other, more important consideration raised in the discussion about education that Cisneros presented is one that must be evaluated more critically. A reward system built into children's education might have unintended consequences. That reward system reminds me of the productivity deals of the sixties wherein workers in factories and workers in the fields, steelworkers and auto workers, were rewarded on the basis of tonnage, the number of cars produced, et cetera. It was a productivity deal: the more you produce, the more money you earn. But we saw a decline in productivity and a struggle against work emerge as a response to that increased pressure.

We may, in this case, do the same thing to children. We have a productivity deal now for children: produce B's, show up on time, attend class, and you will be rewarded. That is a different kind of incentive than children have had in the past, an incentive that is not a moral incentive. And we are streamlining our kids into this type of program. I am concerned about that, because it might be the wrong message to send them at that age. It is experimental, I understand, but we must proceed carefully with programs such as these.

R. Nathan: I was a member of a group that was brought together by the American Enterprise Institute, a fairly moderate, conservative group. The group was interested in social policy and was composed of academics from across the intellectual spectrum, some fairly liberal people and some conservative people. We wrote a statement with the theme "the new consensus," and I urge you to read this report. *The New Consensus* is based upon the theme of mutual obligation. If you are serious at school, we will make sure you go to college. If you try to get training and get a job, we will give you services on welfare. If you will try to learn skills and are part of a highly disciplined program, we will put you in a special corrections program where you will learn skills that may get you ahead in the labor force. This is different from the sixties' attitude and represents a change. Social programs now are conveying the values of family, responsibility, education, and work. Those are the values that are imbedded in these new initiatives, especially the ones that are getting some response, such as the Boston Compact and the Baltimore Commonwealth Program.

I believe that in a society where jobs and family and responsibility to the community are valued by the society, we cheat young people unless we convey that message. It is important to underline that it is possible, even in this conservative period, to get money and support for social programs like the ones we are talking about. Among Tom Wolfe's wonderful books about the sixties, *Mau-Mauing the Flak Catchers* is my favorite. Wolfe argued that it was wrong to say to people, "Look, there is something wrong with you. Let us help you. You come in, and we will give you a lot of support." It is better to say to a person, "It is right for you to go to school. It is right for you to support your kids. It is right for you to pay if you are a father of a child." We can get more support for social policy if we build it on the values that this country respects. Every poll shows this. Thus, we should put our hopes where the legislatures might be willing to put their money.

TOP (Left to right):
Harry Pachon, Milton Mooris
MIDDLE LEFT: *Lena Guerrero*
MIDDLE RIGHT: *Rodolfo de la Garza*
BOTTOM RIGHT: *Margaret Simms*

PART IX

Political Feasibility of New Policy Initiatives

PART IX

Introduction

Rodolfo de la Garza: Our panel has been asked to comment on the suggestions presented at the conference and to suggest new ideas about the political feasibility of these policies. Let me begin with two very short observations—one is something I find striking, and the second one is a question. One of the factors that has affected every issue discussed today, but which has not been mentioned at all, is immigration. I find it rather curious that people from New York, who live immigration, people from California, who live immigration, and people in other cities who have seen their cities transformed by immigrants, have not talked about what immigration implies for cities in transition.

A second point is puzzling, because I was confronted with it recently in a debate with Roger Connor, who is the chairman of FAIR, Federation of Americans for Immigration Reform. He asked me, "How many people do you want to let in?" The question has meaning for this conference because there is an unarticulated assumption that the quality of life that many of us have or aspire to have is what we would want all people to have. Bringing these two points together—immigration and quality of life—raises two additional questions: What are the resources available to this society in the future, and how are we going to create new resources or redistribute existing resources?

With those questions in mind, let us begin with Margaret Simms, who is presently with the Joint Center for Political Studies. She has been a scholar at the Urban Institute as well as a Brookings Fellow.

Setting Priorities

Margaret Simms: I decided to see if I could sum up some of the proposals we have talked about and discuss the meaning for implementation of those proposals. I will also discuss the probability of getting any of these initiatives through the appropriate government processes.

What we have heard in the last two days is that, far from moving away from two societies into "One nation, indivisible," we may have become three or more societies, and we feel uncomfortable with that. We have heard policy proposals that are designed, we think, to move us in the right direction—policies concerning improvements in the educational system, improvements in employment and training, health care provision, and changes in the welfare system.

We have heard less about that which is most important in terms of political feasibility. Which proposals come first? What are our priorities? Which level of government should have responsibility for each of these proposals? To what degree should the private sector be involved in any or all of these activities? We know that the private sector should be involved in education and in training, but we did not discuss the degree or the division of responsibility.

What method of financing is most appropriate for these proposals? Thus far, we have gotten mostly bad news on that score. However, I would like to provide perspective on the way I see the good news/bad news. Two factors make it likely that we can promote some changes. One is the concern with the competitive edge that was brought up both yesterday and today. There is a real concern that the United States is slipping in world competition and production and that somehow we have to get a grip on this decline and return to the forefront. Doing this means spending money and changing some activities.

Another factor that helps is movement to accept the need to expand public sector activities in a number of ways, particularly in education. This mood may extend to housing and child care as well. This movement is occurring because these problems are touching not just the disadvantaged, but the majority as well. There was a comment suggesting that Dukakis changed the housing discussion from one about the underclass to one about the middle class. My recollection is that he changed this discussion from a discussion about people on the fringe to people in the middle. For example, he talked about homelessness among families, which is an issue that people can rally around. There is also a danger of this advantage. Possibly, this shift will mean benefits have to be spread too far. That policy is in opposition to Bob Reischauer's argument that we can maximize resources if we target them more carefully.

More generally, I would like to comment on three main issues. One is the question of what level of government is to bear primary responsibility for implementation of policies to improve our cities. Yesterday there was a discussion about the fact that political power is now concentrated more at the state and local levels. This statement is particularly true for Hispanics, because their populations are concentrated in particular states. However, there is a danger of encouraging too much concentration of power at that level. There are variations in fiscal capacity across states. This is more clearly evidenced in the black experience, because blacks are not nearly as likely to be concentrated in states with adequate or expansive resources. Living in Mississippi does not provide the same advantage as living in California. There is another danger, and that is the question of the minimum standard issue and variation across states. That means that citizens in different states do not have access to similar opportunities.

The second issue is the one of dedicated resources. This works fine for environmental and pollution cases in which you can tie the revenue to the benefit. If you dirty the air, then you pay to clean it up. But what is the dedicated source for education? What is the dedicated source for some of the other areas, such as homelessness and inadequate health care? If we lean too much on dedicated resources, we will lose the whole question of the common societal good that we are promoting with many of these proposals.

The last issue is the question of people versus places. Again, this an issue that has been discussed off and on in the last two days. We can move away from place-oriented policies to people-oriented policies, but, again, I am not sure whether this approach works very well for all of the services, because then you lose the mechanism for service delivery. What is the mechanism for delivering training services if you tie funding to the individual? What kind of standards or regulations do you impose in order to ensure that the voucher or whatever form of payment to the individual receives is, in fact, used to good effect?

I think we have to look at ways in which we can take advantage of new approaches. Still, we must not implement small changes to the detriment of proposing a basic improvement in the services that we are concerned with enhancing.

R. de la Garza: Regarding the political feasibility of new policy initiatives, our next speaker is uniquely qualified to speak to that. Representative Lena Guerrero, member of the Texas State Legislature, was also a member of the Democratic Platform Drafting Committee. Thus, she knows quite well how one combines political reality with dreams.

Building Coalitions

Lena Guerrero : You know, there are probably advantages and disadvantages of being a Hispanic woman in the Texas House. The obvious disadvantage is that I rarely get invited to go hunting, which is where half of all the decisions are made in the Texas House. Also, I rarely get invited to go into the men's room, which is where the other half of the decisions are made.

The advantage of my being elected to the Texas Legislature is that there was never before elected a young Hispanic woman, so no one knows what to expect. They have such low expectations that anything I say or do could actually exceed them. I figured that they did not know what to expect the first term, but after they had seen me in action, they got ideas about what I was really going to be like. So the second term I just got pregnant. I got pregnant, and they got protective. It was a most interesting process. I vowed to get pregnant every session, but that was a joke.

Seriously, realistic options to create change and the political feasibility of implementing those changes mean some very systematic things. When I view these options, obviously, as a politician, I consider strategies, how to make something occur. I do not really have a formula, but I have some ideas.

The first thing I do in a situation in which I want to achieve something is to assess the proposition's strengths and weaknesses. I find out who would be for it, naturally, and who would be against it. While I am concerned about those who are for it, I tend to concentrate on these who are against. it. Then I proceed to actually work on strategies. I begin by thinking about what it is that those who oppose the proposition would do if they were in my position. I have found that education through public relations is an important way to promote an initiative. When I have spare time in the legislature—and it is a full-time job even though they do not consider it and surely do not pay you for a full-time job—I always think about implementing policy in terms of gaining momentum and support by assuring that people understand what the problem is.

The difficulty with that strategy is that there are numerous problems. Given a certain situation in certain communities, the problem could be highlighted in different ways. The important thing is to begin to educate people about what the true picture is. I use public mediums to convince people that a problem exists and there is this sense of urgency to solve it or to bring forth some important solutions.

The second aspect, and it is probably the most essential element in bringing about change in an effective way, is building coalitions. I like to begin with the ones that nobody thinks I could get. The individuals or groups least likely to be for the cause are the ones I go after, because once I am able to tear down some of the barriers, people begin to think, "Even they are for it? Well, if they are for it, it must not be all that bad." And suddenly the tougher opposition begins to follow through, supporting the concept of strange bedfellows in politics. I go after those groups that I think would not likely support something.

Another aspect is who I get to speak for the proposal, who sponsors it, or who is to be the leader in the media campaign. Those are important considerations. I must determine whether someone is believable. It is interesting to me that, in Texas, if you want someone to endorse your cause and you want a balanced commercial, you might get Henry Cisneros and Barbara Jordan to endorse something in the same commercial. If you did, obviously, you have a good coalition, and you are able to address the issue from two people who are very well respected. So it is important to think about who will speak for an issue and who will be the symbolic leader of the proposal.

Credit and praise are also important elements in effecting feasible change, as well as including as many people as possible and making them feel as if they are part of the solution. I would like to use one example of the way this strategy worked in the last legislative session. Teenage pregnancy is a very serious problem. The United States is the number-one developed country in the world in terms of teen mothers under the age of nineteen. Texas has the distinction of being third in the union in the number of pregnant young mothers under the age of nineteen, but first in the union with young mothers under age fifteen. The new aspect of teenage pregnancy is that the mothers are much younger. In many states across the union we are talking about twelve-, thirteen-, and fourteen-year-old mothers who do not want to be mothers, who do not know how to be mothers, and who have children who fit in the category of "children at risk." These children are at risk of not developing fully and not having the educational potential to finish high school. Thus, children who live in poverty face a number of other problems that have been discussed in this conference.

This issue has become very important to me. I would swear to everybody who knows me that I did not get pregnant because of it, but I will tell you that, having been pregnant in the process, I understood how it might be if you were twelve or thirteen and were having to go through an incredible change in your life, and you did not really want that baby, and you did not know how to deal with it. Nonetheless, I wanted to deal with this issue in the state legislature. We graduate hundreds of thousands of young people from high school in this state who cannot balance a check book and cannot change a diaper, as if those things do not really happen. Family life education is taught in the public schools in this state, but it is not taught to very many people. Family life education comes under a very specialized category called home economics, which is vocational education. So if you choose the home as a vocation, you are going to learn about family life. If not, you will never learn to sew a button. And the truth is that all of us in this room have had to sew on a button at one time or another or have needed someone to do it for us.

I wanted to address this issue in the legislature, and I used the elements I outlined earlier to do that. The first thing, everybody told me, was, "Lena, what you need is a study." I responded, "I don't need a study. I know what the problems are." They said, "No. You see, in the legislature you really need a study," So I introduced a resolution and got the interim chair for a study. As I began to do the study, I thought it was silly, but it is part of the process. The more I thought about it, the more I decided I needed to use the study in an advantageous way. I held major press conferences. I had young twelve- and thirteen-year-olds with their tiny babies come to my committee and go on record about what they had experienced. I had interviews with television and newspapers and had articles written. We literally exploited the study process. Not only was I able to get an excuse to combine all of the information I needed, but I also made the press understand that they had to be part of the study process. They had to tell people what we were studying.

The second strategy was to make a big to-do about releasing the results. In the process, we began to build coalitions, and we began to convince different groups to support our efforts. For the first time in seventy-plus years the Congress of Parent-Teachers, which is the PTA in Texas, endorsed sex education in the public schools. They had a big fight over it within their own organization, but they endorsed it. They were the one anchor group we felt we needed to have, and we got them. Then we pulled together the Texas Medical Association, a powerful lobby group in Texas, and the Texas Nurses Association. These two groups are almost never on the same side. We began to pull together educators, parents, students, mental health communities, social service agencies, government employees, and a number of other groups to build those coalitions.

Then came the strategy on proposals. The first one had to be something to deal with the immediate problem. The second one had to be something that the bull would go after, "the red flag." The third one represented our long-range goals. The first proposal passed. It was aimed at my colleagues who tell me that we do not need to solve this problem, because it is not a problem. Teen pregnancies do not happen in their area. This is what they told me. So I passed a bill to keep statistics by legislative districts, so that next session I will be armed with data that show that teen pregnancies do, in fact, occur in their districts. The second bill proposed adult education for parents. The bill proposed to help adult parents learn how to talk to their kids about contraceptive education. I put "the word" in it, and the pro-life groups had a big press conference and wanted to kill the bill. It became the "red flag" the bull went after. Last, the third proposal was for sex education in the public schools, which we will reintroduce. All in all, elements that I discussed here were used in this process. Now, we are armed with statistics to use for the long-range goal, which is sex education.

I think, for minorities, we need three things. First, we need more appointed and elected officials in policymaking positions. Second, it is important for us to learn the rules and to learn to strategize within them. And, third, I think it is important for us to persist. If we do, we can prevail.

R. de la Garza: Our third speaker, Harry Pachon, is Kennan Professor of Political Studies at Pitzer College. He formerly worked on the staff of the Appropriations Committee working with California Congressman Ed Roybal and is currently the executive director of the National Association of Latino Elected Officials (NALEO).

Using Political Processes

Harry Pachon: When I was asked to comment on political feasibility of new policies for the cities, I remembered my old political science texts that say that "politics is the art of the possible." And if I look at that definition, art cannot be transmitted, because it is not a science, and people have different expertise insofar as artistic skills are concerned. If I were a true artist, if I were the artist of political feasibility, I would have my shingle on Connecticut Avenue in Washington, D.C., and I would be receiving those one-million-dollar consulting contracts that you hear about in the news. In spite of those caveats, let me talk about some themes that emerged from this conference.

The first of these themes was the language of how we legitimize our goals—not whether or not our goals are legitimate, but how we legitimize our goals. A second theme was one of technical clarity of the objects we wish to accomplish. Mayor Cisneros, when he spoke about the problems of minority education in the city, explained that one of the biggest successes he has had in making minority education a large-scale issue is to cast the problem in terms of a majority society issue. By the year 2030, when large percentages of our population reach retirement years, we will have an undereducated population that will be expected to achieve full productivity. This problem will then become a majority problem, not just a minority problem.

I hear the Honorable Mr. Dinkins talk about the issue of set-asides and the necessity of avoiding such terms as "quota" in preference for the term "set-aside" for political appeasement. We do know that for every billion dollars spent on government contracts in minority communities, we generate anywhere between thirty thousand and fifty thousand jobs in our communities. Thus, legitimizing our language may be one way to increase the feasibility of any proposals that this group or any other group puts forward.

The second issue that I was looking at insofar as language was concerned is the pervasiveness of the technobureaucratic language. Technobureaucratic language is a jargon of its own. We have heard such terms as "reconciliation" and "recision." Government and analysts produce grant allocation formulas that are sometimes forty or fifty factors long. I am involved in immigration, and the discussion in that policy area right now focuses on SLIAG caps in different states and how important it is to have a $450 cap or a $650 cap when discussing how far SLIAG funds can go to reach amnesty applicants. So there has been an increased complexity of technical jargon. I call it technobureaucratic language.

I was disappointed, to be truthful, by two things during this conference. One was that our papers and our presentations use statistics, and yet we are still engaged in the misuse of statistics. Some of our presentations still talk about black and white comparisons in American society, and that is one of the most damaging things that we can do to the black population or to the Hispanic population. We do damage to the black population because we minimize the differences between blacks and whites in the society when we include Hispanics in the white population. We hurt the Hispanic population by making them invisible, by not asking, "Are there any significant differences among blacks, Hispanics, and whites?"

We have also been talking these past two days about cities, and I wonder if we have unconsciously used the term "city" in the image of a northeastern city or maybe a Texas city, not recognizing the phenomenon of suburbanization that has occurred in western states like California. For example, at NALEO we are just finishing an analysis of the amnesty applicants, and the stereotype is that the amnesty applicants in California are located in East Los Angeles, not in the suburban areas. That is not the case in Southern California. Amnesty applicants can be found everywhere from Beverly Hills to Santa Ana, and the city with the second-largest number of amnesty applicants is Santa Ana in Orange County, California. Consequently, I wonder if we shouldn't be trying to specify our language. What do we do about policies for cities when cities are not single structural entities? When they are really fragmented governmental structures? Again, let me use one last example of Los Angeles County. There are eighty cities in Los Angeles County. Chicano and black populations are not concentrated in the central city itself. In the southern parts of Los Angeles, we have seen a phenomenon where blacks moved in the early eighties and since have been displaced by Central American immigrants. We have had, really, two waves of immigrants coming through some of these suburban places.

Another question that is raised when we consider the political feasibility of new policies in the cities is, what networks do we use to accomplish our policy objectives? If I look at the carriers of our message or of our battle plans, I see fewer than 3,300 Hispanic elected officials and slightly over 6,000 black elected officials. That is approximately 9,000 minority elected officials in the United States out of a population of 490,000 elected officials. Less than 2 percent of our elected officials are minority elected officials. I believe this number will change in 1992. Let's say that it doubles in size, from 9,000 to 18,000. What does that mean for policy articulation or implementation for minorities in the central cities and in the suburban ring around our cities?

Additionally, if we look further to determine where the minority appointees are in the executive branch at the federal level, there is a very dismal record. One of the factors that has been ignored is the number of minorities in appointed positions. We hit an all-time low in the Reagan administration of less than 125 Hispanic political appointees. The high point was 300, but, again, this number is from a pool of 8,000 political appointments.

In the Bush administration, are we really going to see a high number of minorities, both black and brown, in significant positions? I have not seen, besides Bill Medina, who was assistant secretary for planning and research in the Department of Housing and Urban Development, any other minority in one of the major analytical departments of the federal government. We have not had a black or a Hispanic in any position responsible for formulating long-term policy objectives of the federal government. There is a serious lack of minorities in policy analyst positions in the federal bureaucracy. One of the things that has come to mind here is that we are talking about long-term impacts and long-term development of policies affecting cities. There is also a tremendous amount of minority underrepresentation in our policy think tanks. Both on the right and on the left, at the Brookings Institution, the American Enterprise Institute, or the Urban Institute, there are few Hispanic and very few black analysts.

The final thing that emerges when considering political feasibility is the question of process. The first priority is establishing the legitimacy of our goals. The second is assuring that we have a network of elected and appointed officials to carry out our goals. The third priority is process. And the political process has changed from twenty years ago. The changes have not occurred as major authorizations and new policy developments but instead have occurred in the budgetary process. Today we experience decreased appropriations and budgetary constraints. Finally, we must talk about the process of implementation. When we know what our objectives are we must then look at the process of implementation and at the giant bureaucracies that currently exist in our urban centers.

R. de la Garza: Our final speaker, Milton Morris, is director of research at the Joint Center for Political Studies. In that capacity, he regularly deals with policy people and thus brings the same double dimension of research and public policy that other speakers have brought to this discussion.

Setting an Agenda for Change

Milton Morris: The problem the final speaker faces is that everything has been said. I want to pause, however, to simply register one last expression of real gratitude and satisfaction for the hosts and planners of this conference. It was rich, well organized, and superb in every respect. Very few conferences seem to reach their peak near the end—I did not say "at the end." This one has held our interest all the way.

I wanted to add just a few comments to the observations about political feasibility. I am of two minds on that subject. I think, first, that we have had, more or less, a complete consensus on what the major problems are, or at least the broad outlines of the problems. I have heard no dissent from the array of specific issues with which we were occupied over the past two days. And while we talked about them in terms of cities or urban areas, one could, in fact, look at them well beyond particular geographic areas and places.

Commissioner Snell's comment about the rural poor reminds us that many of the problems of housing, health care, inadequate education, and so forth that plague central-city people are also present outside central cities. And, to a very great extent, I suspect that over time we will have a combination of place-oriented types of responses to problems and people-oriented types of responses to problems, rather than one or the other.

What strikes me is that, in approaching the question of feasibility, we need to bring together two seemingly contradictory types of sentiments or convictions. One is an informed realism about the resources and the will that exist for change, and the other is a firm commitment to the creation of a caring society, one concerned about human needs.

I want to first emphasize the problems of limited resources and limited will. Not a great deal of effort has been expended in looking at public attitudes, and those attitudes are important. One speaker today criticized the presidential campaign and the candidates for their lack of attention to the weighty issues of our cities. What is most disturbing is that political candidates take this posture precisely because that is what it takes to win elections. That is what most of America and your neighbors want. There is not an enormous ground swell of interest in and support for the issues that concern us here.

At the Joint Center we conduct a survey each year in which we have national samples of black and white populations. And while I agree with Harry Pachon, the realities of surveys dictate that we do some of these artificial comparisons. What is striking is that the area in which there is the widest divergence in black and white political attitudes has to do with perceptions of the role of government in addressing the problems of the poor. There is an almost complete reversal in views on this issue. While the overwhelming majority of blacks think that government should do more to help the poor, the overwhelming majority of whites think that government should do less to help the poor. That is striking, because what it suggests is that, for a very large segment of the population, there are a set of attitudes and a set of values that are, frankly, not encouraging when we think about addressing some of the problems of our cities.

Then, of course, there is the problem of resources. Dick Nathan assured us—and since he is a Republican, he knows—that we will not see a dramatic change or shift toward the programs of earlier administrations. I agree with him. In fact, I think that, regardless of who wins the presidential election, the long, dark shadow of the Reagan revolution will haunt us for quite some time. We will, for the next several years, be talking about the politics of budget cuts rather than planning for improvements, changes, and programs that reflect important and significant investments in people and in solving problems. Thus, when one thinks about feasibility, one must think about an environment in which there is very limited opportunity to spend, very limited will to spend, and a preoccupation with cutting back.

There are other problems as well. While we have had a number of the problems discussed at this conference with us for a long time, we still have not found effective ways to handle them. Then there are some problems that, frankly, we have not talked about very much at all. We did not talk much about immigration or much about drugs. We cannot think about cities or urban problems without addressing the enormous changes that are being brought about by the presence of a new drug culture in our cities, a culture that is in some ways massively distorting the economy and distorting the institutions within cities. That drug culture is an important part of the equation. On that front, we have very few answers. In fact, we have been struck with such suddenness that we are still making futile gestures at a problem and wondering what to do next. We do not have as many of the answers as we would like to have to address the drug problem.

Finally, the problems we have talked about are all big-money problems. We have not addressed any issues that require a relatively modest investment. I wondered what would have happened if we had had somebody with a calculator in the back of the room punching in the numbers as we rattled off the kinds of needs we have. These are big problems, and, as a society, I do not believe that we are prepared under the present circumstances to address them head on.

Thus, in looking at what is feasible and what is likely to be implemented, I suspect we are going to find some incremental adjustments in some areas that will reflect at least partial attempts to deal with the most urgent problems in the areas of education and housing, for example. There will be small gestures in those directions but not the kind of gestures that are likely to represent significant substantive change.

That said, we have some things to be optimistic about. One is that, while we do not know a good deal about how to solve some problems, there are others that we know a good deal about how to solve. Latino and black scholars like yourselves have been engaged in research over the years that provides fairly convincing answers to some of the important social problems, and that is an important step.

Second, from listening to Mayor Cisneros and other people here, we have indications of numerous successful strategies at work. We have focused here on the federal government, and we have only occasionally turned to the state and local governments. Yet, one of the major changes in the last decade has been in the quality of state and local government. A bit more than a decade ago we began with an enormous degree of paranoia. We were convinced that state and local governments were insensitive and unresponsive, that minorities were largely closed out of those arenas, and that state and local governments had to be watched every step of the way if any benefits were going to be delivered. Things are far from perfect in state and local government, but a number of changes have occurred. One change, of course, is the increasing presence of minorities at these levels. Harry Pachon is right: we are still far from adequately represented. The sad part of it is that, at least among blacks, the numbers of elected officials are increasing at less than 2 percent per year, so it will be a long time before we have anything approaching significant representation. Nonetheless, the point is that many state and local governments have become much more creative and more aggressive than they have been, so some solutions to problems are likely to come at these levels.

What will happen in the future depends, to a great extent, on what blacks and Latinos are able to do in the way of coalition building, in the way of creating a new set of values and a new set of priorities for society. It is a large burden to assume, but my impression is that we have some significant work to do.

First off, we have had a respite from struggle, maybe forced by the massive wave of conservatism of the last decade. During that time, much has changed. Again we must pick up the cause and crusade on a number of fronts for political empowerment and for change in the kinds of attitudes and values that now dominate our society. A large part of that effort is ours.

Second, we have to commit ourselves to an unwillingness to accept the constraints imposed by the present political situation, particularly the politics of the budget. You know as well as I do that the budget process is a political process. With blacks at the bottom, I am uncomfortable with the notion of operating within the constraints of the budgetary environment left by the Reagan administration. I believe, for example, that we need to work for significant tax overhauls that provide new monies to spend for solving problems. Furthermore, we must be aggressive and assertive in making those demands for new monies rather than helping people to shave here and there to find dollars.

Perhaps most important, and maybe not entirely different from something said earlier, is a point of emphasis: The future is ours, especially in terms of the minority community. We have to help society to seize upon a new set of values as the values apply to human needs, to the quality of life, and to human capital development. There are new opportunities, and the politics of the next decade and of the next century are going to be determined on that ground. We must be prepared to lead the struggle in shaping values and in initiating and implementing policies that reflect those values.

R. de la Garza: A powerful point was articulated again: that is, we have to legitimize our goals, and that is distinct from taking on goals that society has already defined as legitimate. We must determine what we want and then how to get our issues on the table. That is something to be hopeful about.

A second point is implied in what Milton Morris said about the notion of political feasibility. Political feasibility is not a simple equation, an obvious $a + b = c$. There have been numerous people who have laid out what was politically feasible, only to fail. The notion of political feasibility is difficult to operationalize, and most of us can only predict the feasibility of an issue in hindsight, after the struggle is over, which is really no prediction at all.

Discussion

David Padilla, Postdoctoral Fellow at Stanford: Professor Pachon, you touched on the question of identity of Hispanics, particularly whether they are different from blacks or not. Does this question of identity also pertain to the subgroups within Hispanics? Are there differences between Hispanic cultural groups and do those differences have any implications for the feasibility of policies? Are we going to consider Hispanics monolithically and just count the number of Hispanic officials, or is it important to determine how such a count breaks down by cultural groups within the Hispanics? What kinds of variations are there within the Latino experience?

H. Pachon: I was referring to the presentation of social problems. I was illustrating that if we simply describe a black/white phenomenon, it hurts both blacks and Hispanics. I am calling for more precision. Unfortunately, when you are dealing with large data sets to describe either beneficiary populations or survey populations, every cut you make costs more money. You will quickly hear outraged screams of anguish, such as, "It is going to cost a million dollars to put a Hispanic category in this particular data set."

D. Padilla: I was just referring to the reality of the situation. There are great differences among the Hispanic subgroups—among Puerto Ricans, Mexican Americans, Cubans, South Americans, and other Latinos—even though for political reasons it would be convenient to count them together at times.

H. Pachon: Clearly.

M. Simms: It is the Census Bureau that puts us in this bind because, for whatever reasons—which they often cite as political—they do not publish Hispanic information separate from the racial totals. They say Hispanic is not a race, it is an ethnicity. They include Hispanics as white or black, depending upon how the Hispanics categorize themselves. We are now getting more information on Hispanic subpopulations through the Census Bureau, but we are not getting the type of information that we might get by making them distinct from blacks or whites. Unless you have the census tape, and you can make the distinctions yourself, you are forced to make these black/white comparisons because of the way the data are presented.

H. Pachon: There are policy implications to that situation. Number one, certainly there are experts out here on children and poverty. We know that 39 percent of all Hispanic children now fall below the poverty line. Yet when you compare black and white children in poverty, the differences between blacks and whites do not appear to be great. If we took out the Hispanic children from the white category, it would really highlight the major income gaps that exist at the present time.

As for policy implications, we as researchers, when we see data like that, have to say it is unacceptable. I know that is not going to get us very far, but I think if we scream long enough, possibly the officials will listen.

M. Simms: We need some legislative folks to help us there, because until the Census Bureau is told differently by someone who can make them change, that is the way the census data are going to be presented.

L. Guerrero: You have highlighted yet another important issue of the next Congress, and that is who they will count in the 1990 census. In Texas, if they do not count everybody who is really here, we stand to lose our fair representation in Congress. That could very well mean, at some point, not one but three congressional seats in this state. So you are right, it is a political problem that can be politically solved if we could address it from that angle.

A point was made earlier—and that is, we need not only to know what the problems are and the possible solutions to them, but we also need some sense of the order in which these problems should be addressed. That is a difficult challenge because everybody has a different idea about which issue is most pressing. If, in fact, you are dealing with the three institutions—education, employment, and social services—it seems that some of the problems and solutions must be addressed together. For example, education and corrections tend to go together for a variety of reasons, and we need to address them both. In Texas we will try to do just that next session.

Max Sherman, LBJ School of Public Affairs: One final word: the Ford Foundation is a unique organization, and we would like to thank William Diaz, Human Rights and Governance, who has been actively involved in bringing all of us together. I would like to conclude by saying that, even though we talked about cities in transition, we are actually in a time of many transitions. There will be a new president on the twentieth of January 1989. There will be a new administration in Washington. There have been a number of elections that possibly will change the leadership in many of our states. Many of our major cities will have elections in the near future. Those transitions are going to happen, and we must be involved in these transitions, advising and actively participating to make our cities a better place for all who live in them in the future.

Frank Bonilla

Afterword: Poverty and Inequality in the 1990s

Poverty and Inequality in the 1990s

Frank Bonilla

PART X

Poverty and Inequality in the 1990s

Frank Bonilla: The 1980s have turned out to be a decade for stocktakings and sobering reckonings about the distance between the legislative and institutional commitments to social equality of the 1960s and contemporary U.S. realities. Aside from the key documents that undergird visions of the Great Society, such as the Eisenhower, Katzenbach, and Kerner Commission reports, which we commemorate in this forum, nowhere are these ideals more clearly articulated than in the writings of Dr. Martin Luther King, Jr. In the early sixties, King proclaimed that the nation's drive to honor its historic economic debt to African Americans had to be coupled with a simultaneous assertion of the economic rights of all individuals victimized by poverty, regardless of color. This vision meant "ultimately coming to see that the problem of racism, the problem of economic exploitation, and the problem of war are all tied together."[1] King believed that the basic material well-being of ordinary people, the harmony of social relations in any community, and peace among nations were all inextricably linked. He asserted that combined peoples' force of every race and ethnicity would muster presidential and federal support, along with the institutional resources of churches, unions, and voluntary associations to sweep away the barriers to jobs and assured incomes for all in the nation.[2] King, in the plans for the Poor People's March on Washington in 1968, projected a basis for the broad multiethnic coalition toward which this forum points.

Latinos and the American Dilemma
In the early sixties, as King was laying the foundation for the Civil Rights Movement and the United States lay on the eve of rioting in black communities around the country, a principal collaborator in the landmark study *An American Dilemma* felt able to affirm that job discrimina-

tion had practically been eradicated in the North and West and that racism would be a mere shadow on the U.S. past by the 1980s.[3] This complacent reading of social conditions reflected the current moral climate in the U.S. and suggested that the American people did not have to take assertive action to diminish racial tensions or poverty.

An American Dilemma, which still constitutes one of the most ambitious efforts to detail the inner workings of racial oppression in the United States, makes practically no reference to Latinos. Cubans and Puerto Ricans are absent from the index. The single reference to Mexican Americans describes a study of labor practices in Los Angeles in the 1920s. In work places where Mexicans were considered "colored," they worked side by side with blacks and often had black supervisors. Where they were considered "white," they worked alongside whites but were rarely in positions of command.[4] Most of us who work, I expect, can find some vestiges of these patterns, however attenuated, in our daily lives. In any case, a major presumption of the Myrdal work was that immigration to the United States after World War II would prove a minor factor in shaping the society. That complacent view of the U.S. condition and future was widely shared in the 1960s. In contrast to the warnings of an increasingly divided America in the Kerner Commission Report, in 1967, Daniel Bell, chair of the Commission on the Year 2000, reassured the nation that the unmatched flexibility of the political system and the extraordinary productive capacity of the U.S. economy left this country well equipped to face any contingency for decades to come.[5] By other authoritative accounts of the time, what remained to be done to knit the society into a seamless whole was merely to clean up some stubborn pockets of poverty and unemployment, and the dilemma posed by Myrdal and his associates was well on the way to a relatively untroubled resolution.

Ironically, as it turns out, a great part of whatever income redistribution has occurred in the United States during the postwar years took place precisely in that decade of explosive social discontent and the decade of Lyndon B. Johnson's War on Poverty. Martin Luther King's insights about the polarization of capitalism were driven home at a time when opportunities for social mobility for the poor in the United States were at a peak. From the mid 1970s on, as the Kerner Report predicted, inequality between men and women as well as whites and nonwhites held steady or grew.

Increasingly, national apprehensions about the future and growing inequalities have focused on Latinos, especially after the 1980 census showed them to be the fastest-growing population of nonwhites. The ongoing "Latinization" of the United States is seen by many as equally as or more threatening to the nation's unity than the persistence of racial segmentation or the heightening of class differences. Latinos are a disquieting presence not only because of their growing numbers but also because of their diversity, their apparent attachment to alien languages and cultures, their marked concentration in particular regions, and their growing political salience. As Cuban Americans are discovering anew, ill will and disdain can be engendered as much by success and accommodation as by the limited social achievement and resistance to assimilation imputed to Puerto Ricans and Mexican Americans. Central America, the Caribbean, Mexico, Cuba, Puerto Rico—Latin America at large—are cognate terms for fearsome images of economic stagnation, extreme inflation, massive debt, soaring deficits, repression and torture, armed insurgencies, a vicious drug traffic, uncontrolled migration, and on and on.

Poignant evidence suggests that Martin Luther King's vision of an empowering political unity between African Americans and Latinos in the United States is as old as the reality of their common bondage and marginality. In the 1930s blacks and Puerto Ricans became the voting majority in a single New York assembly district in East Harlem. They fought together, as local insurgents in the Democratic party, for a place in the party machine. The response from "the regulars" included intimidation and violence at polling places.

The leaders of this Latino-African American coalition chronicled that early failure in a pamphlet they titled *The Tragedy of the Puerto Ricans and the Colored American*. On the cover two male figures, naked from the waist up, bound and manacled by a single chain, stand before a backdrop of the New York skyline. A number of vultures hover overhead. The text recapitulated the familiar litany of self-criticism that has followed on all such misfires in coalition building—internal divisions, contention for place among leaders, the indifference of intellectuals, weak organization, ideological naiveté, the resources and ruthlessness of entrenched power. King, too, agonized about organizational cleavages and personal rivalries within the movement .

But now, fifty years later, African Americans and Latinos have become or imminently will become voting majorities in scores of localities around the country. And the conditions from which there may well spring a united rejection of present levels of deprivation and denial in economic, political, and cultural arenas are undeniably in place.

Economic Rights in the 1980s

King observed that, from the early days of the nation, the African Americans' share in social goods stood roughly at half that of whites, while their share in social liabilities had been almost double that of whites.[6] This situation is as true today for income, unemployment, and poverty rates as it was in the 1960s. Research now under way within the framework of an interuniversity network of Latino scholars, as well as other work, indicates that over recent decades, especially in the 1980s, the fortunes of Latinos, in particular Puerto Ricans, have closely followed those of African Americans. The proportion of whites affected by poverty and underemployment also seems to be growing. This forum is partly intended to analyze the fine-grained variations in the experiences of Latinos and African Americans and to encourage discussion of the causes of their present situations. What is most important and alarming about the new evidence of persistent and growing inequality is that it occurs in a period of moderate, but sustained, economic expansion and is not being effectively offset by existing social programs.

King's shift of focus from race to basic economic arrangements brought him a rain of criticism. But, as a matter of fact, his central assertions about the workings of capitalism only echoed those made decades earlier by John Maynard Keynes, who agreed that "the outstanding faults of the economic society in which we live are its failure to provide full employment and its arbitrary and inequitable distribution of income."[7]

Keynes's theoretical labors were intended to show that the key to steady growth was the generation of decently paying jobs to sustain mass demand. Assured growth and the meeting of human needs, he added, would lay a solid foundation for world peace, for "if nations can learn to provide for themselves with full employment by their domestic policy there need be no important economic forces calculated to set the interest of one country against that of its neighbors."[8] King himself balked at articulating a legislative blueprint for full employment and guaranteed incomes. To do so, he asserted, would lend validity to a false image of a benevolent government awaiting well-delineated schemes for the resolution of long-standing inequities. King argued that the poor should not be required to have thoroughly calculated, relatively cost-free schemes already in hand before aggressively advancing claims on government. His Economic Bill of Rights for the Disadvantaged remained a general statement of principles and goals.

Thus, it is not happenstance that the Black Legislative Caucus has spearheaded a 1980s drive in Congress to rouse the nation to develop strategies that emphasize the right of each citizen to work and earn decent wages. It is a symptom of the time that far-reaching legislation seeking to inject new life into full-employment goals has been put before the Congress repeatedly in recent years, although such efforts have generally been ignored by the media. The Congress has before it a substantial package of legislation under the umbrella of an Economic Bill of Rights (HR 2870) and the Quality of Life Action Act (HR1398). These initiatives affirm principles active in U.S. politics at least since Franklin D. Roosevelt's

State of the Union message in 1944: principles partially enacted into law in the Employment Act of 1945 and the 1978 Humphrey-Hawkins Bill. These dispositions have simply been put aside by the Reagan administration. The 1988 Economic Bill of Rights incorporates legislation on the minimum wage, trade policy, housing, health, and school improvement and would commission research to inform the nation and federal government on all aspects of this cluster of problems and remedies.

These initiatives bring into view the scope of the institutional transformations that will be required to bring these goals nearer to reality. To begin with, the proposed legislation forbids any federal agency, including the Board of Governors of the Federal Reserve System, "to promote, directly or indirectly, recession, stagnation or unemployment as a means of curbing inflation." The initiatives recognize the international dimension of unemployment by instructing the federal government to act within the United Nations and the Organization of American States to ensure coordinated economic measures that do not impose sacrifices on the most needy of any nation. Further, proposed legislation requires that every public budget include estimates of its impact on the distribution of income and wealth.

To some it may appear utopian or reckless to propose legislation of this scope and complexity in the present economic crisis and ideological climate. As the proceedings of this symposium show, both politicians and policy specialists are skeptical about the present viability of initiatives invoking full-employment and guaranteed-income goals. Talented and trained individuals with firm roots in our communities will have to do a major part of the new analysis required to validate these national goals. At the same time, the unmeasurable costs of the massive waste of human resources and the social tragedy all around are setting in motion the forces that King envisioned. Churches, unions, regional and community organizations, local governments, and peace activists are on a new quest for economic rights.

Latinos represent a very low profile in this movement at the present time, although we are better prepared than ever in national and local organizations, voting power, and intellectual and technical resources to contribute to the drive for economic justice and peace. To do this we will have to join with others, as King exhorted, to break through a pluralism in which people dwell together but remain locked in worlds apart, in which, as time passes, people know less rather than more about one another. We will also have to dare, in today's more conservative and intimidating climate, to question, as did King, the most taken-for-granted bases of prevailing social arrangements. We might then take more seriously not just the poverty of our own country but its unity with that of other peoples and other nations.

There is a powerful message in these conference proceedings and a striking account of the magnitude and persistence of problems confronted by Latinos and blacks in the transformed and still-transitioning context of our cites. The addresses by politicians, particularly Henry Cisneros and Barbara Jordan, are compelling formulations of the complexity of the problems this conference sought to address. While the recommendations may not constitute a major policy breakthrough, the proceedings register a new moment in the challenges faced by policymakers and a historic coming together of uniquely diverse perspectives.

Notes

1. James M. Washington, ed., *A Testament of Hope* (San Francisco: Harper and Row, 1986), p. 250.
2. Martin Luther King, Jr., *Why We Can't Wait* (New York: Harper and Row, 1963), pp. 137ff.
3. Gunnar Myrdal, *An American Dilemma* (New York: Harper and Row, 1967), p. xliv.
4. Ibid.
5. Daniel Bell, "The Year 2000: The Trajectory of an Idea," *Daedelus* 96, no. 3 (1967): 639-41.
6. Washington, *Testament*, p. 245.
7. John Maynard Keynes, *The General Theory of Employment, Interest, and Money* (New York: Harcourt, Brace and World, Inc., 1964).
8. Ibid.

CONTRIBUTORS

Bernard Anderson
Managing Partner, Urban Affairs Partnership Program; Director, Manpower Demonstration Corporation, and the Pennsylvania Economic Development Partnership; former Economist, Bureau of Labor Statistics, U.S. Department of Labor

Gonzalo Barrientos
Texas State Senator, District 14; former Texas State Representative; Chair, interim committee to study dropouts; member, Education Committee, Texas Sunset Advisory Commission, and interim committee to study the state welfare system

Frank Bonilla
Professor, Ph.D. Program in Sociology and Political Science, City University of New York; Thomas Hunter Professor of Sociology and Director, Center for Puerto Rican Studies, Hunter College, CUNY; Executive Director, Inter-University Program for Latino Research (IUP); member, IUP/SSRC Committee for Public Policy Research on Contemporary Hispanic Issues

Lynn C. Burbridge
Research Associate and Policy Analyst, Urban Institute; formerly on the research staff of the Joint Center for Political Studies; member, Board of Directors, National Economic Association

Henry Cisneros
Mayor, San Antonio, Texas (1981-89); National Chairman, U.S. Saving Bonds for Cities; Past President, National League of Cities and the Texas Municipal League; syndicated columnist, *Los Angeles Times*

Ernesto Cortés

Director, Texas Interfaith and Industrial Areas Foundation; founder, Communities Organized for Public Service (COPS), San Antonio; MacArthur Fellow

David Dinkins

Mayor, New York City (1989-); former Manhattan Borough President; member, Board of Estimate in New York City, Urban League of Greater New York, and National Conference of Black Lawyers; founder, Black and Puerto Rican Legislative Caucus

Leobardo Estrada

Associate Professor, Architecture and Urban Planning, University of California at Los Angeles; member, IUP/SSRC Committee on Public Policy Research on Contemporary Hispanic Issues; advisor, U.S. Bureau of the Census on the Hispanic population in the United States

Rodolfo de la Garza

Professor, Government, University of Texas at Austin; Director, Center for Mexican American Studies; Chair, IUP/SSRC Committee for Public Policy Research on Contemporary Hispanic Issues

Bernard Gifford

Chancellor's Professor and Dean, Graduate School of Education, University of California at Berkeley; author, *History in the Schools: What Shall We Teach?* and *Politics of Testing and Opportunity Allocation*

Lena Guerrero

Texas State Representative, District 51; member, House State Affairs Committee, Government Organization Committee, and Sunset Committee; member, Southern Regional Council of Legislators

Barbara Jordan

Lyndon B. Johnson Centennial Chair in National Policy, Lyndon B. Johnson School of Public Affairs, University of Texas at Austin; former member, U.S. House of Representatives; former member, Texas Senate

Nicholas Katzenbach

Former U.S. Attorney General and Undersecretary of State; head, Mayor Dinkins's Study Group on Drug Abuse in New York City

Arturo Madrid
President, Tomás Rivera Center; Director, Fund for Improvement of Post Secondary Education, U.S. Department of Education; former Professor and Dean, University of Minnesota

Edwin Melendez
Assistant Professor, Urban Studies and Planning, Massachusetts Institute of Technology; Principal Investigator, IUP/SSRC grant project to study Puerto Rican female head of household labor force activity

Harry J. Middleton
Director, Lyndon Baines Johnson Library and Museum; Executive Director, Lyndon Baines Johnson Foundation; former White House Special Assistant to President Lyndon B. Johnson

Joan Moore
Professor, Sociology, University of Wisconsin-Milwaukee; member, IUP/SSRC Committee for Public Policy Research on Contemporary Hispanic Issues; Consulting Editor, *The American Sociologist*; Past President, Society for the Study of Social Problems (SSSP)

Milton Morris
Director of Research, Joint Center for Political Studies, Washington, D.C.; former Senior Fellow, Brookings Institution

Richard Nathan
Professor, Public and International Affairs, Woodrow Wilson School of Public and International Affairs, Princeton University; Director, Princeton Urban Regional Research Center; author, *Social Science in Governments: Uses and Misuses*

Gary Orfield
Professor, Political Science, Public Policy, and Education, University of Chicago; author, *The Reconstruction of Southern Education: The Schools and the 1964 Civil Rights Act*

Harry Pachon
Executive Director, National Association of Latino Elected and Appointed Officials (NALEO); Kennan Professor of Political Studies, Pitzer College, Claremont, California; Consultant, Carnegie and Ford Foundations and the Agency for International Development

Paul Peterson
Professor, Government, Harvard University; Chair, Social Science Research Council Committee for Research on the Urban Underclass; former Director, Governmental Studies, Brookings Institution; author, *A Case for a National Welfare Standard*

Robert Reischauer
Director, Congressional Budget Office; member, IUP/SSRC Committee for Public Policy Research on Contemporary Hispanic Issues; former Senior Vice President, Urban Institute; former Senior Fellow, Brookings Institution; former Deputy Director, Congressional Budget Office

Ricardo Romo
Associate Professor, History, University of Texas at Austin; Director and Scholar, Tomás Rivera Center; author, *East Los Angeles: History of a Barrio*

Max Sherman
Professor and Dean, Lyndon B. Johnson School of Public Affairs, University of Texas at Austin; former Texas State Senator

Margaret Simms
Deputy Director of Research, Joint Center for Political Studies; former Director, Minorities and Social Policy, the Urban Institute; former Brookings Institution Policy Fellow, U. S. Department of Housing and Urban Development

Carol B. Thompson
City Administrator/Deputy Mayor for Operations, Government of the District of Columbia; former Deputy Mayor for Economic Development and Director, Department of Consumer and Regulatory Affairs; Historic Preservation Officer, Washington, D.C.

Guadalupe Valdés
Professor, Graduate School of Education, University of California, Berkeley; (1989-90) Visiting Professor, Spanish and Portuguese, School of Education, Stanford University; recipient, West Haser Award for Outstanding Research, New Mexico State University

Robert B. Valdez
Assistant Professor, School of Public Health, University of California at Los Angeles; Resident Consultant, Economics and Statistics Depart-

ment, Rand Corporation; coauthor, *California without Health Insurance: A Report to the California Legislature*

Rafael Valdivieso

Vice President, Programs and Research, Hispanic Policy Development Project, Washington, D.C.; editor, *The Research Bulletin,* Hispanic Policy Development Project; former Director, Special Programs for the Institute of Education Leadership

About the Editor

Harriett Romo received her Ph.D. in sociology from the University of California, San Diego, and has taught at San Diego State University and The University of Texas at Austin. She has been Project Coordinator for the IUP/SSRC Committee at the UT Austin Center for Mexican American Studies since the committee's inception in 1985.

During the 1989-90 academic year, Dr. Romo held a National Institute for Mental Health (NIMH) fellowship at Stanford University in the Department of Sociology. She is currently involved in several research projects at the Center for the Study of Families, Youth, and Children at Stanford University and is coprincipal investigator of a project funded by the Hogg Foundation for Mental Health focusing on Latino students at risk of dropping out of school. Dr. Romo has published work on immigration, ethnic diversity, student course-taking patterns in high school, and minority education issues.

SPONSORS

IUP/SSRC Committee for Public Policy Research on Contemporary Hispanic Issues

The Inter-University Program for Latino Research (IUP) is a collaborative effort of four university research centers: the Centro de Estudios Puertorriqueños, Hunter College, City University of New York; the Center for Mexican American Studies, The University of Texas at Austin; the Chicano Studies Research Center, University of California, Los Angeles; and the Stanford Center for Chicano Research, Stanford University. The IUP combined its expertise in Latino research with the experience in research grants and research development of the Social Science Research Council (SSRC) to form the IUP/SSRC Committee for Public Policy Research on Contemporary Hispanic Issues. The IUP/SSRC Committee, with funds provided by the Ford Foundation, is committed to supporting sound Latino-oriented research that addresses policy issues and to stimulating informed debate between researchers and policymakers. The committee has sponsored nationwide grants competitions, summer institutes for Latino faculty and graduate students, postdoctoral fellowships, working groups on Hispanic program participation and the changing structure of the Latino family, and public policy forums.

Joint Center for Political Studies

The Joint Center for Political Studies, a nonpartisan, nonprofit institution, was founded in 1970 to help black Americans to participate fully and effectively in the governance of our society and, in the process, contribute to the formation of "a more perfect union." The center conducts studies and analyses of the political, social, and economic status of black Americans to improve the socioeconomic status of black Americans, to increase their influence in the political and public areas, and to facilitate the building of coalitions across racial lines to achieve consensus on public issues. Through publications, conferences, and commentaries, the center helps to illuminate major public policy debates and to establish a continuing framework for the pursuit of racial justice.

Lyndon B. Johnson School of Public Affairs
The Lyndon B. Johnson School of Public Affairs, a graduate component of The University of Texas at Austin, trains men and women of exceptional promise for professional careers in government, business, and nonprofit institutions. The LBJ School offers an innovative approach to education for public service, combining academic coursework in policy studies with applied research and internships in actual policy settings. In addition to its academic program, the school is involved in a wide range of public service activities, including training programs for public officials, conferences and workshops, and a publishing program.

Lyndon Baines Johnson Library
The Lyndon Baines Johnson Library is located on the campus of The University of Texas at Austin and is one of eight presidential libraries administered by the National Archives and Records Administration. It was established to preserve and make available for research the papers and memorabilia of President Lyndon B. Johnson. In addition, the library actively collects the papers of Johnson's contemporaries and conducts an oral history program designed to supplement the written record. The library also sponsors and promotes symposia and lectures dealing with issues of national concern. The museum exhibits of the library provide a detailed story of the Johnson years from the 1930s through the 1960s to the more than 400,000 people who visit each year. The library is a public institution open to all researchers on an equal basis.